SIDNEY'S POETICS

SIDNEY'S POETICS

IMITATING CREATION

MICHAEL MACK

THE CATHOLIC UNIVERSITY OF AMERICA PRESS
WASHINGTON, D.C.

Copyright © 2005
Reprinted in paperback, 2013
The Catholic University of America Press
All rights reserved

The paper used in this publication meets the minimum requirements of American National Standards for Information Science—Permanence of Paper for Printed Library materials, ANSI Z39.48-1984.

∞

LIBRARY OF CONGRESS CATALOGING-IN-PUBLICATION DATA

Mack, Michael, 1963–
Sidney's poetics : imitating creation / Michael Mack.
p. cm.
Includes bibliographical references and index.
ISBN 0-8132-1388-6 (alk. paper)
ISBN 978-0-8132-1388-0 (cloth: alk. paper)
ISBN 978-0-8132-2116-8 (pbk: alk. paper)
1. Sidney, Philip, Sir, 1554–1586—Aesthetics. 2. Sidney, Philip, Sir, 1554–1586. Apologie for poetrie. 3. Creation (Literary, artistic, etc.) 4. Poetics—History—16th century. 5. Aesthetics, Modern—16th century. 6. Aesthetics, British. 7. Poetry. I. Title.
PR2343.M23 2005
808.1—dc22
2004002315

To my mother and father

CONTENTS

Preface ix

Introduction 1

1. The History of Creativity 17

2. Sidney's Fiction and the Allegorical Tradition 34

3. The Idea of Poetry 54

4. The Imitation of Creation 81

5. From Creation to Regeneration 109

6. The Imitation of Cyrus 137

7. Creativity and the Origins of Modernity 157

Appendix: The Text 191

Bibliography 195

Index 211

PREFACE

This book is a study of Sidney's poetic theory and its role in the development of the idea of human creativity. Although the *Apology* has often been identified as a landmark along the path from poetry understood as imitation to poetry understood as creation, critics are far from agreeing on the defining features of Sidney's transitional theory. Attending to the still close relationship of theology and poetics in the period, I examine the ways in which theological considerations shape Sidney's synthesis of the literary-critical tradition and lead him to the then-daring assertion of poetic creativity. Examining Sidney's belief that the poet is a "maker" made in the "likeness" of the "heavenly Maker"—and drawing out the logical conclusions implicit in this "saucy" comparison of poetry to divine creation—I show how Sidney develops an innovative poetic theory that is at the same time an innovative conception of human nature and of the place of human beings within the world. Far more than an artful compendium of Renaissance literary theory, Sidney's *Apology* makes claims no less bold than those of Pico in his *Oration*.

While offering a new interpretation of Sidney's elegant and influential treatise, this book also makes a case for a new understanding of the historical process by which human beings were first thought to be endowed with the power to create—a power previously reserved to God alone. Entering into the debate over the origins of modernity, I show that the standard theories of the transfer of divine powers such as creativity to human agents cannot account for Sidney's theory of poetic creativity. Seeking a better explanation of the origin of Sidney's idea of poetic creativity, I offer a version of the birth of modernity in which sacred and secular values are not necessarily opposed. Unlike previous accounts, mine accommodates what are now recognized to be the continuities between medieval and Renaissance culture, between the Renaissance and the romantic period, and between theological speculation and literary theory.

In my attempt to help modern readers see Sidney's ideas as new—new to them, at least—I use tools of analysis that are hardly new or original. My method, to the extent that I have one, is philological and hermeneutical. This is to say nothing more, really, than that I try to make sense of Sidney's words, one by one and all together. And taking his words seriously means, for me, taking his ideas seriously. As will soon be evident, if not already so, I make use of and attempt to contribute to the wide-ranging and learned endeavor known as "the history of ideas." Since it is an endeavor that has been under attack for some time now, before beginning my study I will provide a brief justification for relying on its findings and employing its methods.

Any such justification must be made vis-à-vis the New Historicism, which has dominated Renaissance studies in recent years. New Historicism is a movement often lauded for its interdisciplinary method and its broad scope, which extends to culture as a whole. Of course, this praise could just as easily be bestowed on the history of ideas. However, anyone conversant with literary trends knows that terms like "interdisciplinary studies" and "cultural studies" are not to be taken at face value. Although the history of ideas is indeed interdisciplinary, in the ordinary sense of the term, no one would think to identify it as such. Nor would anyone think of extending the protective mantle of "cultural studies" to the history of ideas, even though it clearly studies culture. In the double-speak to which literary criticism is prone, "culture" has come to mean "material culture," and "interdisciplinary studies" has been redefined to mean those approaches that have recourse to sociology and social history rather than those allied with philosophy and intellectual history. Insisting quite rightly that the older top-down perspective provides only a partial view of a culture, New Historicism has brought a bottom-up perspective to cultural studies. Of course, this new perspective is no less partial. That it too has introduced a bias that draws new studies toward the same perspective does not, of course, discredit the new methodology. It does, however, explain how the history of ideas can be out of favor through no fault of its own, and how the older approach, with its now marginalized perspective, could be more valuable than ever.

It no doubt is true that many in the past, some associated with the history of ideas, produced a historical picture that was too neat, paying attention almost exclusively to ideas and committing what is now decried as "totalizing essentialism." But it is also quite clear that New Historicists are susceptible to an equal and opposite error, which might be called "totalizing materialism." This is, however, to put the matter too nicely. Grounded in Althusserian Marxism, New Historicism is not susceptible to totalizing materialism, it is committed to it—by definition, as is evident from its overseas alias, "cultural materialism." It is hard indeed to imagine a more totalizing view of Elizabethan culture than that of Alan Sinfield, undoubtedly the most influential of the New Historicists to have written on Sidney. Sinfield propagates what might well be called the "early modern world picture": "In early modern England . . . an ideology of ineluctable, unified hierarchy and value, with a precise, ideal position for each subject, was propagated through what we now call art and literature."[1] This is basically the "Elizabethan world picture" presented by E. M. W. Tillyard—but without the nuance. Unqualifiedly affirming the outline of Tillyard, whom he vilifies, Sinfield simply supplies his own ideological coloring. Although Sinfield decries Tillyard's "essentialist humanism," with its "affirmation of a transhistorical human condition" (to borrow the words of Sinfield's colleague Jonathan Dollimore), he asserts a no less essentialist historicism that absolutely denies any transhistorical human condition.[2] Instead of human nature, Sinfield essentializes culture and elevates it to a lofty transhistorical

---

1. "Sidney's *Defence* and the Collective-Farm Chairman: Puritan Humanism and the Cultural Apparatus," in *Faultlines: Cultural Materialism and the Politics of Dissident Reading* (Berkeley and Los Angeles: University of California Press, 1992), 181–82.

2. Jonathan Dollimore, "Introduction: Shakespeare, Cultural Materialism and the New Historicism," in *Political Shakespeare: Essays in Cultural Materialism*, ed. Jonathan

status.[3] Sinfield's method yields a conclusion that is nothing short of fantastic: he finds in the *Apology* an "aesthetic absolutism" identical in its formal features to that propagated by Stalin and affirmed by Leonid Brezhnev in 1981.[4]

Of course, no methodology is to be blamed for every error and excess of its practitioners. On the contrary, both the New Historicism and the history of ideas should be judged on the basis of their best examples, not their worst. There are indeed many learned and sophisticated scholars who have shown how much each approach has to offer. Certainly, the best in each kind know that there are more things in texts than are dreamt of in any one methodology. In the end, the justification for trying to follow in the great footsteps of scholars such as Ernst Robert Curtius, Erwin Panofsky, and Ernst Kantorowicz will have to be this work itself. I hope that it will demonstrate by example that the variegated tradition going back to A. O. Lovejoy and George Boas can still produce good fruit.

Dollimore and Alan Sinfield (Ithaca, N.Y.: Cornell University Press, 1994), 4. Those who dismiss the history of ideas almost always cite E. M. W. Tillyard's *The Elizabethan World Picture* (London: Chatto & Windus, 1943)—as if this short handbook for undergraduates represents the sum of the whole scholarly endeavor. Rarely do they mention the foundational work of the tradition by Arthur O. Lovejoy and George Boas, *Primitivism and Related Ideas in Antiquity* (Baltimore: John Hopkins University Press, 1935), which is roughly equivalent to dismissing New Historicism without mentioning Stephen Greenblatt's *Renaissance Self-Fashioning: From More to Shakespeare* (Chicago: University of Chicago Press, 1980).

3. To complete the comparison, it should be noted that whereas Lovejoy famously identified thirty-four meanings for "Nature"—and warned that his taxonomy is not exhaustive—in their short piece that serves as a manifesto of cultural materialism, Dollimore and Sinfield identify precisely *two* senses of "Culture," the "evaluative" (bad) understanding, which is responsible for such notions as "high culture," and their own objective (good) "analytic sense" ("Forward to the First Edition: Cultural Materialism," in *Political Shakespeare*, viii). I could happily subscribe to their objective definition of culture—"the whole system of significations by which a society or a section of it understands itself and its relations with the world"—and I have no doubt that literature is, as Sinfield insists, but "one set of signifying practices among others." I am unwilling, however, to believe with Sinfield that cultural materialism is the one key that unlocks the "signifying practices" of every segment of every society. To me it seems better to try to understand each set of "signifying practices" on its own terms, the *Apology for Poetry* included.

4. "Sidney's *Defence* and the Collective-Farm Chairman," 181.

Although I believe the method to be sound, I am under no illusion that this work is free from at least its share of peculiarities and limitations. The most obvious, perhaps, is that a study focused on a brief passage in a rather small work should have such a broad scope. In my attempt to follow Sidney's language back to sources that influence, enable, or adumbrate his poetic theory and ahead to works on which the form and pressure of his theory can be felt, I have ventured into regions of intellectual history far removed from Elizabethan poetics. To a certain extent this is of course unavoidable. Sidney was at home even in seemingly distant intellectual lands, and to understand his work it is necessary to become familiar with what was familiar for him. If I travel beyond the limits of what seems necessary, it is largely because I do not believe that Sidney's poetics can be fully appreciated apart from the historical development of the idea of poetic creativity. If an adequate history of poetic creativity existed, I would happily abbreviate the parts of this study that constitute what might be called "notes toward a history of the idea of human creativity." Unfortunately, no such account exists—nor can one be written without an accurate and in-depth treatment of Sidney's poetics of creativity. Given this scholarly conundrum, I have attempted to do two jobs at once in the hope of making it possible to see Sidney's *Apology* as the cradle of poetic creativity.

A brief outline of the book is no doubt in order. The study begins with a short introductory chapter, after which I offer an overview of the idea of human creativity, bringing together a history of the accounts of divine creation and a history of the ways in which human beings have thought of themselves as the image of God. In the second chapter, I turn to poetic theory in the sixteenth century and show how Sidney draws together the rhetorical and the allegorical strains in contemporary poetic theory, uniting them in the poet's "*Idea* or fore-conceit." The third chapter shows how this famous formulation is also found in contemporary accounts of divine creation, and the fourth examines those accounts of divine creation in order to see more clearly the analogous features in Sidney's theory of human creativity. In the fifth chapter, I show how Sidney's theory of poetic creativity anticipates those of Coleridge and Wordsworth and is in its essence a theory of poetic regeneration. The sixth chapter focuses on the imitation of Cyrus as the means for the renewal of the reader and the "brazen" world according to the Idea in the mind of the maker. Having previously situated the *Apology* in relation to earlier and later Platonic renaissances, I turn, in the final chapter, to the place of the *Apology* in the debate over the origin and nature of modernity. Attending to the interplay between theories of human creativity and theories of modernity, I show how they shape one another and how they shape the way we see ourselves.

Before beginning, I have many debts to acknowledge, some of them weighty. This book began with a summer at the Huntington Library and was finished with many a day at the Folger Shakespeare Library; I am grateful to both institutions and to their talented staffs. I am also deeply grateful to my own institution, The Catholic University of America, and in particular to my colleagues in the English Department, for providing me a truly happy home for scholarship and teaching. I owe special thanks to the Dean of Arts and Sciences, Larry Poos, for his generous support in the final stages of the project; to Anne O'Donnell, S.N.D., for suggestions early on and for reassurance toward the end; to Virgil Nemoianu, for his incisive comments on the work in manuscript and for his good counsel throughout the project; and to Chris Wheatley and Ernie Suarez, whose friendship and encouragement I could not have done without. I also wish to thank Marc Berley, who brought his high standards to bear on an early version of the manuscript, and R. V. Young, who offered numerous corrections and improvements in the final stages. My teachers continue to be an inspiration to me, especially Kathy Eden, James Mirollo, and Anne Lake Prescott, who all offered guidance when I first began the project. To Ted Tayler I owe the most. He continues to teach me with his notes in the margins, and I am grateful beyond expression for his wisdom and unfailing generosity. Anything that this work accomplishes, it is thanks to those I have mentioned; only its infirmities can I claim as my own. My final thanks goes to Orysia; though she came late to the project, she has been my most dedicated reader and a helpmeet fit.

SIDNEY'S POETICS

INTRODUCTION

Sir Philip Sidney's *Apology for Poetry* occupies a central and even a pivotal position in both the history of literary theory and the history of ideas. It is, however, a work that easily could have gone unwritten. Poetry was, as Sidney says in the *Apology*, his "unelected vocation."[1] Sidney's chosen calling was the active pursuit of the cause for which he believed England, and its queen, was destined: European Protestantism. Happily for English literature, if not for Sidney, the pragmatic Elizabeth did not share Sidney's zeal, nor did she hesitate, when he displeased her, to deprive him of political and military service to the state. After writing Elizabeth a letter of advice on the matter of her prospective marriage to Alençon and then challenging the earl of Oxford, his social superior and a supporter of Alençon, Sidney was effectively cut off from all public employment. Thus, in the autumn of 1579, the twenty-five-year-old Sidney retired from the court, and he remained effectively unemployed until mid-1584. It was during this period of semienforced rustication that Sidney composed—in addition to his prose romance, the *Arcadia*, and his sonnet sequence, *Astrophil and Stella*—the short defense of poetry that would prove to be a landmark in literary history.[2]

Sidney never bestowed a title on his defense of poetry, referring to

---

1. *An Apology for Poetry*, ed. Geoffrey Shepard (London: T. Nelson, 1965), 95. Unless otherwise noted, all subsequent citations of the *Apology* refer to Shepherd's edition and are cited parenthetically.
2. The date of the *Apology* remains uncertain. Although many have argued that Sidney composed the work as early as 1579, it probably was written around 1582. On the dating of the *Apology*, see Shepherd, ed., *Apology*, 2–4, and Katherine Duncan-Jones, *Sir Philip Sidney: Courtier Poet* (New Haven, Conn., and London: Yale University Press, 1991), 230–32.

it rather, with his characteristic irony, as an "ink-wasting toy" (141). Nor is there any evidence that he ever considered having it printed. It remained unpublished for almost a decade after his death, until 1595, when it appeared in two separate editions, Olney's *Apologie for Poetrie* and Ponsonby's *Defence of Poesie*. The work did, however, circulate in manuscript prior to its publication, and it is clear that Sidney wrote for more than a small coterie of family and friends.[3] Neither the form of the work—a classical oration—nor its rhetorical style befit a small private audience. On the contrary, running throughout the *Apology* there is what might be called an evangelical impulse. Whether it is the soaring eloquence in his presentation of a fictional Cyrus who can make "many Cyruses," the plaintive insistence of his digression on the bleak landscape of English literature in his day, or the beguiling charm of his persona, Sidney seeks at every point to enamor his audience with his expansive vision of poetry, and with virtue. Deprived of any diplomatic or military responsibility, Sidney did not turn his sights away from God's "great work . . . against the abusers of the world."[4] Rather, laboring in the defense of his "unelected vocation," he contributed to

---

3. Perhaps responding to the power of Sidney's prose, A. C. Hamilton, in *Sir Philip Sidney: A Study of His Life and Works* (Cambridge, U.K.: Cambridge University Press, 1977), goes so far as to call the *Apology* a "manifesto" in which Sidney "declares his emergence as a public poet" (17). See Martin Garrett, in *Sidney: The Critical Heritage* (London: Routledge, 1996), 36–37, who cites internal evidence indicating the "public context" of the *Apology*. For a different view, see Peter C. Herman, "When Is a Defense Not a Defense?: Sidney's Paradoxical *Apology for Poetry*," in *Squitter-Wits and Muse-Haters: Sidney, Spenser, Milton and Renaissance Antipoetic Sentiment* (Detroit: Wayne State University Press, 1996), who believes that Sidney intended the *Apology* only for private consumption, and that the views he wished to be made public are to be found in two letters, one to Edward Denny and the other to his brother Robert.

4. From a letter to Sir Francis Walsingham, in *The Prose Works of Sir Philip Sidney*, ed. Albert Feuillerat, 4 vols. (Cambridge, U.K.: Cambridge University Press, 1962), 3.167. Sidney is expressing his faith that the Protestant cause would advance despite Elizabeth's unwillingness: "If her Majesty were the fountain I would fear considering what I daily find that we should wax dry, but she is but a means whom God useth and I know not whether I am deceived but I am faithfully persuaded that if she should withdraw her self other springs would rise to help this action. For methinks I see the great work indeed at hand, against the abusers of the world, wherein it is no greater fault to have confidence in man's power, then it is too hastily to despair of God's work."

that great work and figured forth an idea of poetry as reformation by other means.

While Sidney's emphasis on moving readers to embrace virtue is well known, the religious underpinnings of his project are seldom noticed, let alone understood. This is not altogether surprising, since Sidney typically handles weighty material with a light touch, choosing not to insist, but rather to beguile. Despite the indirection of his method, evidence of the religious component of his thought is hardly lacking. In the *Apology*, biblical allusions are present throughout, and especially at critical junctures. Beyond the *Apology*, there is abundant testimony to his interest in religion and theology, beginning with his translations not only of some of the psalms but also of parts of Du Bartas's *Divine Weeks* and Mornay's *The Trueness of the Christian Religion*. Notwithstanding the hagiographical coloring of Fulke Greville's *Life of Sidney*, there is no reason to doubt Greville when he records that his friend "made the religion he professed the firme *Basis* of his life" and followed the example of William of Orange, "whoe never devided the consideration of estate from the cause of religion."[5] If Greville's recollections are accurate and Sidney the statesman did not divide his religious ideals from his politics, it seems unlikely that Sidney the poet would choose to divide "the cause of religion" from his poetics.

This tendency to give short shrift to the religious foundations of Sidney's poetics has been addressed by recent studies employing the methods of New Historicism. Alan Sinfield has argued forcefully and repeatedly for the importance of religion in understanding the *Apology*.[6] Sinfield is, however, relentlessly ideological, and his understanding of Sidney's religious commitments is willfully reductive. Although less polemical and programmatic, the New Historicists who follow

---

5. *The Prose of Fulke Greville, Lord Brooke*, ed. Mark Caldwell (New York: Garland, 1987), 23. On Sidney's long-recognized frustration and idealism, see esp. Edward Berry, "The Poet as Warrior: *A Defence of Poetry*," in *The Making of Sir Philip Sidney* (Toronto: University of Toronto Press, 1998), 142–62.

6. See "The Cultural Politics of the *Defence of Poetry*," in *Sir Philip Sidney and the Interpretation of Renaissance Culture: The Poet in His Time and in Ours: A Collection of Critical and Scholarly Essays* (London: Croom Helm, 1984), revised as "Sidney's *Defence* and the Collective-Farm Chairman: Puritan Humanism and the Cultural Apparatus."

Sinfield in emphasizing the religious elements of the work nevertheless share his predictable habit of finding unresolved contradictions in Sidney's religious commitments.[7] As Robert Stillman has recently shown, some of the key contradictions that they discover have their origin not in late-sixteenth-century culture but in their own faulty assumptions about religion in Sidney's time. Sidney's brand of Protestantism was not, as Sinfield and those who rely on him assume, strict Calvinism. It was rather the more optimistic strain developed by Melanchthon and held by Sidney's mentor, Hubert Languet.[8] This more ecumenical Protestantism is, as Stillman demonstrates, perfectly compatible with what Sidney writes in the *Apology*.[9]

Interested in the cultural context far more than the text of the *Apology*, New Historicist studies have been of little help in resolving the interpretive cruxes that vexed earlier critics. Indeed, they have done nothing to elucidate either the nature of the "zodiac" that Sidney lo-

7. See, e.g., Robert Matz, "Heroic Diversions: Sidney's *Defence of Poetry*," in *Defending Literature in Early Modern England: Renaissance Literary Theory in Social Context* (New York: Cambridge University Press, 2000), who sees Sidney unsuccessfully attempting in the *Apology* to reconcile "activist Protestantism" with the courtly culture to which Sinfield finds it opposed. The influence of the New Historicism can also be felt in the more traditional recent study by Brian Cummings, *The Literary Culture of the Reformation: Grammar and Grace* (Oxford, U.K.: Oxford University Press, 2002); Cummings relies heavily on the authority of Sinfield to support his claim that although "Sidney takes extraordinary theological risks," in the final analysis he "does not resolve his theology" (270, 265).

8. "Deadly Stinging Adders: Sidney's Piety, Philippism, and the Defence of Poesy," in *Spenser Studies: A Renaissance Poetry Annual* (2002). On Sidney's belief, also see Blair Worden, *The Sound of Virtue: Philip Sidney's "Arcadia" and Elizabethan Politics* (New Haven, Conn.: Yale Univesity Press, 1996), 34–37, who describes Sidney's providential view without trying to make it conform to a particular religious confession.

9. On the New Historicists' habit of hunting for contradictions, which they uncover with the same predictable regularity as the New Critics discovered paradox and irony, see Stanley Stewart, "Reading Donne: Old and New His- and Her-Storicisms," in *Reading the Renaissance: Ideas and Idioms from Shakespeare to Milton*, ed. Marc Berley (Pittsburgh, Pa.: Duquesne University Press, 2003). Of course, finding contradictions in the *Apology* is hardly new. A generation ago O. B. Hardison Jr., in "The Two Voices of Sidney's *Apology for Poetry*," *English Literary Renaissance* 2 (1972), reprinted in *Sidney in Retrospect: Selections from "English Literary Renaissance*," ed. Arthur Kinney (Amherst: University of Massachusetts Press, 1988), 45–61, argued that Sidney unsuccessfully attempts to reconcile humanism and classicism in the *Apology*. Although the terms have changed, the problem of interpretation remains.

cates in the "wit" of the poet or the status of the *"Idea* or fore-conceit" that is the origin of the poetic work—to mention only two of Sidney's elegant but enigmatic locutions still calling out for explanation. The interpretive difficulties presented by the *Apology* are indeed considerable. Cultural fault lines aside, it remains an open question among critics whether Sidney even presents a coherent poetic theory in the *Apology*. More than a century ago, Joel Spingarn identified the wide array of authorities that makes the *Apology* a treasury of classical and continental poetics, and scholars ever since have been frustrated by the eclecticism of Sidney's treatise.[10] The rich allusiveness of the *Apology*, which was very attractive to contemporary English readers eager for imported theories, makes it difficult for modern critics to distinguish Sidney's own theory from those he cites. To be sure, Sidney's inclusiveness often makes him appear to hold antithetical positions. While he is rightly credited with introducing the Aristotelian and Horatian strains to English criticism, at the same time he can be seen to extend the quite different humanist poetics developed by Dante and Boccaccio. Similarly, the *Apology* seems to propose a rhetorical approach to poetry, of the kind that predominated in classical antiquity, while at the same time relying on the medieval strategy of emphasizing the similarities between poetry and theology. The disparity is considerable: the former approach makes Sidney look neoclassical, the latter protoromantic.

Despite these apparent contradictions, the *Apology* is not at odds with itself. What to postmodern eyes may look like epistemic discontinuities or ideological fault lines are, at least in the case of the *Apology*, the signs of a work that is transitional in character. No more self-contradictory than are the two faces of Janus, the *Apology*, like the Renaissance itself, looks ahead by looking back. It looks back to literary theories centered on imitation and looks ahead to those revolving around creativity. In an often quoted passage, Sidney explicitly defines poetry as imitation—citing Aristotle's definition of poetry as *mimesis;* in some of his most memorable locutions, however, he clearly has in mind something more than Aristotelian imitation. Moving well be-

10. *A History of Literary Criticism in the Renaissance* (London: Macmillan, 1899), 163–64.

yond the already idealized understanding of imitation that was at the heart of the Aristotelian poetics of the cinquecento, Sidney describes the poet not as imitating nature but as going "hand in hand with Nature." Imitating nothing outside of himself, Sidney's poet has recourse only to the "zodiac of his own wit." And working with the "force of a divine breath," the poet has a power not only to figure forth an ideal fictional world but also to move his audience to make that "golden" world real. With this twofold proposal, that poetry has its origin only in the poet's "Idea" and that poetry has the power to reform the world, Sidney transforms the classical ideal of poetry as imitation into something the world had not yet seen, a theory of poetic creativity (100–101).

The brief but especially rich passage that I have been quoting and to which I return throughout the book is well known by all who have studied the *Apology*. It is the climax of the introductory section, which is generally referred to as the *narratio* since Sidney structures his defense of poetry as a classical judicial oration.[11] In order to show the specific nature of Sidney's understanding of poetic creativity, it is necessary to put great analytical pressure on this rather small portion of the *Apology*. For the convenience of the reader, I have included an edited version of the passage, with original spelling and critical apparatus, as an appendix to the present study.

In this climactic passage, Sidney argues that whereas all the other arts merely imitate nature, "the poet, disdaining to be tied to any such subjection, lifted up with the vigour of his own invention, doth grow in effect into another nature, in making things either better than Nature bringeth forth, or, quite anew" (101). The poet "goeth hand in hand with Nature, not enclosed within the narrow warrant of her gifts, but freely ranging only within the zodiac of his own wit." Whereas the world Nature produces is "brazen," the poets "deliver a golden" world, one that includes all that "may make the too much loved earth more lovely." What is more, the power of poesy extends

---

11. See Kenneth Myrick, *Sir Philip Sidney as a Literary Craftsman* (Lincoln: University of Nebraska Press, 1965), 46–83, who first showed that the *Apology* has the structure typically found in a classical forensic oration.

beyond the fictional world to the real world. The "delivering forth" of the poet's "*Idea* or fore-conceit" "is not wholly imaginative," for the "*Idea*" "worketh" "substantially," "not only to make a Cyrus, which had been but a particular excellency as Nature might have done, but to bestow a Cyrus upon the world to make many Cyruses, if they will learn aright why and how that maker made him." Nature produced one Cyrus; the poet, inspiring his audience to imitate the virtue they see in his fictional hero, produces many such heroes.

This desire to imitate Xenophon's Cyrus recalls the brief opening section of the *Apology*, the *exordium*, which directly precedes the *narratio*. Opening with the memorable example of how John Pietro Pugliano's love for his own art, horsemanship, had almost persuaded Sidney "to have wished [him]self a horse," Sidney asks the reader to bear with him if he "followeth the steps of his master," Pugliano (95). In the dazzling conclusion of the *narratio*, Sidney offers an equally memorable panegyric to poesy that goes so far as almost to persuade readers to wish themselves a poem. However, unlike the anecdote of Pugliano, this passage is not delivered as a jest. Sidney quite seriously wishes for his audience to find in the heroic example of Xenophon's idealized Cyrus a model for their own lives. His intention is that his audience transform themselves into other Cyruses, and in language that is itself creative Sidney envisions poetry as an art that can create a nation of heroes.

For Sidney, this poetic skill, which can transform not only the world but humanity itself, is the "highest point of man's wit." Not only does it give the poetic maker the "efficacy of Nature," but it makes him like God, "the heavenly Maker." The divine potency of human beings, which extends over all of "that second nature," is seen "in nothing . . . so much as in Poetry, when with the force of a divine breath [the poet] bringeth things forth far surpassing her doings, with no small argument to the incredulous of that first accursed fall of Adam." "With the force of a divine breath," poesy has the power of none other than the Holy Spirit, whose "argument" has unparalleled rhetorical "force," persuading even the "incredulous" to believe in the fallen condition of humanity. Sidney concludes this lofty opening argument for the dignity of poetry by acknowledging that his argument, though forceful, "will by few be understood, and by fewer granted." Consequently, he turns to "a more ordinary opening"(101). The need for "a more ordinary opening" is understandable, given the state of literary criticism in England at the time. Not only did Sidney's audience suffer what was then understood as the clouded vision that is the common inheritance of fallen humanity, it quite simply had never seen a treatise on poetry that was anything but prosaic. The "ordinary" approach to poetry of the decade prior to the composition of the *Apology* is exemplified in George Gascoigne's *Certayne Notes of Instruction Concerning the Making of Verse or Ryme in English* (1575). Unaffectedly plain in style, *Certayne Notes* does not pretend to be more than a handbook written by a poet for other poets, offering practical advice for keeping audiences entertained. Despite its humble aspirations—or perhaps because of them—the work is not merely derivative. Besides its contribution to prosody—solidifying the iamb as the standard meter—the Horatian spirit of the *ars poetica* is a noteworthy contribution to English poetics. More important still is its quasi-Aristotelian theory of invention, emphasizing ingenuity and surprise (which will be taken up later in relation to Sidney's treatment of the poet's "*Idea* or foreconceit"). But despite these qualities that mark *Certayne Notes* as transitional in character, in its overall style and substance it remains unrelentingly ordinary. The instructions Gascoigne gives for avoiding trite and obvious metaphors and his shortcuts for finding rhymes are thoroughly pedestrian, especially when seen in contrast to Sidney's high-flown arguments about poetry as the highest art known to mankind.

More theoretical than Gascoigne's "notes of instruction" is Thomas Lodge's defense of poetry, probably entitled *Honest Excuses* (1579). Written as a response to Stephen Gosson's *Schoole of Abuse* (1579), Lodge counters Gosson's Puritan attack on poetry, music, and the stage by marshalling an impressive array of authorities. Calling on the authority of the Church Father Lactantius, for example, Lodge makes the traditional defense that poetry, like Sacred Scripture itself, is often allegorical. Although he resembles Sidney in drawing on many sources, he handles his sources with far less sophistication. Simply reiterating the arguments of predecessors, his defense is purely conventional, possessing none of the easy erudition or synthetic originality found in Sidney's *Apology*. Since the *Apology* is still often said to have been written as a response to Gosson, this contrast with Lodge's direct rebuttal is important. It illustrates how far the *Apology* is from being, in any strict sense, an answer to Gosson. Sidney does not, for example, take up the subject at the heart of Gosson's attack: the moral dangers of stage plays. As Geoffrey Shepherd puts it, "what Gosson was attacking, Sidney is not defending."[12]

Considerably more speculative than Lodge's treatise is a slightly earlier defense of poetry, Richard Willis's *De re poetica disputatio* (1573). Although not written in English, it is the first work of the kind written in England. This short scholarly treatise engages contemporary continental poetics, setting itself apart from the traditional rhetorical approach to literary theory in England at the time. Instead of taking rhetorical practice as the principal ground for literary theory and practice, Willis emphasizes the ideal quality of poetic imitation. In a way not seen in the writings of English humanists such as Ascham, whose *Scholemaster* (1570) illustrates the typical approach to imitation as the imitation of language and style, Willis shows an Aristotelian rather

12. Shepherd, ed., *Apology*, 2–3. Despite Shepherd's authority and the ample evidence he presents, many studies still press for a close connection between the *Apology* and *The Schoole of Abuse*. Without even an acknowledgment that some may disagree, Matz, in "Heroic Diversions: Sidney's *Defence of Poetry*," 60, simply states that "Sidney's work almost assuredly replies to the *Schoole*." In his footnote "on the likelihood that the *Defence* constitutes a reply to Gosson," Matz refers the reader to Duncan-Jones, *Sir Philip Sidney*, 232–33, without mentioning that she quite plainly is of the opinion that the "*Defence* is *not* a reply to *The Schoole of Abuse*" (emphasis added). Similarly dubious is the scholarship of Herman, who in "Squitter-Wits" acknowledges that some "Sidney critics dispute Gosson's instigation of Sidney's *Apology*" but simply dismisses them as a "minority" (221, n6), without pausing to consider that the minority in question happens to include the editors of the two standard editions of the *Apology* (Shepherd, Duncan-Jones), one of whom is also the author of the current standard biography of Sidney (Duncan-Jones). Rather than addressing the "minority" position, Herman relies quite heavily, as does Matz, on the authority of a dated work by Arthur F. Kinney, "Parody and Its Implications in Sydney's Defense of Poesie," *Studies in English Literature 1500–1900* 12 (1972): 1–19, in which Kinney overlooks the fact that when Sidney most resembles Gosson, he is drawing on commonplace arguments, such as the antiquity of poetry, which were available to both men through many sources.

than a Ciceronian (or anti-Ciceronian) approach to imitation. He also sets himself apart from the humanist pedagogues by sharing the continental interest in poetic inspiration. Offering a surprisingly subtle treatment of the subject, he anticipates Sidney's emphasis on the inspiration of the audience rather than of the poet. But although Willis precedes Sidney in treating these topics in less ordinary ways, he does not begin to develop his arguments or integrate his materials as fully or as delightfully as does Sidney.[13]

When it comes to the language in which poetry is justified, Sidney has one predecessor who deserves special recognition. Although published in 1589, the dating (not to mention the authorship) of Puttenham's *Art of English Poesie* remains a matter of debate.[14] But whether or not the first book, *Of Poets and Poesie*, preceded or followed the *Apology*, Puttenham unquestionably is to be credited with being the first to use the word "create" to describe the work of the poet. Although Puttenham begins his treatise by bestowing the conventional appellation of "maker" on the poet, he quickly notes that we may "by way of resemblance and reverently" give God the same name. Going further, he says what no one else had dared to write in English before, that poets are "as creating gods"—though he inserts quickly that this is said "by maner of speech."[15] The poet, like God, does not rely on "any foreine copie or example." Rather, just as God "made all the world of nought," so too the poet "makes and contrives out of his own braine."[16]

As suggestive and rich as the analogy is, however, Puttenham does not draw any further consequences from this likeness of the poet and God.[17] Even though Sidney's terminology is more humble than that of

13. For a more detailed description of Willis's *Disputatio*, see J. W. H. Atkins, *English Literary Criticism: The Renascence* (New York: Barnes & Noble, 1968), 104–11.
14. On the difficulty of dating the work, see Gladys Doidge Willcock and Alice Walker, "Introduction," in *The Arte of English Poesie*, ed. Gladys Doidge Willcock and Alice Walker (Cambridge, U.K.: Cambridge University Press, 1936), xliv.
15. George (?) Puttenham, *The Arte of English Poesie*, ed. Gladys Doidge Willcock and Alice Walker (Cambridge, U.K.: Cambridge University Press, 1936), 4.
16. *The Arte of English Poesie*, 3.
17. For another view, see Derek Attridge, "Puttenham's Perplexity: Nature, Art,

Puttenham, his claim, when examined carefully, is in fact far more daring. Whereas Puttenham uses the analogy of God and the poet only to describe what the poet does not do—he does not copy a work as a translator would—Sidney goes on to develop the positive consequences of the resemblance, giving the poet a share in the power of God. Going well beyond Puttenham, Sidney understands that God's creative power is seen nowhere more clearly than in the power to redeem fallen humanity. With grace and wit, Sidney attributes to poetry the God-like power to transform audiences, a power that is, in everything but name, creative.

The daring and originality of Sidney's claim is not only missed but often denied by those studying the *Apology*. Over a hundred years ago, Spingarn led the way, going so far as to declare authoritatively that "there is not an essential principle in *The Defence of Poesy* which cannot be traced back to some Italian treatise on the poetic art."[18] Since Sidney does borrow much material from the Italian criticism of the previous half century, it is easy to treat him, as Spingarn does, basically as a conduit. Though the first robust example of its kind in England—the first of what Spingarn calls the "philosophical and apologetic criticism"—the *Apology* is belated by international standards. Indeed, the very accomplishments that set Sidney apart have become for us the characteristic features of the age. Even Sidney's style, which seems to be all his own, winds up making him, more than anyone else of his age, the representative Elizabethan.

Although Spingarn is right to see Sidney as a major importer of Italian literary theory, he does not go far enough in recognizing the differences between Sidney and his Italian predecessors. Like his learned predecessors, Sidney borrows freely, and like them he is not only eclectic but also synthetic. But his style is less scholarly and far more lively than that of, say, Minturno or Scaliger, and the *Apology* is a

---

and the Supplement in Renaissance Poetic Theory," in *Literary Theory/Renaissance Texts*, ed. Patricia Parker and David Quint (Baltimore: Johns Hopkins University Press, 1986), 274, who finds greater continuity in Puttenham's work and believes that "the analogy between nature's creativity and the artist's" "is a culmination of one thread" that runs through "Puttenham's whole argument."

18. *A History of Literary Criticism in the Renaissance*, 257–58.

much greater literary achievement than any of the Italian treatises to which it is indebted. Unlike its predecessors, the *Apology* is a work *about* literature that itself *is* a work of literature. Like any great work of art, it ultimately defies paraphrase. So too it retains about itself a certain mystery, which beguiles otherwise cautious readers into thinking that through careful scholarly exploration they might discover, like Stanley and Livingston, some literary equivalent of a Lake Victoria.[19] Of course, some of this kind of genetic research simply seeks to be useful, serving as an introduction to the work. Indeed, it is very helpful for the student to be aware, for example, that the *Apology* includes "three strains": the Horatian poetic tradition, the Ciceronian rhetorical tradition, and the Platonic philosophical tradition.[20] But more often than not, source studies express the unspoken hope that having discovered where Sidney is coming from, we will know where he is going. What this conviction reveals, I would argue, is that even though Sidney's is a traditional work, it is somehow, despite Spingarn's authoritative dictum, also original.

Other scholars, accepting the *Apology* as a web of traditional arguments, have chosen not to try to untangle the borrowed strands but to search for the single pattern that Sidney weaves with them. The diversity of these discoveries is striking. Whereas Forrest Robinson believes Sidney's poetics can best be understood in terms of Ramist "visual epistemology," Ronald Levao thinks he discovers in Sidney an applica-

---

19. A few of the more recent examples: S. K. Heninger Jr., "Sidney and Serranus' Plato," in *Sidney in Retrospect: Selections from "English Literary Renaissance,"* ed. Arthur F. Kinney (Amherst: University of Massachusetts Press, 1988), argues persuasively for Sidney's use of de Serres's preface to the *Ion* in Henri Estienne's three-volume folio of Plato; M. J. B. Allen, "Sidney's *Defence* and the Image Making of Plato's Sophist," in *Sir Philip Sidney's Achievements* (New York: AMS Press, 1990), argues that Sidney could have found in the *scholion* for Plato's *Sophist* a reference to "divine phantastic art" that would have provided him with a way to reconcile icastic and phantastic poetry; having conceded, with good cause, that "one hesitates to descry yet another set of Sidneian tracks in the snow of his classical and Renaissance predecessors," Anthony Miller, in "Sidney's *Apology for Poetry* and Plutarch's *Moralia*," *English Literary Renaissance* 17 (1987), goes on to show how Sidney formulated many of his points by differing with the less lively formulations of arguments in Amyot's preface to his translation of Plutarch's *Moralia*.

20. The formulation is that of Shepherd, ed., *Apology*, 45.

tion of the Cusan art of conjecture. Whereas Andrew Weiner believes that Sidney espouses a humble Protestant poetics, Alan Sinfield sees Sidney "appropriating literature to earnest protestant activism." In contrast to both, S. K. Heninger Jr. believes that Sidney models his poetics on Pythagorean and Platonic cosmogonies. Calling into question the unity of the *Apology*, O. B. Hardison argues that two conflicting poetics, humanist and neoclassical, can be found, unresolved, in the *Apology*. This puts him at odds with Kenneth Myrick, who in his much earlier study argues that the unity of the *Apology* is to be found not in its content but in its rhetorical form.[21] Following Myrick's approach, others argue that the unifying principle of the *Apology* is Sidney's persona, which becomes the real substance, the real interest and novelty of the rhetorical performance. More recently, New Historicist studies have focused on the same performative elements but analyzed them from psychological or sociological perspectives, emphasizing the role of social and political pressures in shaping Sidney's performance.[22]

21. Forrest G. Robinson, *The Shape of Things Known: Sidney's "Apology" in Its Philosophical Tradition* (Cambridge, Mass.: Harvard University Press, 1972); Ronald Lee Levao, *Renaissance Minds and Their Fictions: Cusanus, Sidney, Shakespeare* (Berkeley and Los Angeles: University of California Press, 1985); Andrew D. Weiner, *Sir Philip Sidney and the Poetics of Protestantism: A Study of Contexts* (Minneapolis: University of Minnesota Press, 1978); Sinfield, "The Cultural Politics of the Defence of Poetry," 124; S. K. Heninger Jr., *Touches of Sweet Harmony: Pythagorean Cosmology and Renaissance Poetics* (San Marino, Calif.: Huntington Library, 1974); Hardison, "The Two Voices of Sidney's *Apology for Poetry*;" and Myrick, *Sir Philip Sidney as a Literary Craftsman*, 46–83. Also see John O. Hayden, *Polestar of the Ancients: The Aristotelian Tradition in Classical and English Literary Criticism* (Newark: University of Delaware Press, 1979), 100–117, who, in contrast to Hardison, describes the intertwining of humanist and neoclassical elements in the *Apology*.

22. See John Hunt, "Allusive Coherence in Sidney's *Apology for Poetry*," *Studies in English Literature* 27 (1987); Martin N. Raitiere, "The Unity of Sidney's *Apology for Poetry*," *Studies in English Literature* 21 (1981); and Catherine Barnes, "The Hidden Persuader: The Complex Speaking Voice of Sidney's *Defence of Poetry*," *PMLA* 86 (1971). An early and influential historicist study is that of Margaret W. Ferguson, *Trials of Desire: Renaissance Defenses of Poetry* (New Haven, Conn.: Yale University Press, 1983), 150–51, who interprets the *Apology* as "a work of quasi-autobiographical allegory" in which Sidney's defense of poetry is really a defense of himself. William Craft, in *Labyrinth of Desire: Invention and Culture in the Work of Sir Philip Sidney* (Newark: University of Delaware Press, 1994), seeks to explain Sidney's poetics in terms of the cultural constraints of Tudor society. Berry, in "The Poet as Warrior," employs the methods of

This brief survey of the criticism not only reveals the wide array of interpretations, it also confirms the conclusion that although Sidney obviously cannot be attempting all of the things the critics see him doing, what he does accomplish has a sophistication that can sustain multiple weighty interpretations. Perhaps the conflicting opinions confirm Shepherd's judgment that "nothing that Sidney writes is trivial," and, moreover, that "his articulations are moments of European self-consciousness."[23] If Sidney's *Apology* does in fact articulate "moments of European self-consciousness," it may also be that the larger interpretive frames—from the Cusan art of conjecture to Ramist visual epistemology to Protestant logocentrism to Renaissance self-fashioning—are not large enough. Indeed, all of these examine the *Apology* exclusively in relation to its cultural antecedents (or, in the case of the New Historicists, in relation to contemporary material culture). Seen in these terms, Sidney's theory cannot help but look derivative rather than original.

An important study that does treat the *Apology* as original, analyzing it not in terms of its sources but *as* a source, is Meyer Abrams's work on the origins of poetic creativity, *The Mirror and the Lamp*. Although quite old now, its argument about the *Apology* has not yet been superseded. Tracing the history of the shift from poetry understood as imitation to poetry understood as creation, Abrams argues that the poet of Sidney's *Apology*, though not yet creative by romantic standards, is practicing an art that does more than imitate nature. Finding that the poet's mind is adequately characterized neither as a mirror

---

New Historicism to argue that "Sidney's persona embodies the predicament of the generation that Stone describes [in *The Crisis of the Aristocracy*]": "'Trained for war yet reduced to writing poetry, [Sidney] attempts to vindicate his new role as poet by projecting upon it the vanishing ideals of his class and holding the court responsible for their loss" (161–62). Similarly, Matz, in "Heroic Diversions," sees Sidney attempting to reconcile activist Protestantism with courtly culture by means of "a nostalgic version of feudal warrior service" (86–87). Offering a feminist perspective on the *Apology* in early modern culture, Mary Ellen Lamb, in "Apologizing for Pleasure in Sidney's *Apology for Poetry*: The Nurse of Abuse Meets the Tudor Grammar School," *Criticism* 36 (1994), argues that Sidney's work "recapitulates" the larger cultural effort to "transform androgynous boys into virile leaders of men" (515, 508).

23. Shepherd, ed., *Apology*, 11.

nor as a lamp, Abrams must come up with a separate category for Sidney. The category he offers is one in which the poem is a "heterocosm, 'a second nature,' created by the poet in an act analogous to God's creation of the world" (272). Although it would seem to follow that Sidney's theory does therefore qualify as a theory of poetic creativity—indeed, Abrams notes that Sidney invokes as a model for his poetics "the Hebraic account of a creation *ex nihilo* by fiat"—he does not believe that Sidney's theory counts. The unstated reason lies in Abrams's identification of the power of "creativity" with the faculty of the "imagination," a faculty apparently absent in the *Apology*, where Sidney speaks not of imagination but of the poet's "wit." For Abrams, there is no full-fledged theory of poetic creativity until the eighteenth century's "psychologizing" of poetic theory, which "took the creative act indoors and delegated it to the faculty of imagination."[24] With his focus on the "creative imagination," Abrams overlooks the fact that although the word "imagination" does not appear in the *Apology*, the idea is virtually present in the sixteenth-century notion of "wit" that Sidney employs. Etymologically kin to *video*, "wit" preserves the association, perhaps as old as the human race, of sight and knowledge. In the sixteenth century, it still encompasses both reason and imagination, and only with Bacon does "wit" begin to be associated with reason *against* imagination. It easily could be argued that the romantic project of reconciling analytic reason with imagination is essentially an attempt to recover what was lost when the wit was broken into reason and imagination.[25]

Given Abrams's identification of the significance of the *Apology* within the development of poetic creativity, it is surprising that Sidney scholars do not have more frequent recourse to the idea of creativity. Of course, there are reasons for this. One is the daunting scope and

24. *The Mirror and the Lamp: Romantic Theory and the Critical Tradition* (New York: Norton, 1958), 274, 75. According to Abrams, it is Addison's "The Pleasures of Imagination" that "compounds" the "suggestions" of Sidney and others and makes them "strongly effective in the critical tradition."

25. On the decay of "wit" into "reason" and "imagination," or "fancy," as it was called, see Edward Tayler, introduction to *Literary Criticism of Seventeenth-Century England*, ed. Edward Tayler (New York: Knopf, 1967), 3–32.

complexity of the topic. Even if a critic sees the connection between Sidney's poetics and the growth of the idea of human creativity, it still is prudent to ask whether a heavy investment in the history of ideas is justified by Sidney's brief and elusive treatment of the topic. Understandably, critics can feel that they need not puzzle out the details of a theory that Sidney himself never fully articulated.[26] The rewards, however, justify the effort, for the *Apology* is in fact far more than a delightful compendium of Renaissance literary theory or an amiable polemic motivated by merely personal or programmatic considerations.

Although Sidney's style is modest, indeed often self-deprecating, his claims are larger and bolder than those of Pico or Vives. Indirectly rather than directly, with an art that hides art, the *Apology* presents a vision of human nature that, while deeply Christian and deeply Neoplatonic, is also new. In comparing the *Apology* to such seminal works as Pico's *Oration* and Vives's *Fable about Man*, I do not wish to turn Sidney's poetics into one more example of a favorite Renaissance topos, the God-like dignity of human beings.[27] Nor do I wish to situate the *Apology* within the often-told story of the "Renaissance discovery of man." Quite the contrary, my aim is to show that when the *Apology* is properly understood, the old story of the "Renaissance discovery of man," with its several variations, cannot stand. Mine is not a Whig interpretation of the history of creativity. Rather than presenting the *Apology* simply as part of a larger intellectual movement, or as a step toward a well-known cultural destination, the following chapters will show that Sidney was interested in destinations of which we are unaware, ends that once were thought to be the essence of creativity but now have been lost to us. Stripping away the veneer of teleology and timeworn generalizations by attending to the language of the *Apology*, I hope to show that, understood on its own terms, the *Apology* presents an idea of creativity that is, even today, original.

26. One notable exception, however, is S. K. Heninger, who identifies important sources for Sidney's locutions. As will become clear in the course of this study, though I draw different conclusions I am greatly indebted to Heninger's work.

27. For ample selections from Italian humanists on the topic, see Charles Trinkaus, *"In Our Image and Likeness": Humanity and Divinity in Italian Humanist Thought*, 2 vols. (Chicago: University of Chicago Press, 1970).

CHAPTER I

THE HISTORY OF CREATIVITY

Locating a single point of origin for an idea is generally difficult if not impossible. Finding that an original idea was anticipated in an earlier period I take to be commonplace. In the case of the Renaissance discovery of human creativity, it might be argued, for example, that Plato's *Symposium* and *Ion*, works of great importance to Ficino's Platonic Academy, present far earlier theories of human creativity. The differences between Plato and his followers are, however, no less important than their similarities. If one acknowledges what separates as well as what unites, the *Symposium* is rightly understood to be about intellectual fertility and *pro*creation, which, though related, is distinct from intellectual creativity. And the poetic fury of the *Ion*, presented with an irony that the Renaissance largely missed, also stands at some distance from any proper understanding of human creativity. Although Plato's accounts of the erotic ascent to the World of Ideas gives the lover access to beauty and truth, neither truth nor beauty for him is the invention of the lover. They are timeless and, in a word, uncreated. Although the *Symposium*, and Ficino's commentary on it, fired the minds of Renaissance Neoplatonists, what those minds produced was a theory of originality that also drew on the more radical Christian doctrine of *creatio ex nihilo*. This idea of humans creating out of nothing had not yet been born—nor had its absence even been felt—in the time of Plato.

Like these ancient anticipations of the Renaissance discovery of human creativity, those of the Middle Ages are instructive chiefly for the contrast they provide. Although medieval poets and artists could and did compare their work to the divine work of creation, examples

18   The History of Creativity

from the period show something fundamentally different from human creativity as conceived in later ages. Whereas the medieval thinkers time and again represent God as a poet and the world as his book, they do not reverse the analogy and speak of the human poet as a God-like creator or of poems as creations. Although they attribute their own powers of art to God, as a rule they do not claim his creative powers for themselves.[1] This is not to say that before the Renaissance people were not creative, but only that they did not think—or at least did not speak—of themselves as such.

The exceptions are few and isolated. The earliest of which I am aware is found in the commentaries of the medieval canonists. As Ernst Kantorowicz has shown, in explaining the legal powers of the pope, the canonists attribute to him the twin powers of creation and annihilation. The establishment of an ecclesiastical jurisdiction or the declaration of an illegitimate person or act to be legitimate would be examples of creation. Rendering a legitimate ruling or title null and void would be annihilation.[2] Certainly significant, this application of the power of creation to human beings is obviously quite limited, being reserved for the pope and used only in legal matters.

Another exception to the rule is found in the philosophy of Nicholas of Cusa. Working out the consequences of the doctrine of man as a microcosm, Cusa found that the human being is "another god," who rules over the earth as God rules over the universe. Whereas the Scholastics accepted the Aristotelian understanding of art as an imitation of nature, Cusa believed in the autonomy of art, an autonomy mirroring the absolute power and freedom of God the creator. Just as creation was an act of "unfolding," whereby the complexity and

---

1. See Robert Hanning, "'Ut Enim Faber . . . Sic Creator': Divine Creation as Context for Human Creativity in the Twelfth Century," in *Word, Picture, and Spectacle*, ed. Clifford Davidson, (Kalamazoo: Medieval Institute Publications/Western Michigan University, 1984), who cites some of the most daring examples of the comparison of divine creation to human art. Though daring, none goes so far as to attribute creation to human beings.

2. "The Sovereignty of the Artist: A Note on Legal Maxims and Renaissance Theories of Art," in *Essays in Honor of Erwin Panofsky*, ed. Millard Meiss (New York: New York University Press, 1961).

variety of creation proceeded logically, even geometrically, from the absolutely simple Idea in the mind of God, so too human art is an unfolding: "The mind, having the free faculty of conceiving, finds within itself the art of unfolding its conceptions." Cusa holds up "potters, sculptors, painters, turners, metal-workers, weavers, and similar artisans" as examples of those who "possess this art." Although humble, these examples all illustrate originality, since the source of the artifact is the mind, and the mind alone. Cusa's famous and homely example of creativity is the spoon maker, who follows no model in nature:

> Outside of the exemplar in our mind [*extra mentis nostrae ideam*], the spoon has no other exemplar [*exemplar*]. For although the sculptor or painter takes exemplars from the things that he wishes to represent, I however do not. I bring forth spoons and bowls from wood and jars from mud. Indeed in doing this, I imitate the forms of no natural thing. In fact such forms as spoons, bowls, and jars are made by human art alone. Hence my art is more of a perfection than an imitation of created forms, and in this it is more similar to the infinite art.[3]

In what unquestionably constitutes a claim for human creativity, Cusa emphasizes the originality of what comes into being. The spoon, he thinks, has no model, no precedent in nature. Art here is not completing what is lacking in nature or discovering what is hidden in it; rather, it is bringing forth something never before seen—just as God brought forth something unprecedented when he created nature.

Despite the obvious differences between the technical and Scholastic legal thought of the canonists and the esoteric metaphysical speculation of Cusa, in both is evident the common influence of late medieval voluntarism. Just as the followers of Ockham emphasize the absolute freedom of God, denying that he is bound by any higher

---

3. From *De mente*, in *Opera Omnia*, ed. L. Baur (Leipzig, Germany: Meiner, 1937), 5.51, as quoted and translated by Pauline Moffitt Watts, in *Nicolaus Cusanus: A Fifteenth-Century Vision of Man* (Leiden, The Netherlands: E. J. Brill, 1982), 135–36. See William Bouwsma, "The Renaissance Discovery of Human Creativity," in *Humanity and Divinity in the Renaissance and Reformation: Essays in Honor of Charles Trinkaus*, ed. John W. O'Malley, Thomas M. Izbicki, and Gerald Christianson (Leiden, The Netherlands: E. J. Brill, 1993), 30, who also discusses this passage.

norms, whether ethical or metaphysical, so too the canonists hold that the pope, as God's vicar, is in certain respects above the law. And similarly, Cusa holds that artists are not bound by preexisting forms, any more than God is bound in creation. Whereas the norms established by Aristotle and affirmed by the Scholastic systematizers had been that both art and the law imitate nature, with Cusa and the canonists art and the law are freed from nature as a norm and model.

This more existential approach is carried forth in the speculation of the Florentine humanists. Indeed, their emphasis on the act of existence is a characteristic feature of the Italian literary theory from which Sidney borrowed heavily. Recognizing that the most radical fact about a thing is not its essence but its existence—not *what* it is, but rather *that* it is—the Italian theorists were more sensitive to, and often fascinated by, the artifact's relation to nonbeing. In his *Commentary on Dante* (1481), Cristoforo Landino sees as a sign of the dignity of the poet that his work "departs from making and comes very near to creating," which is to say that the work is composed almost though "not entirely out of nothing." Showing no interest in the theory of divine Ideas, Landino is interested in the material—or, more precisely, the lack thereof—out of which the work is formed:

> And the Greeks say "poet" from the verb "piin" [sic], which is half-way between "creating," which is peculiar to God when out of nothing he brings forth anything into being, and "making," which applies to men when they compose with matter and form in any art. It is for this reason that, although the feigning of the poet is not entirely out of nothing, it nevertheless departs from making and comes very near to creating.[4]

---

4. *Opere di Dante degli Alighieri . . . col Comento di Cristoforo Landini* (Vinegia, 1484), "Preface," fol. a [vii]v, as quoted and translated by Abrams, in *The Mirror and the Lamp*, 273. Landino repeats this argument in his commentaries on Horace (1482) and Virgil (1487), in both cases emphasizing the ability of the poet to make a poem "nearly out of nothing." Landino's claim that "ποιέω" (his odd transliteration, which many have remarked, is "piin") "is half-way between 'creating' . . . and 'making'" is mistaken. He amends his argument, however, in his *Commentary on Virgil*, and instead of presenting ποιέω as between creating and making, he calls ποιέω ambiguous, meaning "now to make something out of something, now to create out of nothing" (*Publius Vergilius Maro, Opera* [Venice, 1491], fol. 70r ff., as quoted by E. N. Tigerstedt, in "The Poet as Creator: Origins of a Metaphor," *Comparative Literature Studies* [1968]: 459, who points

The History of Creativity   21

Landino has in mind the analogy between divine creation and poetic quasi-creation:

> God is the supreme poet, and the world is his poem. And as God organizes creation, *idest*, the visible and invisible world which is his work, with a recourse to number, measure, and weight, and therefore the prophet said *Deus omnia fecit numero, mensura et pondo*, so the poets with the number of the feet, the measure of brief and long syllables and the weight of the maxims and of the sentiments compose their poems.[5]

In his *Commentary on Virgil*, Landino gives a less striking but more detailed explanation of the essence of poetic creativity, as he understands it. Although God is a poet, it does not follow for Landino that the poet is God:

> For God produces out of nothing whatsoever He will, which we call "create." But men, on the contrary, are not able to make anything but out of given matter. The Poet, however, though he does not quite make a poem without any matter—for Virgil chose to sing of the misfortunes and wars of Aeneas—nevertheless, thanks to the story which holds the whole work together, he, covertly and cunningly, includes into this story, nearly out of nothing, the deepest meanings. They, however, who perceive them, understand how a man born to glory, purified step by step from folly and various faults, can attain the Supreme Good.[6]

For Landino, the reader should not look to the quasi-historical facts of the life of Aeneas for the truth in the poem; rather, the "deepest meanings" will be found in the story that connects the historical facts, which is made "nearly out of nothing." For Landino, the "deepest meanings" are to be found in what is most fictitious—as Shakespeare would later have one of his wise fools put it, "the truest poetry is the most feigning." It follows that God is the "supreme poet," and that his

---

out this development in Landino's theory and suggests that it was Ficino who pointed out the earlier mistake).

5. *Scritti critici e teorici* (Rome: Bulzoni, c. 1974), 1.142, as quoted and translated by Danilo Aguzzi-Barbagli, in "Humanism and Poetics," in *Renaissance Humanism: Foundations, Forms, and Legacy*, ed. Albert Rabil Jr. (Philadelphia: University of Pennsylvania Press, 1988), 94.

6. *Opera* (Venice, 1491), fol. 70r ff., as quoted and translated by Tigerstedt, "Poet as Creator," 459.

creation—of everything out of nothing—has the deepest meanings possible since it is an uncompromised act of feigning. With Landino, the Platonic denigration of imitative art is thus turned upside-down. Whereas Plato's ontological criticism saw art as departing from reality and approaching nothingness, Landino's theory of creativity praises art for having its origin in nothing and extols the artist for taking on a resemblance to the Supreme Poet.

In his *Poetics* (1561), from which Sidney borrows heavily, Scaliger draws out conclusions implicit in Landino. Whereas Landino calls God "the supreme poet," Scaliger reverses the analogy and calls the poet "almost . . . a second deity." Like Landino, Scaliger employs many of Aristotle's strategies, such as that of opposing poetry to history, yet arrives at formulations that never would have occurred to Aristotle. Describing the ability of poetry to show forth "images more beautiful than life," Scaliger does not emphasize the universal or ideal; instead, he argues that the poet delivers "images of those things which are not." The Christian and existential character of Scaliger's thought comes through clearly in the famous passage in which he argues that, in contrast to other artists, who "represent things just as they are," the poet presents a "speaking picture" in which he

depicts quite another sort of nature [*naturam alteram*], and a variety of fortunes; in fact, by so doing, he transforms himself almost into a second deity [*Deum alterum*]. Of those things which the Maker of all framed [*opifex condidit*], the other sciences are, as it were, overseers; but since poetry fashions images of those things which are not, as well as images more beautiful than life of those things which are, it seems unlike other literary forms, such as history, which confine themselves to actual events, and rather to be another god, and to create [*sed velut alter deus condere*].[7]

---

7. Translated by F. M. Padelford in Hazard Adams, ed., *Critical Theory since Plato* (San Diego, Calif.: Harcourt, 1971), 140–41. The original is available in Julius Caesar Scaliger, *Poetices Libri Septem* (Stuttgart, Germany: Friedrich Frommann Verlag, 1964), 3: "*Sola poesis haec omnia complexa est, tanto quam artes illae excellentius, quod caeterae (vt dicebamus) res ipsas, vti sunt, representant, veluti aurium pictura quadam. at poeta & naturam alteram, & fortunas plures etiam: ac demum sese isthoc ipso perinde ac Deum alterum efficit. Nam quae omnium opifex condidit, eorum reliquae scientiae tamquam actores sunt: Poetica vero quum & speciosius que sunt, & quae non sunt, eorum speciem ponit: videtur fane res*

Not tied to "actual events," the poet depicts "another sort of nature," and in so doing "transforms himself almost into a second deity," that is, "another god," *"alter deus."* The poet has the power not only to imitate a subject but to produce things that do not yet exist. It should be noted that the postromantic translation of Scaliger's Latin uses "create" rather freely, since Scaliger himself employs not *"creare"* but *"condere,"* which might more accurately be rendered "to found" or, as is the case earlier in the same paragraph, "to frame." Like Sidney, Scaliger shows lexical restraint while at the same time praising the poet by noting that as a "Maker," his name, by providential design, is the title of God.

Sidney's debt to this passage in Scaliger has often been noted. The "speaking picture," the rivalry of the Sister Arts, and the notion of the poet as a second deity producing ideal images "more beautiful than life" all inform Sidney's theory of poetry. Sidney's claim for the poet is, however, more radical than that of Scaliger, whose interest is more purely literary. Whereas Scaliger emphasizes the excellence of the poet as an artist, surpassing other "literary forms," Sidney makes a broader claim for the excellence of the poet as a human being. Taking up as a premise the idea that the poet is a "maker" "made" by the "heavenly Maker," Sidney claims God-like powers for the poet even beyond what Scaliger bestowed. Created in God's "own likeness," the poet not only "bringeth things forth far surpassing" what is found in the natural world, he does so "with the force of a divine breath" (100–101). This "divine breath" of Sidney's "maker" evokes both creation narratives in Genesis: in the first, God sends his "Spirit" over the waters; in the second, God breathes the breath of life into Adam's nostrils. Reserving for later chapters a fuller explanation of these claims for the poet, as well as further justification for my interpretation, it is enough here to see that in drawing an analogy between poetic making and divine making, Sidney attributes to poetry a forcefulness not less than that of the Holy Spirit.

---

ipsas, non vt aliae, quasi Histrio, narrare, sed velut alter deus condere: vnde cum eo commune nomen ipsi non a consensu hominum, sed a naturae prouidenta inditum videatur."

Needless to say, this assertion of the divine effectiveness of poetry goes far beyond the most daring claims of the Italian theorists. It also is a far bolder claim than that of Sidney's contemporary Puttenham, who, though he employs the word "create," feels compelled to add that he is only speaking figuratively, "by maner of speech."[8] Equally important for the present discussion, Sidney's assertion that poetry has the power of the Holy Spirit, the power to bestow grace on audiences, is something that few Sidney scholars have understood, and even fewer granted. Foremost among those who simply cannot believe that Sidney could believe such a thing is Andrew Weiner, who attributes to Sidney a severe Calvinism incompatible with such a position.[9] Of course, Weiner and those who also embrace his disbelief have great difficulty explaining away Sidney's claim for the power of poetry. What forces them into this interpretive bind is that they mistake both Sidney's brand of Christianity—which, as Robert Stillman has definitively demonstrated, is not a strict Calvinism at all—and also the theological tradition that Catholic and Protestant Christians alike inherited.[10]

Sidney was hardly the first to believe that human beings have a God-like potential. On the contrary, his claim that the poet is a "maker" whom the "Heavenly Maker" "made . . . to His own likeness" invokes a tradition that extends back through Renaissance humanists, Scholastic philosophers, and Church Fathers into the deepest roots of the Hellenistic and Hebraic traditions.[11] Along with the literary-historical tradition of imitation, a recognition of this theological tradition of the *imago dei* is necessary for a proper understanding of Sidney's claim for poetic making. Sidney's literary innovation is also a radical theological innovation, and neither the literary nor the theological aspect of Sidney's theory can be understood apart from the other.

8. See the previous chapter for a more detailed discussion of Puttenham's use of the term "create."
9. *Poetics of Protestantism*. See also Sinfield, "The Cultural Politics of the *Defence of Poetry*," who relies on Weiner.
10. "Deadly Stinging Adders: Sidney's Piety, Philippism, and the *Defence of Poesy*."
11. See Jules Gross, *La Divinisation du Chrétien d'après les Pères Grecs* (Paris: Librairie Lecoffre, 1938), for the most thorough study to date of the bifurcate background.

The obvious origin of this theological tradition is the creation narrative in the first chapter of Genesis, where the absolutely transcendent God, who so far surpasses his creation that his very name is not to be uttered, creates an "image" of himself. From this point on, there can be seen a running, sometimes systematic, commentary on the idea of man as made in the image of God. In the Christian Scriptures, notable developments are found in several passages of St. Paul. Attending to the "glory" of the "image," Paul develops, quite fully, an anthropology in terms of light and reflection: "But we all, with open face beholding as in a glass the glory of the Lord, are changed into the same image from glory to glory even as by the Spirit of the Lord."[12] This elaborate mirror trick results in a participation in the divine, a spiritual regeneration of human nature that the Fathers of the Eastern Church not infrequently referred to as "deification."

Among the Church Fathers who developed the idea of deification, Gregory of Nyssa stands out in the East, whereas Augustine commands the field in the Latin West. Both make use of Paul's specular device, which by their time had already assimilated the Greek idea of the visible world as an imitation or reflection of the invisible intelligible world.[13] The Greek Fathers go further with the Platonic distinction, especially its denigration of material existence. For Gregory, although human nature is the mirror in which the image of God can be seen, that image is darkened and defaced by involvement in temporal existence. The purification of the soul from sin and from material attachments is like the polishing of the mirror, so that its original clarity and brightness is restored. In contrast, for Augustine, although vestiges of the triune God can be seen in all of creation, the "rational or

---

12. 2 Cor 3:18. See also Col 1:15 and 2 Cor 4:4, where it can be seen that the "glory of the Lord" is the creative light that first shone in the darkness and that now is visible in the sanctified human person. Reflected in human persons this glory transforms them into the image of Christ, who in turn is the "image of the invisible God."

13. On the convergence of Pauline and Platonic traditions in the three great Cappadocian Fathers, Basil, Gregory of Nyssa, and Gregory of Nazianzus, see Jaroslav Pelikan, *Christianity and Classical Culture: The Metamorphosis of Natural Theology in the Christian Encounter with Hellenism* (New Haven, Conn.: Yale University Press, 1993), 120–35.

intellectual creature which is made after the image of God" is like a "glass" in which human beings can behold, as clearly as is possible in this world, "the Trinity which is God, in our own memory, understanding, and will."[14] In this theological anthropology can be seen a more general, and what will prove to be more lasting, contribution. Confirming by the example of his own work the Pauline doctrine that we can "behold and understand His invisible things . . . by those things which are made," Augustine establishes a method of reasoning by analogy from the visible to the invisible, from the creature to the Creator, and specifically from God's image to God's nature.[15]

To appreciate Sidney's theological innovation, it is necessary to understand how the recourse to the analogy of God and human beings became a basic tool of speculative theology in the Latin West. In their development of the Augustinian synthesis, the Schoolmen greatly refine this analogical method. Instead of searching for traces of the three divine persons throughout creation, Aquinas develops a far more subtle theory of the "analogy of being" *(analogia entis)*, which understands the contingent being of creatures as a participation in the absolute being of God. With the support of this metaphysical framework, which ensures that all claims for the similarity of creatures to the Creator (e.g., the resemblance between the beauty of a creature and the beauty of God) are properly qualified with a recognition of the absolute disproportion between the finite and the infinite, Aquinas is able to be more bold than Augustine, who never asserted the resemblance of creatures to God without, almost in the same breath, protesting that God, because of his divine transcendence, is much more different than similar to any of his creatures.[16]

---

14. *De Trinitate* 15.20.39, in Philip Schaff, ed., *Nicene and Post-Nicene Fathers (First Series)*, 14 vols. (Peabody, Mass.: Hendrickson, 1994), 3.220–21; hereafter *Nicene and Post-Nicene Fathers* will be abbreviated as NFPF.

15. *De Trinitate* 15.20.39. Augustine is alluding to Rom 1:20: "For the invisible things of him from the creation of the world are clearly seen, being understood by the things that are made."

16. See, e.g., *De Trinitate* 15.20.39: "But I have warned him [who speculates on the divine nature] . . . that he should discern in that likeness, of whatever sort it be, a great unlikeness also." Aquinas also modifies Augustine's idea of the soul, with the same

With this strong sense of the analogy of God and human beings firmly established, Sidney and other Renaissance authors extend the speculative method by turning it on its head. Rather than looking to creatures in order to learn about God—St. Paul's recommended method—they look to God in order to learn about creatures. That the inversion of this or any analogy should lead to new insights is admittedly far from obvious. Indeed, one might suspect that it would almost certainly result in circular reasoning. But history indicates otherwise. In cases in which the inversion of an analogy is preceded and followed by long enough stretches of time, new insights are in fact discovered. It was the formidable body of sacred science that had been built up over the centuries that allowed Renaissance philosophers and then poets to discover, implicit within their theological patrimony, the Godlike qualities of human beings.

In Renaissance England, the continuity with the earlier Scholastic speculative method—as well as a fundamental alteration in its application—is nowhere as evident as in the poetry of John Donne. Adept at manipulating the theological tradition for effect, Donne makes theological sophistication the price of admission for anyone who would understand his poetry. Like Augustine, Donne is able to use human realities to understand divine realities, presenting divine love in human terms. However, he also frequently shows human love to be something divine.[17] Whereas Donne did much to divinize human love, oth-

---

effect of strengthening the analogy of God and human beings. Turning from Augustine's tripartite conception of the soul to the soul endowed with reason and will, which he found in William of Moerbeke's translation of Aristotle's *De anima*, Aquinas sees that these powers of knowing (intellect) and loving (will) explain the spiritual activity not only of human beings but also of God (*Summa theologiae*, ed. Thomas Gilby [New York: McGraw-Hill, 1964], Ia, q. 27, aa. 2–3). Applying human psychology to the Divinity, Aquinas infers nothing less than an explanation for the procession of the persons of the Holy Trinity: the generation of the Son takes place through God knowing himself, and the generation of the Holy Spirit takes place through God loving himself. Thus, even while abandoning Augustine's elaborate taxonomies of created trinities and shifting away from triadic and toward dyadic formulations for human and divine psychology, Aquinas preserves and enhances Augustine's central insight into the analogy of God and the human soul.

17. An example of the former would be his famous sonnet "Batter my heart three-personed God." Although many examples could be cited to illustrate the latter (the

ers occupied themselves with the divinization of the intellect. Medieval writers, finding it highly suggestive to think of the divine intellect in human terms, had spoken of God as a poet, and the world as his poem. Renaissance authors, reversing the flow of thought, imagine how the poet is like God the Creator and how the poem is, in Donne's words, "a little world made cunningly," or in Sidney's, a "golden" world. Although Sidney does not put his theology on display in the way Donne does, the theological substance of his claim for the poet is no less important. Whereas the medievals used the analogy to make discoveries about God's creative goodness and the poetic order of nature, Sidney uses the analogy to discover the poet's creative goodness and the divine efficacy of human art.

Before Sidney and Donne, the inversion of the master analogy can be seen in the seminal works of Renaissance humanism. As is well known, works such as Pico's *Oration* and Vives's *Fable of Man* present human nature as essentially Protean. What is less often recognized in their theological anthropology is that in resembling all things and having no fixed nature of its own, humanity resembles God.[18] In this Christian and Neoplatonic existentialism can be seen a transposition of the existentialism of Aquinas. Whereas Aquinas frees God from all constraint by identifying his essence with his existence, Pico and Vives loosen the constraint of reductive definitions of human nature.[19] Ini-

---

first to come to mind might be "The Canonization" and "The Extasie"), one worthy of more attention is "The Relique," in which Donne uses the method of apophatic theology—designed for speculating on the nature of the inscrutable God—in order to describe his lover.

18. See Giovanni Pico Della Mirandola, "Oration on the Dignity of Man," in *The Renaissance Philosophy of Man*, ed. Ernst Cassirer, Paul Oskar Kristeller, and John Herman Randall (Chicago: University of Chicago Press, 1965): "And if, happy in the lot of no created thing, he [man] withdraws into the center of his own unity, his spirit, made one with God, in the solitary darkness of God, who is set above all things, shall surpass them all" (225); and, in the same volume, Juan Luis Vives, "A Fable about Man": "As he [Jupiter] of gods the greatest, embracing all things in his might, is all things, they [the other gods] saw man, Jupiter's mime, be all things also" (389).

19. Although too much has been made of the role of the late Scholastic emphasis on divine freedom in the birth of modernity, it is true that the existential freedom of man is modeled on an analogous freedom, long recognized, in God.

tially, it would appear that Sidney is far more modest in his claims than were Pico and Vives. For Sidney, man is neither a "chameleon" nor a "great amphibium." Nor is humanity capable of ascending the Great Chain of Being, passing through the angelic realm to the identification with God as a pure spirit. Nevertheless, Sidney's claim, properly understood, is no less bold. As subsequent chapters should make clear, Sidney sets his poet on an even higher peak than Pico's magus. Of the wonders worked through magic, none shows forth divine power more fully than poetry, as Sidney conceives it, which not only mirrors the Incarnation by providing humanity an ideal model for imitation, but also resembles grace in its ability to move humanity to embrace the good it presents.

In general, Renaissance authors who elicit admiration for humanity have no interest in denigrating the divine nature. On the contrary, they see man's marvelous nature as a sign of the goodness of the God who created it. As Sidney says, the greatness of the human "maker" is reason to "give right honour to the heavenly Maker" (101). This Christian humanism, in which the glory of human beings gives glory to God, is obviously quite different from today's secular humanism. In the newer version, the analogy between God and human beings has vanished into identity, and the glory of human beings is seen as all their own. With God marginalized, the way of seeing the world is changed: no longer is analogy a captivating tool for thought. Although many would characterize this change as a liberation of human thought, it is, arguably, an impoverishment. In merging the human and the divine, secularism bears an odd resemblance to the earlier phenomenon of anthropomorphism. This earlier, though hardly extinct, tendency to think of God (or the gods) too much in human terms mirrors the modern tendency to think of human beings as supreme. In both cases, what is lost is the willingness, if not the ability, to see similarity between the human and divine while still recognizing fundamental differences and giving each its due.

Although recourse to analogy became less habitual after the Renaissance, in later periods there also can be seen attempts, from time to time, to reclaim the proper use of analogy as a tool for thinking. In

England, after the French Revolution, just such an effort was mounted by those referred to, for the sake of convenience, as the romantic poets. Writing at a time of crisis, in which a rupture between the real and the ideal was acutely felt by some, the romantic poets strove, each in his own way, to reunite ordinary and elevated experience. Like Sidney, they did not confine their theorizing to the art of poetry. Rather, they gave human nature—and its relation to the transcendent—as much prominence as technical matters, engaging in what amounts to poetic and theological anthropology. Of course, the great stretch of history—economic and political as well as intellectual—that stands between Sidney and the romantics makes comparison all but impossible. Much of what most concerned the romantics was unknown to Sidney—from the social problems arising from industrialization to the philosophical problems arising from empiricist epistemologies. Nevertheless, there also were fundamental similarities uniting the periods. Like the Renaissance, the romantic period was a time of enthusiastic rediscoveries of Neoplatonism, naturalism, and humanism—perennial and Protean movements that have contributed to intellectual flourishing in other periods as well. Although the romantic poets looked to and "romanticized" the Middle Ages, their continuity with the Renaissance is at least as important. Indeed, their true affinity is seen nowhere more clearly than in their common exaltation of the genius of Shakespeare, Spenser, and Milton. Perhaps the similarity and difference can best be seen together in the romantics' attempt to reclaim the ability, seriously atrophied by the end of the eighteenth century, to see the world analogically.

The romantics' wish to reclaim analogy is particularly clear in their thinking about poetic creativity. Looking back to the Renaissance, Shelley cites "the bold and true word" of Tasso: *"Non merita nome di creatore, se non Iddio ed il Poeta* [None deserves the name of Creator except God and the Poet]."[20] Although one might assume that Shelley

20. *Shelley's Poetry and Prose: Authoritative Texts, Criticism*, ed. Donald H. Reiman and Sharon B. Powers (New York: Norton, 1977), 505–6. Shelley is recalling not the exact words but the substance of Tasso's *Discorsi del poema eroico* (1594). Thinking of creation as drawing order out of chaos, Shelley claims that poetry "makes us the inhabi-

invokes Tasso to claim creative power for the poet, his purpose, rather, is to deny it to any but God and the poet. Shelley realized that what once seemed extraordinary—that the human mind can create—had come to be taken for granted. Coleridge was particularly well aware of how poetic theory had invaded theology and made some of its terms its own. Like Shelly, he reacts to the indiscriminant use of "creation." Contrasting the higher *"modifying* Power" of the "Imagination" with the merely *"aggregating* power" of the "Fancy," Coleridge praises the imagination as "a dim Analogue of Creation." The word "dim" in this formulation is particularly important. Writing at a time when the analogy between human and divine powers was, he thought, too readily granted, Coleridge saw fit to draw attention to the shadowy quality of human creation alongside that of God.[21]

Sidney's concern, it should be noted, was just the opposite: he was not afraid that the analogy would be taken for granted but that it might "be deemed too saucy a comparison." Whereas Sidney knew he would face resistance if he were "to balance the highest point of man's wit with the efficacy of Nature," Coleridge did not see any reason to hesitate in calling Shakespeare "nature humanized." Whereas Coleridge wanted to restore nuance to the analogy of poetry and creation, Sidney was simply hoping that some might not dismiss the comparison out of hand. Although standing at opposite ends of an arc extending from the emergence of poetic creativity as a questionable innovation to its retrieval from the scrap heap of worn-out metaphors and commonplace ideas, Sidney and Coleridge think of poetry in very similar terms. Both rely on the analogy of God and human beings. For Coleridge the mind is "made in God's Image, and that, too, in the sublimest sense, the *Image of the Creator.*"[22] Quite explicit about the Chris-

---

tants of a world to which the familiar world is a chaos" and "creates anew the universe after it has been annihilated in our minds by the recurrence of impressions blunted by reiteration."

21. In a letter to Richard Sharp, dated 15 January 1804, Coleridge writes that the imagination is "not all that we can *believe* but all that we can *conceive* of creation" (Samuel Taylor Coleridge, *Imagination in Coleridge*, ed. John Spencer Hill [Totowa, N.J.: Rowman & Littlefield, 1978], 50).

22. Letter to Thomas Poole, 23 March 1801, in Coleridge, *Imagination in Coleridge,*

tian theological underpinnings of his poetics, Coleridge calls the primary imagination, of which the secondary is "an echo," "the living Power and prime Agent of all human Perception," "a repetition in the finite mind of the eternal act of creation in the infinite I AM."[23] Although Coleridge develops his theory of creativity much more fully than does Sidney, his starting point is the same. It is the oldest idea in the book: that man is made in the image of God.

Pivotal in the transformation of poetic imitation into poetic creativity is the idea of the imitation of God. In Sidney's transitional poetics, art is at once the mirror of nature and a mirror of the divine art of creation. When poetic creativity receives a fuller treatment in the romantic period, this double mirroring remains at the heart of creativity. As is the case with Sidney, for Wordsworth and Coleridge art still imitates nature, and the mind, though creative, is still a mirror. The difference is that the mind not only mirrors the world, but the world also mirrors the mind. Wordsworth sees "man and nature as essentially adapted to each other, and the mind of man as naturally the mirror of the fairest and most interesting properties of nature."[24] But in his version of ideal imitation, the mind, like the natural world, is active rather than passive, and the relation between the two is not static but dynamic. Escaping the older "servile imitation," which is merely a "blind copying of effects," the new understanding of poetic imitation, as described by Coleridge, achieves a "free and rival originality," and is the "true imitation of the essential principles." As Coleridge explains,

---

35. Relying on the belief that the mind is the image of God, Coleridge seeks to prove that the Imagination must be active and creative, and that Newton, a "mere materialist," must be mistaken in thinking of *"Mind"* as something "passive," "a lazy Looker-on on an external World."

23. Biographia Literaria 13, in *Imagination in Coleridge*, 126.

24. "Preface" to *Lyrical Ballads*, in *Selected Poems and Prefaces*, ed. Jack Stillinger (Boston: Houghton Mifflin, 1965), 453. The importance of the mirror in the romantics' speculations on creativity runs against the general argument of Abrams in *The Mirror and the Lamp*. These formulations indicate that the shift in epistemology—seen in the shift in the dominant metaphor for the mind, from mirror to lamp—is the effect rather than the cause of the new poetics of creativity. The fundamental cause is the new understanding of the ways in which human beings can mirror God. The birth of creativity takes place not by abandoning the image of the mirror but by doubling it.

The History of Creativity 33

these essential principles are found not in created nature, *"natura naturata,"* but in creating nature, *"natura naturans."*[25] Because the poet imitates *natura naturans,* poetic creation is thus not opposed to poetic imitation: it is its perfection. Poetic creation is imitation in its truest form.

Although Sidney does not express himself in philosophical terms, he relies on the same distinction employed by Coleridge. When Sidney makes his "saucy . . . comparison" and "balance[s]" "the highest point of man's wit with the efficacy of Nature," this efficacious "Nature" is *natura naturans.* It stands in contrast, later in the same sentence, to "that second nature" over which God gave human beings dominion. This "second nature" is, of course, the created world, *natura naturata.* For Sidney, as for Coleridge and Wordsworth, the poet imitates creating rather than created nature, and he finds creating nature not by looking to the world around him but by looking into "the mind of man." Indeed, the "wit" of Sidney's poet contains what Coleridge calls the "essential principles" of *natura naturans,* and they are crystallized in the poet's *"Idea* or fore-conceit," which Sidney believes to be the ultimate origin of the poetic work.

This *"Idea* or fore-conceit" has proved a puzzling formulation for critics. It is a formulation that is difficult to locate with any precision within the history of creativity that I have just outlined: the word "Idea" is everywhere, and "fore-conceit," Sidney's own neologism, is nowhere. To understand the term as Sidney uses it, it is necessary to locate it not only within the broad sweep of the history of creativity but also within the more local context of the history of sixteenth-century poetic theory. In the next chapter I will show how, with the "Idea or fore-conceit," Sidney synthesizes the allegorical and rhetorical traditions he inherited, refashioning them into a novel theory of fiction making.

25. *On Poesy or Art,* in *Biographia Literaria, with Aesthetic Essays,* 2 vols., ed. John Shawcross (Oxford, U.K.: Clarendon Press, 1907), 2.257–58. On Sidney's reliance on the distinction between *natura naturans* and *natura naturata,* see John Ulreich, "'The Poets Only Deliver': Sidney's Conception of Mimesis," *Studies in the Literary Imagination* 15 (1982).

CHAPTER 2

SIDNEY'S FICTION AND THE ALLEGORICAL TRADITION

In his artful defense of poetry, Sidney draws on a remarkable array of sources, an array that includes works not only from different periods and places but from divergent poetic traditions. Borrowing from his humanist predecessors, especially Boccaccio, Sidney justifies poetry by arguing that the first philosophers were poets and that Christ taught in parables. Calling on classical authorities, Sidney cites Aristotle's definition of poetry as an art of imitation, as well as Simonides' metaphorical naming of poetry as a "speaking picture." He invokes Horace's twin aims of poetry, profit and delight, which he merges with the three ends of the Ciceronian rhetorical program: teaching, delighting, and moving. Throughout the *Apology*, Sidney turns to these and other classical authorities directly, and also indirectly through his contemporary sources, most notably the authors of the Pléiade and the theorists of the Italian cinquecento, such as Fracastoro, Minturno, and especially Scaliger.

Despite the variety of available classical and contemporary influences, it can safely be said that Sidney, like other English writers in the sixteenth century, inherited two general approaches to poetic theory: the allegorical and the rhetorical.[1] The humanist tradition, looking back to Dante and Gregory the Great, was the primary conduit for allegorisis, while the continental neoclassicists revived and disseminated

---

1. See Spingarn, *A History of Literary Criticism in the Renaissance*, 166.

the rhetorical approach to poetics prevalent in antiquity.[2] Sidney draws on both traditions, and in doing so he draws them together. They are yoked in his central device for poetic making, the "*Idea* or fore-conceit." Whereas "*Idea*" comes from the realm of philosophy and suggests the more serious allegorical poetic tradition, "conceit" is drawn from the vocabulary of rhetorical invention. Uniting and transforming the characteristic features of allegorical and rhetorical poetry, Sidney formulates a theory of fiction in which the poetic work can be, like allegory, fraught with meaning for our real world and, like an oration, charged with the power to move audiences to take action in that world.

Sidney's debt to the rhetorical tradition is widely acknowledged. The extent to which sixteenth-century poetic theory draws on rhetorical theory is evident in the work of Sidney's plain-style predecessor, George Gascoigne. In his *Certayne notes of Instruction concerning the making of verse or ryme in English* (1575), Gascoigne presents a theory of poetic invention whose debt to rhetorical invention is obvious. Instructing the would-be poet to "stand most upon the excellencie of [his] Invention, & sticke [hesitate] not to studie deeply for some fine devise," Gascoigne stresses, as did many rhetorical theorists in his day, the more dialectical canons of rhetoric: invention and arrangement.[3] When he continues by saying that when these are found, "pleasant woordes will follow well inough and fast inough," he is again thinking in rhetorical terms, siding with those rhetoricians who stress *res* over *verba*. Indeed, if one did not know that the subject was poetic invention, one could just as easily assume that Gascoigne is discussing rhetorical invention.

The most memorable passage of *Certayne notes*, in which Gascoigne gives instruction on the right way and the wrong way to praise

---

2. See Wilbur Howell, *Poetics, Rhetoric, and Logic: Studies in the Basic Disciplines of Criticism* (Ithaca, N.Y.: Cornell University Press, 1975), 89–90, 105ff., whose discussion of the close alliance between poetic and rhetorical theory in Renaissance England does not overlook the very real distinctions between the methods of the poet and the orator.

3. George Gregory Smith, *Elizabethan Critical Essays*, 2 vols. (Oxford, U.K.: Clarendon Press, 1904), 1.48. I have silently emended the u/v.

a woman, could just as easily be featured in a handbook on epideictic rhetoric. In order to praise a woman, according to Gascoigne, one should not speak of her "christal eye" nor her "cherrie lippe," for these things are *"trita et obvia,"* trite and obvious. Instead of these worn-out, commonplace metaphors, Gascoigne would have the writer take an unusual and unexpected approach, such as finding a "supernaturall cause" for the lady's natural beauty, or turning her "imperfection" into perfection. These contrivances, which delight by calling attention to their own ingenuity, are a traditional staple of the rhetoric of praise and blame. Gascoigne also relies heavily on the treatment of metaphor in rhetorical handbooks in his description of the "good and fine devise" as one that finds similarity in dissimilarity in a fresh and unexpected way.[4] Perhaps nowhere is Gascoigne's alliance with the rhetorical poetics and distance from the allegorical mode more clear than when he counsels the use of allegory—not in order to convey deep truths, but to entertain audiences with the ingenuity of the invention.[5]

A comparison of Sidney and his accomplished predecessor is instructive. As a professional poet writing a technical handbook for poets, Gascoigne's primary objective is to give instruction on how to please patrons and to avoid producing what "will appear to the skilfull Reader but a tale of a tubbe." Like most followers of Horace, Gascoigne subordinates instruction to delight; in his description of the poet's principal aim as the "making of a delectable poeme," Gascoigne echoes Horace's *"delectare"* while omitting mention of *"prodesse."*[6] In contrast, Sidney stresses the didactic function of poetry. More akin to Aristotle than to Horace, he believes that the greatest pleasure comes from learning something new. In addition to delight and knowledge, Sidney adds a third end, that of moving his audience. In his desire for the poet to move his audience "to take . . . goodness in hand" and to "make them know that goodness whereunto they are moved," Sidney

---

4. See, e.g., Aristotle's *Rhetoric* 3.10–11 and the companion passage in *Poetics* 22.
5. *Elizabethan Critical Essays*, 1.48.
6. *Elizabethan Critical Essays*, 1.47. On the long tradition of confusing Horace with Aristotle, see Bernard Weinberg, *A History of Literary Criticism in the Italian Renaissance* (Chicago: University of Chicago Press, 1961), 111–55.

gives further evidence of a moral seriousness not evident in Gascoigne (103). As St. Augustine had done long before in his *De doctrina christiana*, Sidney adapts Cicero's three aims of rhetoric—to teach, to delight, and to move—for his own program of edification.[7]

Although the "fore-conceit" clearly occupies the place of the poet's invention, it cannot be explained simply in terms of the rhetorical poetics of Sidney's day. Whereas the rhetorical tradition held that the invention, or "conceit," is the key to a good oration and must precede the other stages of crafting an oration, Sidney's addition of the prefix "fore-" suggests that the poet's conceit preexists even the first stage of the rhetorical process. This suggestion is in fact confirmed later in the *Apology*, when Sidney once again intentionally flies in the face of the canons of rhetoric. Whereas the traditional rhetorical instruction sent the orator into the subject matter to see what he might discover or "come into" (the etymology of "invention"), Sidney asserts that the poet "doth not learn a conceit out of a matter, but maketh matter for a conceit" (120). Rather than relying on the traditional aids for invention, such as the topics, Sidney's poet follows the method of God, who created matter out of nothing to "figure forth" what certainly would qualify as his *"Idea* or fore-conceit"(100).[8]

Reserving for later a discussion of the relationship between the Ideas of God and those of the poet, I presently wish to examine a different association, that of Sidney's *"Idea* or fore-conceit" with allegorical poetics. A number of learned studies of the allegorical tradition find Sidney indebted to it, from Rosemund Tuve's *Allegorical Imagery*, published almost four decades ago, to recent works by Mindele Anne Treip and Kenneth Borris.[9] These works have not, however, convinced

7. On Augustine's earlier synthesis of Ciceronian, Horatian, and Platonic principles, and its relation to the *Apology*, see Shepherd, ed., *Apology*, 69–71.
8. See Thomas Wilson, *The Arte of Rhetorique* (Gainesville, Fla.: Scholars' Facsimiles and Reprints, 1962), 18, who follows Aristotle's association of rhetoric with probabilistic thinking when he defines "[t]he findying out of apte matter, called otherwise Invencion, [as] a searchying out of thynges true, or thynges likely, the whiche maie reasonably sette furth a matter, and make it appere probable."
9. Rosemund Tuve, *Allegorical Imagery* (Princeton, N.J.: Princeton University Press, 1966); Mindele Anne Treip, *Allegorical Poetics and the Epic: The Renaissance Tradition to*

Sidney scholars, who still generally hold that the *Apology* represents a departure from, if not an outright rejection of, allegory. Despite the strong arguments of those specializing in allegory, the consensus in Sidney studies, originally formed by important scholars such as Geoffrey Shepherd, A. C. Hamilton, and Michael Murrin, has not to this date been challenged from within.

In the introduction to his fine edition of the *Apology*, Shepherd argues that Sidney does not follow the old allegorical approach practiced by Boccaccio and his followers, who "in exalting poetry had reduced it to serious fable-making."[10] Although Sidney's approach to poetry certainly differs in significant ways from that of Boccaccio, one nevertheless cannot help noticing how very often Sidney cites the arguments of Boccaccio and his followers, and how often he cites serious fables as examples of just the kind of poetry he has in mind. In comparing the poet to the philosopher, Sidney does not hesitate to deploy Boccaccio's argument that the parables of Christ are true poetry—in Sidney's terms, "right" poetry (108–9). And in the conclusion of the same passage, Sidney reaffirms Plutarch's allegorical approach to poetry, claiming that the poet "is indeed, the right popular Philosopher. Whereof Esops Tales give good proofe, whose prettie Allegories stealing under the formall Tales of beastes, make many, more beastly than beasts, begin to hear the sound of vertue from those dumbe speakers" (109).

Indeed, Sidney concludes his section on the "works" of poesy by sealing his case with two examples, both of which are fables. The first, Menenius Agrippa's tale of the belly, shows the Roman mob the foolishness of its rebellion. Not only does Boccaccio defend this kind of didactic allegory, he defends precisely this one. Arguing that "it is rather useful than damnable to compose stories," Boccaccio calls upon the example of Menenius Agrippa quieting the Roman mob "all by means of a story" to show that not all poets are liars.[11] Al-

---

"Paradise Lost" (Lexington: University Press of Kentucky, 1994); and Kenneth Borris, *Allegory and Epic in English Renaissance Literature: Heroic Form in Sidney, Spenser, and Milton* (Cambridge, U.K.: Cambridge University Press, 2000).

10. Shepherd, ed., *Apology*, 29–30.

11. *Boccaccio on Poetry: Being the Preface and the Fourteenth and Fifteenth Books of Boc-*

Sidney's Fiction and the Allegorical Tradition   39

though the subject is not strictly theology, it clearly is didactic and has the same goal as the parables of Christ: the amendment of life. Just as Agrippa's tale made the mob recognize itself and feel shame for its conduct, so too Nathan's tale of the man whose beloved ewe was taken from him "made David . . . as in a glass . . . see his own filthiness." Although "the discourse itself [is] feigned," "the application" of the story is "most divinely true": the ewe is Bathsheba, and the thief is David himself (115). The right poet Nathan instructs the divine poet David and brings about in him a sudden change of heart by means of an allegory.

Given Sidney's use of allegories to exemplify his theory of poetry, it should not be surprising that those who attempt to distance Sidney from allegory are unable to disassociate him altogether. Although he sees the *Apology* participating in the decline of allegory, Michael Murrin nevertheless acknowledges that Sidney shares several beliefs of the allegorists. In addition to locating the value of poetry in its Idea, Sidney believes that verse is not essential to poetry; that a figure like Cyrus should be a pattern for imitation; and that poetry is superior to philosophy.[12] But despite these similarities, Murrin finds Sidney at odds with the allegorists on several important points, including his emphasis on poetic genius, his denial of divine inspiration, and his appeal to a popular rather than to an elite audience. What ultimately decides the matter for Murrin is that the allegorists begin with truth, whereas Sidney begins "not with truth but with the fact of making."[13] Emphasizing Sidney's commitment to poetry as making, Murrin argues that for Sidney the poet is not concerned with the truth, and therefore is not interested in allegory.[14] However, the correct implica-

---

caccio's *"Genealogia Deorum Gentilium,"* ed. Charles Osgood (New York: Liberal Arts Press, 1930), 50.

12. *The Veil of Allegory: Some Notes toward a Theory of Allegorical Rhetoric in the English Renaissance* (Chicago: University of Chicago Press, 1969), 185.

13. *The Veil of Allegory,* 168–69.

14. What Murrin considers his strongest argument is quite forcefully contradicted by Sidney himself, who explicitly and repeatedly speaks of the poet's ability to reveal truth. Indeed, Sidney shows nothing less than a passion for truth when he praises "Achilles, Cyrus, Aeneas, Turnus, Tydeus, and Rinaldo," "who doth not only teache

tion of Sidney's reiteration of the old argument that the poet "nothing affirmeth, and therefore never lieth" is not that the truth and truthfulness do not matter, but that they do—otherwise a defense against untruthfulness would be unnecessary (123). That Sidney's maker does not affirm a proposition is simply to say that he does not proceed as one would do in an oration, moving from statement to proof in order to "affirm" the truth. It is not allegory but rhetoric from which Sidney is differentiating poetry. Unlike the orator, the poet does not "affirm" the truth with an argument, he embodies it with a fiction.

Closest to acknowledging Sidney's debt to the allegorical tradition is A. C. Hamilton, who offers a rather subtle and interesting formulation of Sidney's theory of the image. What distinguishes Sidney from the allegorists is, for Hamilton, that the meaning of an allegory lies "behind" the fiction, whereas the meaning of Sidney's image is found "within" it. Although Hamilton admits that Sidney's fiction may (and does) point *"beyond"* itself, he argues that "it first points insistently *to* itself."[15] As Hamilton explains, because the fiction "points insistently to itself," Sidney's theory is "usually seen as opposed to the allegorical tradition." He, however, resists the simple dichotomy between allegory and the new poetics and explains that in pointing *"beyond"* itself, the fiction in fact "includes" the allegorical tradition.[16] Although Hamil-

---

and move to a truth, but teacheth and mooveth to the most high and excellent truth" (119). Furthermore, a large part of the *narratio* is indebted to the humanist argument that poets were the first philosophers, giving knowledge under the veil of allegory until their people were ready for philosophy proper, which draws back the veil and looks at truth directly. Reiterating the arguments of generations of humanists before him, Sidney speaks of poetry as "the first light-giver to ignorance," and as the "milk" that nourished noble nations until they were able "to feed" on "tougher knowledges" (96).

15. *The Structure of Allegory in the "Faerie Queene"* (Oxford, U.K.: Clarendon Press, 1961), 12, emphasis added. This nuance is, unfortunately, not generally appreciated, even by those who cite Hamilton's distinction, such as W. R. Davis, who silently turns a conjunction into a disjunction and says that for Sidney "the value of poetry or fiction resides in itself, *not* in something it points to" (*Idea and Act in Elizabethan Fiction* [Princeton, N.J.: Princeton University Press, 1969], 28, emphasis added).

16. Unfortunately, Hamilton undermines this useful distinction and confuses matters by adding another, very odd, distinction, arguing, that "[t]hough Sidney does not use the allegorical tradition, it is implicit in his central doctrine that the poet's fictions are [in Sidney's own words] 'things not affirmatiuely but allegorically and figuratiuelie

ton accurately describes the poetic image as understood by Sidney, his formulations do not point, as he thinks, to a new poetics. On the contrary, what he describes is simply typology, a kind of allegory at least as old as Homer and the Bible.

Although typology is a standard literary device in Sidney's time, even the best scholars overlook it when analyzing the *Apology*.[17] Indeed, those who mention allegory in relation to the *Apology* rarely differentiate typology from other, often cruder, forms of allegory. One important distinction within the rich and varied tradition, as Rosemund Tuve demonstrated some time ago, is that between classical and Christian allegory. Whereas the former gives little or no importance to the literal sense, the latter emphasizes *figura*, or typology.[18] When the classical allegory, which saw signs and things as separate, was assimilated by the Christian tradition, things were understood also to be signs. Since things do not cease to be things by being signs, the literal meaning must be given its due alongside the allegorical

---

written'" (17). Why Sidney "includes" the allegorical tradition without "using" it remains mysterious, as does Hamilton's description of allegory as "implicit" in Sidney's theory when his own quotation of the *Apology* quite explicitly identifies allegory as a positive element of that "central doctrine."

17. This is due in large measure to the impoverished understanding of allegory that has followed on Coleridge's influential denigration of the technique. See Treip, *Allegorical Poetics*, 45–47; and Borris, *Allegory and Epic*, 110–14. On the prestige allegory still enjoyed in the eighteenth century, see Abrams, *The Mirror and the Lamp*, 288–89, who shows that allegory and personification were seen as the central techniques employed by the creative imagination. Addison, for instance, thought of the personification of virtue and vice, of Fame in Virgil, of Sin and Death in Milton, as the essence of poetic creativity; for him the invention of "similitudes, metaphors, and allegories" "has something in it like creation. It bestows a kind of existence, and draws up to the reader's view several objects which are not to be found in being. It makes additions to nature, and gives greater variety to God's works" (*Spectator*, nos. 419 and 421, as quoted by Abrams, *The Mirror and the Lamp*, 288).

18. *Allegorical Imagery*, 122. Although in recent times types and allegories have been presented as opposites, in their long histories the two are actually closely related. On the opposition between "good" myth and "bad" allegory, a more recent version of the opposition between symbol and allegory, see Angus Fletcher, *Allegory, the Theory of a Symbolic Mode* (Ithaca, N.Y.: Cornell University Press, 1964), 14–15. As the title of his work indicates, he rejects these distinctions. See also Borris, *Allegory and Epic*, and Treip, *Allegorical Poetics*, both of whom understand typology as a part of allegorical poetics.

sense. The literal sense is not lost in the allegorical; rather, it participates in it. In becoming something more, the historical fact does not cease to be what it is. Isaac carrying the wood for his own sacrifice is a figure of Christ carrying the cross; but in prefiguring Christ, he does not cease to be Isaac. Nor does Cyrus cease to be a historical figure because he is, for Cicero and for Sidney, *"effigiem iusti imperii,* 'the portraiture of a just empire'" (103). As Tuve rightly claims, Sidney's theory, in which "particulars shadow universals," is indeed a version of typology, as is the allegory of the *Faerie Queene*.[19]

In his "Letter to Raleigh," Spenser describes an allegorical method that is rightly classified as typology. Sidney's acquaintance acknowledges that some will find his allegorical method "displeasaunt," and would "rather have good discipline delivered plainly in way of precepts, or sermoned at large . . . then thus clowdily enwrapped in Allegoricall devices." However, he replies by showing how "much more profitable and gratious is doctrine by ensample, then by rule" by contrasting Plato, who "in the exquisite depth of his iudgement, formed a Commune welth such as it should be," to Xenophon, who "in the person of Cyrus and the Persians fashioned a governement such as might best be." Xenophon is to be preferred because he provides in Cyrus an "Allegoricall device" that is also an "ensample," which is precisely what Spenser says he has "laboured to doe in the person of Arthure."[20] In Arthur, Spenser provides both an allegory and a model for his Christian and English readers. For Spenser's readers, understanding Arthur the allegory is the same as understanding Arthur the exemplar—and is the same as understanding themselves. Formulated more simply, Arthur is the type of the Christian and the type of England.

Like Spenser's Arthur, Sidney's Cyrus provides a moral mirror in

19. *Allegorical Imagery,* 122. For very good bibliographies on typology, see Sacvan Bercovitch, *Typology and Early American Literature* (Amherst: University of Massachusetts Press, 1972), 245–337; and Stephen Barney, *Allegories of History, Allegories of Love* (Hamden, Conn.: Archon Books, 1979), 29–55.

20. Edmund Spenser, *The Faerie Queene,* ed. Thomas P. Roche (New York: Penguin Books, 1987), 16.

which readers can examine their own lives. In Cyrus, they will see an allegory for themselves as they should be.[21] The scheme is obviously Neoplatonic: the world is an allegorical mirror, a glass in which we see a reflection of the Idea in the mind of God. Just as the world can only mistakenly be taken to hold its full significance in itself, so too Sidney's fictional world, though it appears self-contained, is in its essence but a reflection of a higher reality: the Idea in the mind of the maker. As a reflection of that Idea, the poetic image illuminates those who behold it with transcendent truth.

The luminous quality of Sidney's "golden" world has often been discussed. Usually it is approached from a rhetorical standpoint, and its *enargia* is noted. But if one admits the interplay between the rhetorical and the allegorical traditions, one can see that Sidney's "golden" world resembles Bonaventure's aesthetic understanding of the real world, which he said was "like a mirror, bright with reflected light of the divine wisdom," "like a great coal radiant with light."[22] According to this Christian Neoplatonic view, the world is a radiant incarnation of the transcendent wisdom in the benevolent mind of God. Sidney's "golden" world has the same brilliance, and the same analogy to the immaterial reality of the divine mind. It does not much matter that Bonaventure is not speaking of a literary creation, since for him the world is God's book. It is to be understood the same way God's other

21. Finding in Xenophon's Cyrus an ideal and an example, Sidney resembles his Italian predecessors. As Baxter Hathaway explains, from Robortello to Tasso—roughly from 1548 to 1585—a lively tradition emphasizes the role of the epic hero as a perfect exemplar for human conduct. Robortello follows Cicero and argues that Plato intended the Ideas to be understood as perfect exemplars, each being "the ultimate form of its kind," and, like Sidney, he proposes Xenophon's Cyrus as just such a heroic pattern. The hero is, in this view, an obvious inspiration to readers: "For what kind of prince is not incited to virtue on reading the education of Cyrus in Xenophon and does not hope that by imitating him he can become like him" (*In librum Aristotelis de arte poetica explicationes* [Munich, Germany: W. Fink, 1968], 296, 91, as quoted by Baxter Hathaway, *The Age of Criticism: The Late Renaissance in Italy* [Westport, Conn.: Greenwood Press, 1972], 145, 146).

22. Etienne Gilson, *The Philosophy of St. Bonaventure* (New York: Sheed & Ward, 1938), 229–30, as quoted by William K. Wimsatt and Cleanth Brooks, in *Literary Criticism: A Short History* (New York: Knopf, 1957), 147.

book is to be interpreted: allegorically. So too for Hugh of St. Victor, for whom "the whole visible world is almost a book written by the hand of God, with each creature standing as a letter therein."[23] If Sidney takes a step away from allegory toward realism, the reality he sees is not the gritty reality that the modern novelist sees. The things of this world are "established by the Divine Will" not simply for their own sake but also "for the manifestation of the invisible wisdom of God."[24] Hugh, unlike Coleridge, sees no need to distinguish between allegory and symbol: "symbolic" and "allegorical" are united rather than divided under the larger rubric "spiritual." To understand the world, one must be able to discern its spiritual sense:

If an illiterate looks on an open book, he sees the forms of the letters but he cannot read. The man who sees only the outside of the creatures and does not realize what there is of a God in them is as dull as an animal; he knows the outside but not the inner meaning. The spiritually gifted man, who understands all things, considers the beauty of the outward form, but also perceives in the inner nature the marvelous wisdom of God.[25]

The world is, for Hugh, an allegory. To interpret the world, one must go beyond the world, to the mind of the Creator, where the true meaning of creation is to be found. For Sidney, the same holds for interpreting the fictional world: "for any understanding knoweth the skill of the artificer standeth in that *Idea* or fore-conceit of the work, and not in the work itself" (101). On the other hand, one who believes

---

23. *Didascalicon*, in J.-P. Migné, ed., *Patrologiae Cursus Completus. Series Latina*, 221 vols. (Paris: Migné, 1844–1865), 176, col. 814: "Universus enim mundum iste sensibilis quasi quidam liber est scriptus digito Dei." The translation is that of D. C. Allen, *Mysteriously Meant: The Rediscovery of Pagan Symbolism and Allegorical Interpretation in the Renaissance* (Baltimore: Johns Hopkins University Press, 1970), 114n.31. Hereafter the *Patrologiae* . . . . *Series Latina* will be abbreviated as PL.
24. *Didascalicon*, PL 176, col. 814, as translated by Allen, 114n.31.
25. *Didascalicon*, PL 176, col. 814, translated by Allen, 114n.31: "Quemadmodum autem si illiteratus quis apertum librum videst, figuras aspicit, literas non cognoscit: ita stultus et *animalis homo*, qui *non percipat ea quae Dei sunt* (1 Cor 2), in visibilibus istis creaturis foris videt speciem, sed intus non intelliget rationem. Qui autem spiritualis est et omnia dijudicare potest, in eo quidem quod foris considerat pulchritudinem operis, intus concipit quam miranda sit sapienta Creatoris."

that the world contains its own meaning, that it is a world unto itself, is like the illiterate man who sees the letters but knows not their sense.

I realize that my discussion runs the risk not only of making Sidney's theory appear more consistent than it really is, but also of making it look superannuated rather than innovative. To counteract such an impression, I would simply point out that it is in looking back to medieval typology that the *Apology* anticipates the romantic worldview, which, like that of Sidney, is more orderly than it initially appears and, unlike ours, is capable of seeing the visible world as

> Characters of the great Apocalypse,
> The types and symbols of Eternity,
> Of first, and last, and midst, and without end.[26]

This symbolic and allegorical view of art and the world, places a heavy hermeneutic burden on readers. Just as Hugh knows that many cannot penetrate the veil of appearances, so too Sidney knows that not all will penetrate to the Idea in the mind of the poet. What is more, he knows that many will fail to understand not only poetic works but also his theory of poetry. And of those who do understand, many will not accept it: "But these arguments will by few be understood, and by fewer granted" (101). Like a good orator, Sidney is attentive to the response of his readers, and he recognizes fundamental divisions within his own audience as well as the audience for poetry. The audience is first divided between those who do not understand and those who do; and then those who understand are divided into those who believe and those who do not.

This division is reflected in the structure of the *Apology* itself. After acknowledging that his opening "arguments will by few be understood, and by fewer granted," Sidney turns to what he calls "a more ordinary opening." Although he seems to leave his opening arguments behind, as C. S. Lewis first pointed out, the argument of the

---

26. *The Prelude*, 6.639–41, in *Selected Poems and Prefaces*, ed. Jack Stillinger (Boston: Houghton Mifflin, 1965).

narratio recurs in Sidney's discussion of the "right poets." According to Lewis, Sidney's "central doctrine"—"the real Sidnean position"—is found in his original argument. The subsequent "more ordinary opening" is designed to win those who found the first argument "too ambitious and metaphysical." Employing a method that is "concessive and strategical," Sidney condescends to present "something 'which no man will denie'" in order to "lure" his audience into agreement with the original position.[27] Indeed, Sidney's claim that the "right poet" "borrow[s] nothing of what is, hath been, or shall be" but instead "range[s], only reined with learned discretion," is identical to his earlier description of the "high flying liberty of conceit" of the poet who goes "freely ranging only within the zodiac of his own wit." As Walter Davis notes, Sidney does not retreat from his original claims but "merely restates them in a more logical manner with more temperate diction."[28] It stands to reason that the *Apology*, as a piece of forensic oratory, would marshal all available arguments in defense of the accused, making strategic use of diverse material in order to provide a range of arguments that will appeal to a diverse jury. What I want to point out, however, is that this is also the strategy of a good allegorist who wishes to accommodate the needs of his varied audience. While the original presentation, with its rather enigmatic formulations, offers the more able minds in his audience some pleasant exercise in interpretation, Sidney's "more ordinary opening"—which is like a shad-

---

27. *English Literature in the Sixteenth Century* (New York: Oxford University Press, 1954), 344. On Sidney's indirection, see Barnes, "The Hidden Persuader: The Complex Speaking Voice of Sidney's *Defence of Poetry*," and Leslie D. Foster, "'I Speak of the Art, and Not of the Artificer': The Logical Structure of Sidney's *Defence of Poetry* and the Concessive Arguments," *Hebrew University Studies in Literature* 5 (1977). Noting the apparent disjunction between the *narratio* and what follows, Hardison, in "The Two Voices of Sidney's 'Apology for Poetry,'" surmises that the *Apology* is unfinished, was written during two periods, and speaks with two contradictory voices—that of an early Sidney influenced by Italian humanists and that of a later Sidney who has fallen under the sway of French neoclassicism. There is, however, no evidence that the *Apology* is unfinished; its elegance suggests, rather, a virtuoso performance in which Sidney argues along two separate lines in order to appeal to two segments of his audience.

28. *Idea and Act*, 32.

ow or type of his ideal opening argument—gives milk to those who are not ready for the rich fare of the *narratio*.

It is quite true that in proposing "a more ordinary opening," Sidney appears to abandon the claim that poetry has something divine about it. Indeed, in the *partitio* he seems explicitly to deny the theological content of the poetry he defends, distinguishing theological and philosophical poets from "right poets" in order to focus his defense solely on the latter. However, on closer inspection, the distinction between the theological and the "right poets" blurs. Although the theological poets clearly have the highest subject matter, the "right poets" have a far more inclusive subject matter, extending to all that "may be and should be." Not only does the scope of the "right poets" exceed and, indeed, encompass that of the divine poets, Sidney calls their "consideration" of that great subject matter nothing less than "divine." This division, which appears to establish the independence of fictional poetry and to abandon the humanist program, which stresses the similarity of poetry and theology, is thus not as stable as it first appears. Sidney distinguishes the right poets from the theological poets in order ultimately to bestow on the right poets all the powers of the theological poets and, by the end of the *partitio*, to identify the "right poet" not only with the theological poet but also the poet as described in the lofty terms of the *narratio*.[29]

Although this sleight of hand might strike many modern readers as disingenuous, in its historical context it can be seen simply as Sidney's attempt to accommodate the differing needs of his heterogeneous audience. The recognition of a divided audience was in his time deeply embedded in the humanist tradition. It finds notable expression in Boccaccio's *Life of Dante*, in which Boccaccio, like Aquinas before him, applies Gregory the Great's analysis of Sacred Scripture to poetry:

In the same account it discloses the text and its underlying mystery. Thus at the same moment by the one it disciplines the wise, and by the other it

29. See Anne Lake Prescott, "King David as a 'Right Poet': Sidney and the Psalmist," *English Literary Renaissance* 19 (1989), who, picking up on Sidney's trick of making distinctions without differences, shows that Sidney's "theological poet" is in the end identical to the "right poet."

strengthens the foolish. It possesses openly that by virtue of which it may nourish little children, and preserves in secret that whereby it holds rapt in admiration the minds of sublime thinkers.³⁰

Hardly an artifact of medieval obscurantism, this ability to hide and disclose truth at the same time is found virtually unchanged in Francis Bacon's discussion of "poesie allusive, or parabolical." "Applied onely to express some speciall purpose or conceit," this form of poetry "*excels the rest, and seemeth to be a sacred and venerable thing; especially seeing Religion it self hath allowed it in a work of that nature, and by it, traficks divine commodities with men.*" In presenting divine truth to men, this kind of poetry is "of ambiguous use, and applied to contrary ends. For it serves for *Obscuration;* and it serveth also for *Illustration:* in this it seems, there was sought a way how to teach; in that an Art how to conceal."³¹

Boccaccio repeats the distinction between the "learned" and the "unlearned" in his *Genealogy of the Gentile Gods*, tagging on the Horatian twofold aim of instructing and delighting: "Such then is the power of fiction that it pleases the unlearned by its external appearance, and exercises the minds of the learned with its hidden truth; and thus both are edified and delighted with one and the same perusal."³² In his *Life of Dante*, he makes it clear that the exercise of interpretation results in more than hermeneutic fitness:

It is obvious that anything that is gained with fatigue seems sweeter than what is acquired without any effort. The plain truth, since it is quickly understood with little difficulty, delights us and passes from the mind. But, in order

---

30. Hazard Adams, ed., *Critical Theory since Plato* (San Diego, Calif.: Harcourt, 1971), 125. Written in 1364, the *Life of Dante* was first published in 1477. Aquinas quotes Gregory the Great (*Moralia* 20.1) to affirm that Holy Scripture can have several senses: "Holy Writ by the manner of its speech transcends every science, because in one and the same sentence, while it describes a fact, it reveals a mystery." Noting that "those things that are taught metaphorically in one part of Scripture, in other parts are taught more openly," Aquinas explains that "the very hiding of truth in figures is useful for the exercise of thoughtful minds, and as a defense against the ridicule of the impious, according to the words *Give not that which is holy to dogs* (Matth. Vii.6)" (*ST* Ia, q. 1, aa. 9–10).

31. *Advancement of Learning*, Book 2, in Tayler, ed., *Literary Criticism*, 148–49.

32. *Genealogy*, 14.9.

that it may be more pleasing, because acquired with labor, and therefore be better retained, the poets hide the truth beneath things apparently quite contrary to it. For that reason they produce fables.[33]

The difference Boccaccio sees between the challenging obscurity in Holy Writ and in poetry is that since it is "addressed to the few" poetry has even more justification for employing obscurity.[34] These theories can be found, virtually unaltered, in Harington:

It sufficeth me therefore to note this, that the men of greatest learning and highest wit in the auncient times did of purpose conceale these deepe mysteries of learning, and, as it were, couer them with the vaile of fables and verse for sundrie causes: one cause was that they might not be rashly abused by prophane wits, in whom science is corrupted, like good wine in a bad vessell. . . . Another, and a principall cause of all, is to be able with one kinde of meate and one dish (as I may so call it) to feed diuers tastes. For the weaker capacities will feede themselues with the pleasantnes of the historie and sweetnes of the verse, some that haue stronger stomackes will as it were take a further taste of the Morall sence, a third sort, more high conceited then they, will digest the Allegorie: so as indeed it hath bene thought by men of verie good iudgement, such manner of Poeticall writing was an excellent way to preserue all kinde of learning from that corruption which it is now come to since they left that mysticall writing of verse.[35]

The arguments of Gregory, Jerome, and Boccaccio were recycled not only by Harington but also by Sylvester and Golding, who praised allegory in prefaces to their translations. And despite its effort to throw off medievalism, the Pléiade still saw a use for allegory; and in the court of Navarre, serious allegory was, with Italian Platonism, very much in fashion.[36] With allegory, and the divisions it presumed among readers,

---

33. *Life of Dante*, 22.6, in Allan H. Gilbert, *Literary Criticism: Plato to Dryden* (Detroit, Mich.: Wayne State University Press, 1962), 211.

34. *Genealogy*, 14.12.

35. "A Preface, or Rather A Briefe Apologie of Poetrie and of the Author," in O. B. Hardison Jr., ed., *English Literary Criticism: The Renaissance* (New York: Appleton-Century-Crofts, 1963), 211–12.

36. See Tuve, *Allegorical Imagery*, 41, 122, 219ff.; Lewis Soens, ed., *Sir Philip Sidney's "Defense of Poesy"* (Lincoln: University of Nebraska Press, 1970), 77–78; and Jean Seznec, *The Survival of the Pagan Gods: The Mythological Tradition and Its Place in Renaissance Humanism and Art* (New York: Harper Torchbooks, 1961), 96–101. On hermeti-

generally went the recognition of some knowing elite, whether the Protestant "elect," the Neoplatonic "enlightened," the courtly aristocracy, or all of these, as in the court of Navarre.

It could be argued that Sidney also intended his work primarily for an elite audience. That he himself did not have the work published could be taken as evidence of such an attitude. And when the work was published posthumously, more evidence could be found in the title pages of both editions. Although not chosen by Sidney, the Horatian epigraph on the title page of the Olney edition leaves little doubt as to what at least was thought by some to be Sidney's attitude: "*Odi profanum vulgus, et arceo.*" Although the *Defence*, published by William Ponsonby, lacks any epigraph, Ponsonby's 1598 folio, prepared under the supervision of Mary Sidney, has an emblem of a boar in front of a flowering plant, which bears the words "*Spiro non tibi.*" But while these Latin tags convey the impression that the work is intended for the few, in fact they are entirely commonplace. Indeed, few readers would have had any difficulty reading the Latin.

The function of the tags is not so much to keep readers *out* as to give them the pleasure of feeling *included* among an elite. Testifying to the existence of an elite knowledge, they serve as gates through which all who would be elite must pass. Like gates, the tags serve a double purpose: keeping people out and letting them in. Sidney's desire is the latter. Rather than wishing to exclude the uninitiated from penetrating to some esoteric meaning, his intention is to show readers the way to the true knowledge of poesy. Whereas the "more ordinary opening" accommodates the weakness of his audience, the tags urge them to recognize a more extraordinary inner sense. They urge them not to be swine, and to recognize the pearls hidden in what they read. Moti-

---

cism and allegory in Renaissance courtly circles, see Sears Jayne, ed., introduction to *Commentary on Plato's "Symposium on Love,"* ed. Sears Jayne (Dallas, Tex.: Spring Publications, 1985), 18, who argues that although Ficino's *Commentary on Plato's "Symposium"* appears to the uninitiated to be a historical account of a banquet that Ficino attended, where the guests gave speeches commenting on the speeches of Plato's *Symposium*, for the courtly elite of the Medici circle, it was understood neither as a historical account nor as a commentary on Plato but, rather, as Ficino's own treatise on love.

vated by a spirit that is evangelical and even ecumenical, they reveal the attitude of the Christian allegorist who, imitating the method of Christ himself, often conceals in order to reveal.

As with the tags, the *peroratio* of Sidney's oration seems to convey the elitist hermeticism that emanated from the court of Florence. Explicitly advocating an allegorical approach to poetry, Sidney "conjure[s]" his audience to "believe" with him "that there are many mysteries contained in Poetry, which of purpose were written darkly, lest by profane wits it should be abused" (141–42). It is impossible, however, to miss the irony of his advocating a veiled approach to poetry in so open a manner. Sidney handles the serious and self-important hermeticist approach with a playfulness that is obvious. Thus Sidney evokes allegorical obscurantism while at the same time establishing an ironical perspective on it. Although this attitude distances Sidney from courtly obscurantism, it aligns him with another tradition, the *serioludere*. In this mode, a playful irony does not rule out a serious purpose. A conventional if complex resource of the oratorical tradition, it allows someone like Erasmus to write a mock-encomium whose principal jest is that the work is written in jest. Operating in the same vein, Sidney uses his facetious tone facetiously. Mimicking the courtly writers who wished to acknowledge a privileged audience in a way that would not expose them or their ideas to the gaze of outsiders, Sidney playfully places his audience in the position of those who have been initiated into the "sacred mysteries of Poesy." Those in his audience who have not understood will think that Sidney cannot be serious, choosing instead to take Sidney at his word when he calls the *Apology* an "ink-wasting toy." Those who have understood, however, will find themselves wittily "conjured" into an inner circle of those who "believe" (141).

When, after "conjuring" the reader to believe, when Sidney moves to the rewards for belief, his examples border on the inane. He promises his imaginary reader that his "name shall flourish in the printers' shops" and that he shall become "kin to many a poetical preface," where he will "dwell upon superlatives." The subsequent examples, however, are less ludicrous. He tells the reader that if he "believes," though he be *"libertino patre natus,"* the mere "son of a freedman" (a term of derision, as used by Horace's detractors [*Satires* 6.6]) he shall grow into *"Herculea proles,"* an offspring of Hercules. Not only does the tone change with this claim, but the content becomes serious as well. This kind of immortality, through adoptive filiation and deification, evokes—in an obscure and yet clear way—the analogous liberation and transformation of the Christian into a child of God. Adding one qualification, *"Si quid mea carmina possunt,"* "If aught my songs avail," Sidney echoes Virgil's ambiguous and poignant claim for the power of poetry to bestow immortality (142; see *Aeneid* 9.446) and allusively implies an analogy between his audience and Nisus and Euryalus, who die heroically and in love. At this point, Sidney's climax has become ecstatic, and he goes on to say that believing in poetry, his reader's "soul shall be placed with Dante's Beatrice, or Virgil's Anchises"—that is, in heaven or in the fields of the blessed. Here Sidney jestingly speaks of fictional beatitude—in order to make a serious point, for those who can understand—about the beatitude fiction can give. He is speaking at once of the power of poetry to bestow mock immortality and the real thing, which is the chief of the "many mysteries contained in Poetry, which of purpose were written darkly lest by profane wits it should be abused" (142).

If readers are conjured into believing Sidney's jest, just as Sidney had almost been persuaded to wish himself a horse, they will wish themselves a poem. Whereas Milton would later say that the poet "ought himself to be a true poem," Sidney would have the audience as well as the poet be true poems.[37] What Sidney's poet knows is not equine but human nature, and the metamorphosis Sidney less jestingly proposes is that his audience wish themselves to be identified with Cyrus, who is both a poem and an exemplary human being.[38] He

37. "Apology for Smectymnuus," in John Milton, *Complete Poems and Major Prose*, ed. Merritt Hughes (Indianapolis, Ind.: Bobbs-Merrill, 1957), 694.
38. To appreciate fully the humor of the contrast between the "self-love" of Pugliano and that of Sidney the poet, one also should recall the commonplace contrast of the medieval logic texts, in which the horse represents the brute animal from which man is distinguished by his specific difference, reason. Seen within this tradi-

would have the audience, like the poet, possess the Idea of Cyrus, so that they too could be Cyrus. Before entering into the imitation of Cyrus by the reader, however, it is necessary to turn to the making of Cyrus, which begins with the poet's Idea.

---

tion, Pugliano leads his audience to identify itself with the lower part of its nature, whereas the poet leads the audience to an identification with Cyrus, who represents human nature at its best. Even into the eighteenth century authors had recourse to this opposition between man and horse; it is, for example, the basis for the wit of Book 4 of *Gulliver's Travels*, with its smart horses, the Houyhnhnms. On this tradition, see Shepherd, ed., *Apology*, 144–5; and R. S. Crane, "The Houyhnhnms, the Yahoos, and the History of Ideas," in *Studies in the History of Ideas, 1600–1800*, ed. J. A. Mazzeo (New York: Columbia University Press, 1962). See also Anne Lake Prescott, "Spenser's Chivalric Restoration: From Bateman's 'Travayled Pylgrime' to the Redcrosse Knight," *Studies in Philology* 86 (1989), who traces the identification of the horse with the will, the desirous part of the soul, from Plato to St. Bernard to the Renaissance.

CHAPTER 3

THE IDEA OF POETRY

Any understanding of Sidney's poetics hinges on the interpretation of a handful of terms, and perhaps chief among them is "Idea." According to Sidney, "the skill of the artificer standeth in that *Idea* or fore-conceit of the work, and not in the work itself. And that the poet hath that *Idea* is manifest, by delivering them forth in such excellency as he hath imagined them" (101). The typographical presentation of *"Idea,"* capitalized and italicized in both of the original editions of the *Apology*, indicates that at least the printer thought of it as a special or foreign word. The reason for this special treatment is not immediately apparent to modern readers. From our current perspective it is difficult to realize how different the word "Idea" would have sounded in the sixteenth century. As accustomed as we are to taking for granted the ability to "have an idea," it is hard to imagine a time in which there would have been something strange in the notion that human beings can have ideas. But this was exactly the case in Sidney's time, when the primary location of ideas was understood to be the divine rather than the human mind. In locating the lofty Idea in the mind of the poet, Sidney is indeed taking a bold step for his time, making an extraordinary claim for the human mind.

Among the critics who recognize that there was something special about the Idea in Sidney's time, there is, however, little agreement on just what that distinctive quality is. Whereas Forest Robinson sees Sidney's *"Idea"* as a component of a Ramist "visual epistemology," D. H. Craig, also focusing on visual epistemology, argues that Sidney's theory of the Idea is a hybridization of the Aristotelian and Platonic doctrines. A number of critics see a connection between the *"Idea* or foreconceit" and the divine Ideas, they construe the relationship variously. Kurt Spellmeyer believes that Sidney is indebted primarily to Plotinus for his idea of the Idea; S. K. Heninger, however, insists that Sidney "unmistakably ha[s] in mind the term *idea* as Plato first had used it." Whereas both give short shrift to the Christian transmission of the Platonic Idea, Ronald Levao places the *"Idea* or fore-conceit" squarely within the Christian Neoplatonic framework, arguing that Sidney asserts a method analogous to the Cusan "art of conjecture." A. Leigh Deneef also believes that the *"Idea"* is a divine Idea; he, however, understands the *"Idea* or fore-conceit" as part of a "linguistic model" for poetic making. In general agreement, John Ulreich believes that Sidney's Idea is ultimately analogous to the divine *logos*. Although he also takes the theological aspect of Sidney's thought seriously, Andrew Weiner believes that Sidney is working to establish a "Protestant Poetics," and, accordingly, would never presume to compare the work of the poet to divine creation through the Ideas. Despite a similar adherence to the belief in a Protestant poetics, M. J. Doherty differs from Weiner and gives the poet access to transcendent knowledge—not through the Ideas but through the inner light of Wisdom. Discounting the importance of contemporary influences such as Protestant theology and Neoplatonic philosophy on Sidney's attitude toward poetry, Wesley Trimpi argues that Sidney is indebted directly to Seneca and Cicero for his idea of the Idea. Taking a similar line, Travis Curtright stresses Sidney's debt to classical sources, arguing that the Ideas are to be understood in terms of Aristotelian rhetoric, as "character types displaying the persuasive effects of *ethos*."[1]

1. Robinson, *The Shape of Things Known;* D. H. Craig, "A Hybrid Growth: Sidney's Theory of Poetry in *An Apology for Poetry,"* in *Sidney in Retrospect: Selections from "English Literary Renaissance,"* ed. Arthur F. Kinney (Amherst: University of Massachusetts Press, 1988); Kurt Spellmeyer, "Plotinus and Seventeenth-Century Literature: A Prolegomenon to Further Study," *Pacific Coast Philology* 17 (1982); Heninger, *Touches of Sweet Harmony,* 295; Levao, *Renaissance Minds and Their Fictions;* A. Leigh Deneef, "Rereading Sidney's Apology," *Journal of Medieval and Renaissance Studies* 10 (1980); A. Leigh Deneef, *Spenser and the Motives of Metaphor* (Durham, N.C.: Duke University Press, 1982), 5–11; Ulreich, "'The Poets Only Deliver'"; Andrew D. Weiner, "Sidney, Protestantism,

This array of learned studies is rich indeed; unfortunately, the diversity of opinions makes only one thing clear: that there is no consensus on what "the *Idea* or fore-conceit" is. One reason for the confusion is the common pitfall of source studies: once they have determined a source, they tend to exclude—prematurely—other possible sources. To avoid this understandable tendency and to arrive at what is at least close to a definitive understanding of Sidney's terms, I will refrain from deciding too quickly on any specific sense or source for Sidney's usage. Deferring a final determination, I will instead undertake a broad survey of the term as it was used in Sidney's time in order to reconstruct the context in which any particular use of the term, whether that of Sidney himself or of one of his sources, must be interpreted.

The journey of the term down to Sidney's time was, as Panofsky has masterfully shown, long and complex.[2] The complicated itinerary of the Idea passes back and forth between points no less distant than the mind of God and the human mind. In the Renaissance the Idea was in a process of transition from the divine to the human realm, a move that the Idea had made many times before, the most famous example of which is Aristotle's modification of the Platonic Idea to fit the confines of the human mind. A later instance is found in Seneca, who draws the Platonic Idea down to the human mind in order to supplement Aristotle's theory of causality with a fifth cause, which he calls the "exemplary" or "Platonic" cause.[3] Cicero attempted a similar

---

and Literary Critics: Reflections on Some Recent Criticism of the *Defence of Poetry*," in *Sir Philip Sidney's Achievements* (New York: AMS Press, 1990), 121; M. J. Doherty, *The Mistress-Knowledge: Sir Philip Sidney's "Defence of Poesie" and Literary Architectonics in the English Renaissance* (Nashville, Tenn.: Vanderbilt University Press, 1991); Wesley Trimpi, "Sir Philip Sidney's *An Apology for Poetry*," in *The Cambridge History of Literary Criticism: The Renaissance*, ed. Glyn P. Norton (Cambridge, U.K.: Cambridge University Press, 1999), 187–98; and Travis Curtright, "Sidney's *Defense of Poetry*: Ethos and the Ideas," *Ben Jonson Journal* 10 (2003): 102.

2. As must be the case with any discussion of the history of the Idea, mine is greatly indebted to Erwin Panofsky, *Idea: A Concept in Art Theory*, ed. Joseph Peake (Columbia: University of South Carolina Press, 1968), which is supplemented by the more recent work of David Summers, *The Judgement of Sense: Renaissance Naturalism and the Rise of Aesthetics* (Cambridge, U.K.: Cambridge University Press, 1987).

3. *Epistulae Morales*, trans. Richard Gummere, Loeb Classical Library (Cambridge,

conflation of the immanent and the transcendent, the Aristotelian and the Platonic, in philosophical writings that served as an important conduit through which Plato passed to the Renaissance. The so-called middle Platonists and Neoplatonists applied the term "Idea" to the superhuman Νοῦς, while at the same time investing the human mind with analogous realities. The Neoplatonic revivals brought about by Scotus Eriugena, the School of Chartres, Ficino, and German idealism gave the human mind similar access to the divine Ideas and, in doing so, were for intellectual culture what the flooding of the Nile is for local agriculture. Written during just such a period of intellectual fertility, the *Apology* thus has a place in a much larger historical process, one that repeats itself as it progresses.

Behind the Renaissance transformation of the Idea is the confusion in the medieval translation of Greek terms. Whereas Aristotle's εἶδος had been rendered, by William of Moerbeke and others, variously as *forma, species, imago, figura,* and *exemplar,* Plato's ἰδέα proved far less easy to translate, and indeed it was generally transliterated rather than translated. A problem arose, however, when it was necessary to explain Plato's term. There was no alternative but to use, judiciously and with qualification, the same group of terms used to translate εἶδος. Aquinas thus explains ἰδέα in terms of *forma:* "The form [*similitudo*] of the house already exists in the mind of the architect. This can be called the idea [*idea*] of the house; because the architect intends to make the house to the pattern of the form [*formae*] which he has conceived in his mind."[4] Although what is in the mind of the architect "can be called the idea of the house," such a denomination obviously runs contrary to thirteenth-century expectations. Aquinas must justify the application of the term to the thought of a human maker; and clearly it is only in reference to the mind of the divine creator that the term Idea had its full meaning: "There must be in the divine mind a form [*forma*], to the likeness of which the world is made; and that is what we mean

---

Mass.: Harvard University Press, 1961), 65.7. See Panofsky, *Idea,* 19–25, who quotes Seneca. See also Wesley Trimpi, *Muses of One Mind: The Literary Analysis of Experience and Its Continuity* (Princeton, N.J.: Princeton University Press, 1983), xv–xvi.

4. *ST* Ia, q. 15, a. 1.

by an idea [*idea*]."⁵ Using human psychology to explain the working of the divine mind, Aquinas never forgets that it is only by analogy that we can know what the divine Ideas are and that the resemblance between *"idea"* and *"forma"* does not make them identical.

This careful distinction is lost, however, in the Renaissance, as can be seen in Thomas Cooper's (1565) definition of "idea" as "the figure conceived in Imagination, as it were a substance perpetuall, beyng as paterne of all other sorte or kinde, as of one seal procedeth many printes, so of one *Idea* of man procede many thousandes of men."⁶ Visible and specific while at the same time being abstracted, intelligible, and universal, Cooper's "figure conceived in Imagination" is not Plato's Idea but Aristotle's εἶδος. With no mention of the Idea as outside of or somehow above the human mind, all that seems to remain of Plato's Idea is the name. However, Cooper cannot completely abandon Plato's transcendent Idea, and with an "as it were," Cooper gives in to the irresistible temptation to think of the Idea in Platonic terms as "a substance perpetuall." Though located safely in the imagination and conceived through sense apprehension, Cooper's Idea nevertheless looks back (via Cicero, whom Cooper cites) to Plato's transcendent Idea.⁷ Like his contemporaries, Cooper ultimately does not embrace the austerity of Aristotle's emphatic rejection of Plato's transcendent ἰδέα in favor of a narrowly defined and completely immanent εἶδος. Nor does he share Aquinas's precision in defining ἰδέα as analogous—but not identical—to *forma*. Instead, for Cooper and his contemporaries, the likeness between the human εἶδος and the divine

---

5. *ST* Ia, q. 15, a. 1. See Panofsky, *Idea*, 86ff.

6. *Thesaurus Linguae Romanae & Britanicae* (Menston, U.K.: Scolar Press, 1565). For a learned and witty history of the idea of the Idea, see Edward W. Tayler, *Donne's Idea of a Woman: Structure and Meaning in the "Anniversaries"* (New York: Columbia University Press, 1991), 25ff.

7. See Tayler, *Donne's Idea of a Woman*, 29, who shows how the Platonic Idea subsumes Aristotle's *species intelligibiles* (the intelligible, as opposed to the sensible, appearance) in the sophisticated writing of Melanchthon and others as well as in popularized presentations like that of Blundeville, whose misunderstanding of Plato could hardly be more obvious when he asserts what he believes to be "the true meaning of *Plato* touching *Idea*, that is, to be perpetuall in the mind, not separate from mans intelligence, as some men faine" (*Arte of Ligicke* [London, 1619], 1.4; p. 7, as qtd. by Tayler, 29).

ἰδέα vanishes into identity. Speaking of the Idea but thinking in terms of Aristotelian psychology, Cooper and his contemporaries ironically bring about the revenge of Plato on Aristotle, restoring his interchangeable use of ἰδέα and εἶδος.

The ordinary sense of "idea" in Sidney's time—and its difference from our present understanding of the term—is evident in Shakespeare's use. The first thing to note is that Shakespeare uses "idea" but a handful of times, which suggests that there was then something special about the term. When he does deploy the word, the sense is closer to our notion of "image." In *Much Ado about Nothing*, Friar Francis predicts that when Claudio hears how Hero

> died upon his words,
> Th' idea of her life shall sweetly creep
> Into his study of imagination,
> And every lovely organ of her life
> Shall come apparell'd in more precious habit,
> More moving, delicate, and full of life,
> Into the eye and prospect of his soul,
> Than when she liv'd indeed.[8]

Although perceived in the "imagination," this image of Hero is *"more moving, delicate, and full of life"* "than when she liv'd." Once seen with corporeal eyes, she now will be seen with "the eye and prospect of his soul." What is seen with the eye of the mind is the image of Hero, but not just Hero as Claudio had last seen her. The "idea of her life" is the image of her *whole* life. This image of Hero in her wholeness has the resplendent quality that the Scholastic philosophers attributed to the universal. This general image has a vividness, an *enargia*, more lively than the living image. Recognizing fully what he has lost, Claudio will know Hero as she really was. In her Idea is her essence, made visible, as it were, to the "eye" of the "soul."[9]

---

8. 4.1.211, 222–30, in G. Blakemore Evans, ed., *The Riverside Shakespeare* (Boston: Houghton Mifflin, 1974). Subsequent quotations of Shakespeare are all from this edition.

9. On Donne's similar use of the term in the *Anniversaries*, see Tayler, *Donne's Idea*

This is the same sense Spenser gives the word in *Amoretti* 45. His "inward self" is a more perfect mirror for his love than her "glasse of christall clene":

> Leaue lady in your glasse of christall clene,
>   Your goodly selfe for euermore to vew:
>   and in my selfe, my inward selfe I meane,
>   most liuely lyke behold your semblant trew.
> Within my hart, though hardly it can shew
>   thing so diuine to vew of earthly eye:
>   the fayre *Idea* of your celestiall hew,
>   and euery part remaines immortally:
> And were it not that through your cruelty,
>   with sorrow dimmed and deformd it were:
>   the goodly ymage of your visnomy,
>   clearer then christall would therein appere.
> But if your selfe in me ye playne will see,
>   remoue the cause by which your fayre beames darkned be.[10]

His heart provides not her visible image but her eternal, essential image. In his heart she will be able to see the reflection not only of her face ("visnomy"), but of her very self, her nature ("physiognomy")—which it turns out is not as "fayre" as her face, having been deformed, or "darkned," by her own "cruelty." As Kenneth Larsen has pointed out in his recent edition, critics have disputed whether "Idea" embodies the Platonic doctrine or simply refers to a "mental image."[11] As I hope is now clear, this dispute cannot have a winner, since the Platonic Idea and the Aristotelian "mental image" were commonly conflated. In Spenser's more precise usage, the conflated Idea-image is St.

---

of a Woman. According to the account of Drummond of Hawthorden, Donne responded to Jonson's complaint that "if [Donne's funeral elegy for Elizabeth Drury] had been written of the Virgin Mary it had been something" by saying that "he described the idea of a Woman, and not as she was" (Ben Jonson, *Ben Jonson*, ed. Ian Donaldson [Oxford, U.K.: Oxford University Press, 1995], 596).

10. In *"Amoretti" and "Epithalamion": A Critical Edition*, ed. Kenneth Larsen (Tempe, Ariz.: Medieval and Renaissance Texts and Studies, 1997), emphasis added.

11. *"Amoretti" and "Epithalamion,"* 174.

Paul's "εἰκών," which is a perfect mirror of the celestial Idea.[12] Although Spenser's handling of it was more precise than usual, the conceit of the icon as the perfect image of the Idea was commonplace. It was, for example, the master conceit of Michael Drayton's sonnet sequence, entitled *Idea's Mirror*.

By the end of the seventeenth century, however, the Idea had for the most part lost its luster. In Descartes's famous (if not wholly consistent) use of the term, the Idea is bound up with the workings of the human mind, though it retains—at least if clear and distinct—the power to point to realities outside and above the mind. With Locke, on the other hand, the Idea is completely psychologized and loses all power of transcending the confines of the human mind. He uses the term merely "to stand for whatsoever is the Object of the Understanding when a Man thinks, . . . to express whatever is meant by Phantasm, Notion, Species, or whatever it is, which the Mind can be employ'd about in thinking."[13] In Locke's influential redefinition, the noetic power of the Idea is severely reduced, and gone completely is its dazzling power as a mental image.

Along with the dulling down of the Idea can be seen a correlative dimming in the idea of the imagination as a power capable of figuring forth not only particular pictures but also the universal Idea of a thing. Whereas reason and imagination were united in that single faculty that Sidney and his contemporaries called "wit," Bacon effected a separation of reason from imagination that proved influential. Nevertheless, even for Bacon, imagination still played an important role in human knowledge, the role of messenger in judging and choosing: "For sense sends all kinds of images over to the imagination for reason to judge of; and reason again when it has made its judgment and selec-

---

12. See Larsen's note for the references to Plato and also for the Pauline use of the term for the "image" of God, to which the poem alludes with its calendrical correspondence to the liturgical readings (174).

13. *An Essay Concerning Human Understanding*, ed. Peter Nidditch (Oxford, U.K.: Clarendon Press, 1984), 47. On the revolutionary character of Locke's definition, see Richard Rorty, *Philosophy and the Mirror of Nature* (Princeton, N.J.: Princeton University Press, 1979), 48, who also gives other references to the "'idea' idea" in the seventeenth century.

tion, sends them over to imagination before the decree be put in execution." And the imagination is more than a messenger for Bacon, for "it is either invested with or usurps no small authority in itself, besides the simple duty of the message." Furthermore, "in matters of faith and religion our imagination raises itself above our reason" since "divine grace uses the motions of the imagination as an instrument of illumination, just as it uses the motions of the will as an instrument of virtue; which is the reason why religion ever sought access to the mind by similitudes, types, parables, visions, dreams."[14] Perceiving realities that are above reason, the imagination in Bacon is identical to the power described by Theseus in *Midsummer Night's Dream*, which "bodies forth / The forms of things unknown" and "apprehend[s] / More than cool reason comprehends."[15] Of course, Theseus is a rationalist, and he is speaking against the imagination. For him, the divine frenzy of the poets is simply madness. But Shakespeare makes Theseus's formulations ambiguous, and, ironically, the character says more than he knows, presenting what in fact is a very beautiful description of the Neoplatonic poetic method.

Whereas Bacon and Shakespeare both poised reason against imagination, the balance was soon tipped heavily in favor of reason. Hobbes, who was influential in the psychologizing of the Idea and the dimming of the imagination, declared that imagination "is nothing but *decaying sense*." This materialistic epistemology prepared the way for Locke's previously inconceivable concept of the Idea, which amounts to the Aristotelian εἶδος voided of its intelligibility. By the time of Dr. Johnson's dictionary (1755), the power of the imagination to mirror transcendent realities is nowhere to be found. Having lost its previous ideal or iconic radiance, it is, in Johnson's definition, simply the product of the mind, a "mental imagination." Only with the romantic poets, when once again the doctrines of Plato and Aristotle are conflated, does the imagination reclaim its lost power.

14. *The Advancement of Learning*, 5.1, in *The Works of Francis Bacon*, 14 vols., ed. James Spedding (London: Longmans, 1868), 4.405–6.
15. 5.1.5–6, 14–15.

With Sidney, clearly both the Idea and the imagination still retain spectacular powers. Nevertheless, when compared to the ordinary idea of the Idea in the period, Sidney's Idea stands apart. Although it shares the conflated ideal and sensible qualities depicted by Shakespeare or Spenser, the origin of Sidney's Idea is more mysterious. Sidney's poet arrives at his Idea neither through the apprehension of the world around him nor through his ecstatic travel to the world of forms. Instead, it is by "freely ranging only within the zodiac of his own wit" that the poet comes up with his Idea (100). As this language indicates, Sidney's idea of the Idea is not merely the product of the usual conflation of the Platonic and Aristotelian approaches. In addition to luminous universality, Sidney's Idea possesses originality.

This idea of the Idea as original has its sources in Italian art theory of the sixteenth century. Although the Idea still would have been thought to be most at home in the mind of God, it was enjoying a certain dual residence in the human mind, thanks to the theories of Italian scholars and critics. The meaning of the term nevertheless remained far from standard. Indeed, the variety of ideas of the Idea among the Italian art theorists is striking. In his use of the term, Scaliger takes the straight Platonic position: there is the eternal and separately existing Idea; the thing, which is an imitation of the Idea; and the picture or word, which is an image of an image.[16] Scaliger's firm adherence to the Platonic doctrine does not, however, prevent him from identifying it with the Aristotelian position in order to locate the Idea also in the mind of the poet. This direct access to the Ideas allows the artist to produce images of things not merely as they are but as they were meant to be.[17] Scaliger thus preserves the Platonic veneration of the Ideas, placing them above the gods, while following Aristotle in circumventing the Platonic denigration of art as an imitation of an imitation.

In contrast to Scaliger's lofty idea of the Ideas, Giorgio Vasari, in

---

16. *Poetices*, 3.1, p. 80.
17. *Poetices*, 3.1, p. 80. For a helpful analysis of Scaliger, see Marijke Spies, *Rhetoric, Rhetoricians, and Poets: Studies in Renaissance Poetry and Poetics*, ed. H. Duits and A. van Strien (Amsterdam: Amsterdam University Press, 1999), 23.

the 1568 edition of his *Lives of the Painters*, gives a comparatively mundane sense to the term. He proposes a watered-down version of the Aristotelian psychology of abstraction, in which the Idea is likened to a "design," which is marked by its "exceedingly regular . . . proportions."[18] In Vasari's usage, "form," "idea," and "concept [*concetto*]" all signify the standard proportion for a certain kind of thing in nature. The "design" is that same Idea figured forth by the hand of the artist. In its regularity, this Idea still has a certain ideal quality, but striking is the almost total substitution of regularity and proportion for transcendence.

Between the senses that Scaliger and Vasari give the term is that of Giovanni Paolo Lomazzo, who is known for his *Trattato dell'arte della pittura* (1584) and his *Idea del Tempio della pittura* (1590). Although these works obviously did not influence Sidney in their published form, Sidney and Lomazzo may have known of each others' ideas through the miniaturist Nicholas Hilliard. Hilliard, with whom Sidney discussed painting, was primarily responsible for having parts of Lomazzo's *Trattato* translated into English.[19] Lomazzo argues that through the impressions of the divine Ideas, the *formulae idearum*, the artist can intuit the ideal world and figure it forth, thus giving the Idea the ideal quality so absent in Vasari's definition of the term.[20] This idea of the Idea, which falls somewhere between the Platonic and the Aristotelian versions, is most properly characterized as Neoplatonic. Indeed, Lomazzo's definition borrows from Ficino's treatment of the Idea and translates Ficino's theory of love and contemplation into a theory of artistic production.

In his *Commentary on the Symposium*, while Ficino explains Plato's account of how the lover gives birth to Ideas in the presence of beau-

---

18. *Le vite de' più eccellenti pittori, scultori ed architettori*, ed. Gaetano Malanesi (Florence: G. C. Sansoni, 1878–1885), 1.168, as quoted and translated by Panofsky, *Idea*, 66. See the discussion of Vasari in Summers, *The Judgement of Sense*, 210.

19. See Shepherd, ed., *Apology*, 64.

20. See James Mirollo, *Mannerism and Renaissance Poetry: Concept, Mode, Inner Design* (New Haven, Conn.: Yale University Press, 1984), 24, on whose explanation of Lomazzo I rely.

ty, he is in fact redefining the Idea in terms of his own philosophical system. Translating Diotima's speech on the ladder of love into his own Christian Neoplatonism, Ficino introduces a Scholastic causal analysis not found in Plato's dialogue:

When the figure [*figura*] of some body meets the eye, and through the eyes penetrates into the spirit, if that figure, on account of the preparation of its matter, corresponds closely to the figure which the divine Mind [*divina mens*] contains in its Idea [*idea*] of the thing, it immediately pleases the soul since it corresponds to those Reasons [*rationibus*] which both our intellect [*mens*] and our power of procreation preserve as copies [*exemplaria*] of the thing itself, and which were originally received divinely.[21]

Although the Ideas are in the divine Mind alone, the mind of the lover contains "Reasons"—copies of the divine Ideas—"which were originally received divinely." Ficino explains the pleasure of seeing a beautiful body as arising from the close correspondence between the "figure," or sensible species apprehended through the standard Aristotelian psychology of abstraction, and the "Reasons," or traces of the divine Ideas, in the human intellect. Bringing together strands from different traditions, Ficino's psychology weds the Aristotelian correspondence theory of knowledge to the Platonic doctrine of *anamnesis*, or recollection.

For Ficino, the ascent from the love of a beautiful body to the love of the eternal Forms is a process of sublimation, as it is for Plato. This movement from the mind of man to the mind of God is not only upward but also inward. Discernible in Ficino's interest in human psychology as a mirror of the divine psychology is a pre-Cartesian "inward turn." For Ficino, the beautiful object is valuable not in itself but in its capacity of conveying the image of the divine Mind to the human mind, where it resembles the image imprinted by the divine Mind at creation. Thus it can be said quite literally that for Ficino, beauty is in the mind of the beholder. The mind is the primary reality, the physical world is of interest only insofar as it displays the mind of

---

21. Marsilio Ficino, *Commentary on Plato's "Symposium on Love,"* trans. Sears Jayne (Dallas, Tex.: Spring Publications, 1985), 6.8, p. 119.

God or affects the mind of man. Ficino's emphasis on the mental and spiritual aspect of love is, arguably, as much a rationalization as a sublimation. But even if he is overly optimistic about the ability to rule unruly passions, he is nevertheless quite genuinely convinced of the fundamental correspondence between the human mind and the mind of God.

In his commentary on the *Phaedrus*, Ficino gives a fuller explanation of the origin of these preexisting "reasons." He takes the standard Scholastic position that Ideas are *"exempla rerum in mente divina"* and gives them a distinctive Christian-Platonic interpretation that allows a commerce between the World of Forms and the human psyche. Whereas Vasari posits Aristotelian abstraction as the origin of the artistic Idea, Ficino understands the source of the artistic Idea to be the divine Ideas, impressed on the human mind at creation.

> By sparks he [God] designates the Ideas . . . and he also thus designates [*designat*] the impressions of these Ideas [*formulas idearum*] innate in us, which, formerly benumbed by lack of use, are rekindled by the breeze of teaching, and they are brightened by the Ideas just as the rays emitted by the eyes [are] by starlight.[22]

The artistic Idea is discovered, or, more accurately, recollected, when it is "rekindled by the breeze of teaching" or "brightened by the Ideas." Looking to the world of Ideas just as one might look to the starry heavens, the student sees the Ideas because of the "rekindled" "formulae" in his mind *and* because of the light by which the Ideas "brighten" the formulae.[23] Ficino preserves the medieval approach to

---

22. *Opera* (Basel, 1576), 2.1574, as quoted and translated by Panofsky, *Idea*, 56–57, who gives the Latin: *"Per scintillas designat ideas . . . designat et formulas idearum nobis ingenitas, quae per desidiam olim consopitae excitantur ventilante doctrina, atque velut oculorum radii emitantes ideis velut stellarum radiis collustrantur."*

23. This complex theory of knowledge combines, on the one hand, two ideas of sight—extramission and intramission of beams—and on the other, a theory of illumination. The same epistemology underlies Sidney's famous sonnet "Leave me, O love which reachest but to dust." Although rather complicated, this intersection of theories of light and epistemology was not uncommon. See, e.g., the illustration from Charles Bovelle, *Liber de intellectu* (1510), 14.8 , f. 85, reproduced in Thomas Browne, *"Religio Medici" and Other Works*, ed. Leonard Cyril Martin (Oxford, U.K.: Clarendon Press,

the physical world as an expression of the divine Mind, as a vehicle for the dialogue between God and human beings, as a visible sign or symbol to be interpreted spiritually by those with eyes to see. But he also adds to the medieval model by placing a new emphasis on the analogy between the divine Mind and human minds. God's Ideas are impressed not only on the world but also on the human mind. Thus the natural world is a book written by God; but so too is the human mind. In it is already present to us—again, if we have eyes to see—the whole book of nature. Whereas the medieval Scholastics gave the human mind the faculties of the divine Mind (reason and will), Ficino gives it the contents of the divine Mind as well.

This epistemology is clearly Augustinian, and it points to Ficino's considerable debt to Augustine's doctrine of the Ideas. Although Augustine does believe that God and the Ideas can be known directly, through a mystical illumination, he believes that there is a much more ordinary kind of illumination, one that shines on all creatures, even those who have turned away from God. Illumined by this invisible intelligible light, the mind does not see the light of God but instead sees *by* the light of God. What the soul sees are not the divine Ideas themselves, but their impressions, imprinted on the soul by the divine light. According to Augustine, the ordinary process of illumination leaves an impression of the divine Ideas on the soul just as a seal leaves its impression on wax.[24] Lest Augustine be blamed for mixing metaphors of light and wax, it should be recalled that Aristotle had done the same in his theory of perception. An important difference between Augustine and Aristotle, however, is that Augustine does not propose a theory

---

1964), 357, in which the sun is *"intellectus,"* shining at once on *"Res in Mundo,"* which the eye perceives by beams it sends out, and *"Res in Memoria,"* which are represented as stars, presumably brightened in the same instant that the corresponding *"Res in Mundo"* is illumined. This is a sun that, in the words of Sidney's sonnet, "doth both shine, and give us sight to see."

24. See *Eighty-Three Different Questions*, trans. David L. Mosher, *The Fathers of the Church* (Washington, D.C.: The Catholic University of America Press, 1982), 80–81; *De Trinitate* 14.21.15, in *Later Works*, ed. John Burnaby, vol. 8 of *The Library of Christian Classics* (Philadelphia: Westminster Press, 1980), 119; and Etienne Gilson, *The Christian Philosophy of Saint Augustine* (New York: Octagon Books, 1983), 66–111.

explaining knowledge of the external world but rather explaining moral knowledge. The impressions are not of what is, but of what ought to be. Augustinian illumination is concerned essentially with wisdom rather than knowledge. The impressions are the rules by which we measure the world. They tell us not what is in the real world, but what should be in it—and what we should be doing in it. For Augustine, the Ideas are the basis for all ethical judgments. Whereas Descartes and his heirs will use "ideas" to explain human knowledge in general and to ground judgments of certainty, Augustine relies on them to explain how we know what is good and what is right—an important function of Sidney's Idea.

Ficino goes further than Augustine in relating Ideas to the conduct of life. At the climax of the sixth speech in his *Commentary on the Symposium*, Ficino explains that the end of human life is to return to the Idea in the mind of God by which man was first created. In this end lies human perfection:

> Anyone who surrenders himself to God with love in this life will recover himself in God in the next life. Such a man will certainly return to his own Idea, the Idea by which he was created. There any defect in him will be corrected again; he will be united with his Idea forever. For the true man and the Idea of a man are the same.[25]

It is evident that in his enthusiasm, Ficino extends the idea of the Idea as a pattern for ethical action beyond what Augustine had intended. Whereas Augustine considered the Ideas the ground for ethical knowledge and action, Ficino makes the Ideas the end as well. Whereas this recovery of integrity, this identification of love of God with the proper love of self, is reserved by Ficino for the next life, Sidney will locate this end point of the Christian moral life in the present world. In one sense more optimistic than Ficino, in another sense less rationalistic, Sidney puts the goal of Christian perfection within the reach even of persons living an active life.

In this belief that the purpose for seeking Ideas is a sort of Platonic apotheosis in which one is united forever with the "Idea of a man," Fi-

---

25. *Commentary on the "Symposium,"* 145.

cino's more strictly Neoplatonic side emerges. Indeed, his debt to Augustine is more than matched by his debt to Plotinus, whose elaborate philosophical and mystical understanding of the universe synthesizes the Platonic, Aristotelian, and later Hellenistic theories of the roles of Ideas within the cosmos. In 1492 Ficino translated the *Enneads*, and its multiple publications attest to the considerable influence of Plotinus on the Renaissance.[26] And Plotinus's influence on art theory cannot be overestimated. Often quoted is Plotinus's defense of the arts, which effectively rebuts Plato's argument against art as an imitation of an imitation. Plotinus argues that art imitates not the visible nature but the "forming principles" of nature, thereby giving art the same ontological status as nature:

But if anyone despises the arts because they produce their works by imitating nature, we must tell him, first, that natural things are imitations too. Then he must know that the arts do not simply imitate what they see, but they run back up to the forming principles [λόγους] from which nature derives; then also that they do a great deal by themselves, and, since they possess beauty, they make up what is defective in things. For Pheidias too did not make his Zeus from any model perceived by the senses, but understood what Zeus would look like if he wanted to make himself visible.[27]

It is not difficult to see how Sidney's theory of poetic making through the "*Idea* or fore-conceit" resembles Plotinus's description of the arts shooting "back up to the forming principles." Indeed, Kurt Spellmeyer argues that "at the heart of the *Apology* is a tenet central to Plotinian aesthetics—that the artist does not imitate objects of sensation only,

26. See Spellmeyer, "Plotinus," 50, who notes that the *Plotini Enneades* was published in 1540, 1559, and 1582.
27. *Plotinus*, trans. A. H. Armstrong, Loeb Classical Library (Cambridge, Mass.: Harvard University Press, 1966), 5.8.1. I quote not from the translation of Stephen MacKenna (which Spellmeyer uses) but from the more recent and more literal translation of Armstrong. Spellmeyer is undoubtedly led astray by MacKenna's free use of "create," which introduces considerable confusion to a reader trying to discern the precise method of artistic production Plotinus has in mind. For example, MacKenna translates "ποιοῦσι" as "creates" ("Still the arts are not to be slighted on the ground that they create by imitation of natural objects"), which results in a confused idea of "creation by imitation." Armstrong's choice of "produce" is clearly more accurate.

but holds the mirror to the Ideal Forms themselves."[28] For Plotinus, art and nature proceed according to the same "reason-principle," but art surpasses nature in its ability to "make up what is defective in things." This seems to square nicely with Sidney's view that the poet, working through his *Idea* or fore-conceit," does not imitate nature but goes "hand-in-hand" with her, making a "golden" world, which is better than the "brazen" one she produces on her own.

One should pause, however, before identifying Sidney's theory too closely with that of Plotinus. Their striking similarities are accompanied by significant differences. When Spellmeyer says that "nowhere is Sidney more obviously Plotinian than in [his] defense of art as primarily creative, and only secondarily imitative, insofar as it images not things but Ideas," he is again unclear at best.[29] Given that Plotinus held a thoroughly emanationist metaphysics—and indeed forcefully denounced the Christian doctrine of creation—it makes little sense to describe his doctrine of the artistic imitation of Ideas as "creative." Spellmeyer unintentionally smoothes over differences between the two, writing, "Not only do Plotinus and Sidney both regard artistic activity as a contemplation of the inwardly visible, but they contend that this activity has moral value because it simultaneously illuminates the understanding while redeeming nature from its initial disorder."[30] Although Sidney and Plotinus share an optimistic attitude toward the human mind, Plotinus is not really interested in poetics (how the work is made), nor does he descend into a discussion of the details of artistic production. And although both believe that art can produce works in which the Ideas show forth more clearly than they do in the works of nature, the notion of "redeeming nature from its initial disorder" would mean something quite different to each. For Sidney, "redeeming nature" means individuals leading heroic lives that transform the real world from one that is "brazen" to one that is "golden." For Plotinus, the goal is not a life of heroic action but one of asceticism and contemplation; his interest is not in "redeeming" the world—to the extent he was familiar with the Christian concept, it was highly repug-

---

28. "Plotinus," 51.   29. "Plotinus," 52.
30. "Plotinus," 52.

nant to him—but in leaving it behind. Although Plotinus rebuts Plato's argument against imitation, he does not question Plato's fundamental position that the material world—both art and nature—is a world of shadows. For Plotinus, the work of art, like the world itself, presents a great danger if its insubstantiality is not always kept in mind. Like the reflection of Narcissus, the work of art is an illusory image whose beauty can draw the naïve beholder to his death.[31]

Of course, this Platonic distinction is hardly alien to Sidney, who knows well that the world and art can lead one astray. However, his response to the dangers of the material world is different from the Plotinian *contemptus mundi*. His remedy is not to turn away from the "too much loved earth," but instead to make it "more lovely" (100). Sidney agrees with Plotinus that art and nature are vehicles for contemplating the higher realities they figure forth; but unlike Plotinus he does not reduce their function and value to this alone. For Sidney, contemplation does not lead one to turn one's back on the work of art or on the world; its leads one, rather, to incarnate (another Christian concept that was anathema to Plotinus) the Idea of the work in one's own life and to redeem the world through heroic moral action in that world. For Sidney, the material world and the active life are both good, and art aids the perfection of both. Thus, with Plotinus as with Sidney's other predecessors, resemblance should not be taken for identity.

Evident in Sidney's Idea are elements from the theories of his precessors, but in a combination and a form never before seen. At once more daring and less esoteric than Ficino, Sidney encapsulates and surpasses his predecessor, giving Ficino's theory of knowledge a witty and inward turn. Ficino believed that the human mind had traces of the divine Ideas, and that the illumination of those "formulas" requires the agency of the divine Ideas and of visible forms that enter the soul through the eyes. Sidney, on the other hand, says nothing about anything outside of the mind. Sidney's poet has no need of sense impressions, for he "bringeth his own stuff, and doth not learn a conceit out of a matter" (120). And instead of distinguishing between

---

31. See 5.8.2.

the Ideas, which are above the human mind, and the traces of those Ideas, which are within, Sidney has only the "Idea or fore-conceit," which he clearly locates in the mind of the poet. Proving himself a true Astrophil (i.e., a "star-lover"), Sidney even locates the starlight with which the Ideas were metaphorically associated by Ficino in the "zodiac" of the poet's "own wit" (100).

When Sidney translates the sun from the external world into his mind in his famous sonnet "Leave me O love," the image is admirable for its elegance rather than its difficulty. Readers have little problem with the association of the Sun with God or with the idea of an inner "light." Much more difficult to understand is the transfer of the zodiac, through which the Sun moves, into the mind of the poet. It is hard indeed for modern readers to appreciate the influence of the zodiac on Renaissance minds. A system for organizing the stars, the zodiac seemed to promise control over the occult influences exerted by the stars, a control that was important for alchemical transformations, for medicinal cures, and for predicting the future. In its association with the stars, the zodiac suggested inclusiveness as well as order. The zodiac marked the entire annual course of the Sun through the heavens, and, like the twelve months, could be used to divide the year. A symbol of cosmic inclusiveness and order, the zodiac was pressed into service as a tool for ordering all that lies beneath it. Whether the task was to arrange the human body into its parts or to divide the memory into places, the zodiac seemed a powerful device for discovering comprehensive and differentiated systems. Encompassing the whole Ptolemaic universe, the zodiac was a perfect symbol for integrating the entire circle of knowledge while differentiating that mental universe into seemingly manageable parts.

This association of the starry heavens with the circle of knowledge was already old in the Renaissance. The traditional division of the epic into twelve books, corresponding to the number of signs in the zodiac, was thought appropriate because of the encyclopedic nature, or at least pretensions, of the genre.[32] Bacon, who was nothing if not an en-

---

32. On the zodiac and the epic, see Alastair Fowler, *Spenser and the Numbers of Time*

cyclopedist, concludes the *Advancement of Learning* by noting, "Thus have I made as it were a small Globe of the Intellectual World."[33] The globe he would have had in mind was a celestial rather than a terrestrial one. The medieval encyclopedist Bernardus Silvestris, identifying the heavens with the *Nous*, holds that all of earthly history is inscribed in the heavens, which are therefore like a book in which all the events that have been or are to come can be read.[34] Using the same metaphor of the book, John of Salisbury locates the inscriptions in the human mind rather than the heavens, describing reason as a book in which both pictures and the divine Ideas are inscribed.[35] Inheriting these traditions of organizing knowledge and locating it in the heavenly mind of God or in the human mind, Sidney does not choose between them. Instead he combines them: locating all knowledge in the zodiac, he then locates that zodiac in the wit of the poet.

It is with this sense of the zodiac as a circle encompassing and organizing all learning that Palingenius named his twelve-book attempt to cover all knowledge the *Zodiacus vitae* (c. 1543). Extending the encyclopedic tradition of Bartholomaeus Anglicus's *De proprietatibus rerum*, Palingenius produces a work that is equally pedantic though significantly more pretentious. Quite popular, it was translated by Barnabe Googe and published in five English editions between 1560 and 1588. The full title in the 1576 edition reveals its encyclopedic aspirations: *The Zodiake of life, writetn* [sic] *by the excellent and Christian Poet, Marcellus Palingenius Stellatus. Wherein are conteined twelve severall labours, painting out moste lively, the whole compasse of the world, the reformation of manners, the miseries of mankinde, the pathway to vertue and vice, the eternitie of the Soule, the course of the Heavens, the mysteries of nature, and divers other circumstances of great learning, and no lesse iudge-*

(London: Routledge, 1964), 51; and J. Michael Richardson, *Astrological Symbolism in Spenser's "The Shepheardes Calender"* (Lewiston, N.Y.: Edwin Mellen Press, 1989), 3.

33. *The Advancement of Learning*, Book 9, in *Works*, 5.118.

34. *The Cosmographia of Bernardus Silvestris*, trans. Winthrop Wetherbee (New York: Columbia University Press, 1973), 87, 92.

35. *Policraticus* 1, 173, as quoted by Ernst Robert Curtius, in *European Literature and the Latin Middle Ages*, ed. Willard Trask (New York: Pantheon Books, 1953), 320.

ment. The connection between knowledge and the stars seems evident in the addition of "Stellatus," meaning "be-starred," to the author's invented name.[36] Encompassing this tradition that is, at least in Palingenius, at once pedestrian and hermetic, Sidney translates the zodiac to the mind of the poet. Shifting the macrocosm into the microcosm, Sidney makes a bold as well as witty claim for the human mind.

Sidereal imagery was, of course, a noticeable feature of the poetry of many of Sidney's contemporaries.[37] For some of them, including Raleigh, Chapman, Spenser, and Marlowe, the interest in the stars was not purely poetic. The "School of the Night" in *Love's Labour Lost* is often taken as a satiric reference to the stargazing nights of Raleigh and his circle.[38] Although the membership and the date of inception of the coterie cannot be determined with much certainty, the involvement of the magus Henry Percy, earl of Northumberland, and Giordano Bruno leaves little doubt that the group entertained hermeticist idealizations of the heavens. Using the zodiac as the basis of his hermetic art of memory, Bruno precedes Sidney in translating the zodiac into

---

36. "Stellatus" also seems to point to the place of origin of Palingenius, who is usually identified as Pier Angelo Manzolli of Stellata. For the biography of Palingenius and the history of the reception of his work in England, see Rosemund Tuve, ed., introduction to *The Zodiake of Life*, ed. Rosemund Tuve (New York: Scholars' Facsimiles and Reprints, 1947).

37. See S. K. Heninger Jr., "Sidney and Milton: The Poet as Maker," in *Milton and the Line of Vision*, ed. Joseph Anthony Wittreich (Madison: University of Wisconsin Press, 1975), 69ff., for his discussion that ranges freely and eloquently between Sidney's *Apology*, Spenser's *Shepheardes Calendar*, and Milton's *L'Allegro* and *Il Penseroso*. Heninger reproduces the well-known woodcut from Bartholomaeus Anglicus's *De proprietatibus rerum* (Lyons, 1485) that has Summer and Winter surrounded by the twelve months, which, in turn, are surrounded by the twelve signs of the zodiac (71). As Heninger explains, the zodiac like the calendar was used to show at once the passage of time and the cycle that encompasses that passage, which can be viewed in a single image, in a single instant. Although the significance of the zodiac in Spenser's *Shepheardes Calender* is a matter of debate, there is no question that one of Spenser's models, *The Kalender of Sheepehards* (1503), brought together the functions of the almanac and the household encyclopedia, while serving as a repository of astrological lore (Richardson, *Astrological Symbolism*, 1–2).

38. "These earthly godfathers of heaven's lights, / That give a name to every fixéd star, / Have no more profit of their shining nights, / Than those that walk and wot not what they are" (1.1.88–91).

The Idea of Poetry   75

the mental world of human beings.³⁹ The zodiac would certainly have evoked images of the magus; and not just Bruno but any magus, whose excellence was manifested in large measure by his knowledge of the heavens. Indeed, the magus contemplating the heavens was an emblem of the Neoplatonic aspiration for wisdom. According to Ficino, astronomy was the "highest" of the liberal arts because the knowledge of the astronomer "is nearly the same as that of the very Author of the Heavens."⁴⁰

Even though Raleigh's circle was not yet active when Sidney was writing the *Apology*, Sidney knew those who would be its members. He at once anticipated the astronomical interests of the so-called School of the Night and saw beyond them.⁴¹ Although Sidney shared their enthusiasm for the stars, he had no appetite for arcana. On the contrary, according to Moffett's account, he had "a certain innate loathing" for astrology, which "he seemed purposely to slight."⁴² Unlike the self-impressed natural philosophy set, whose ambition was to rise above earthly limitations, Sidney wanted to bring heavenly lights to bear on human affairs. And he did so with a sense of irony toward the elusiveness of siderial aspirations. This attitude, altogether lacking in those given to astrology, can be seen in Sidney's locating heavenly

---

39. See Frances Yates, *The Art of Memory* (Chicago: University of Chicago Press, 1966), 208ff.; and Mary Carruthers, *The Book of Memory: A Study of Memory in Medieval Culture* (Cambridge, U.K.: Cambridge University Press, 1990), 321.

40. *Théologie Platonicienne*, ed. Raymond Marcel (Paris: Société d'Édition Les Belles Lettres, 1964), 2.226. See also Plato, *Timaeus*, ed. R. G. Bury, Loeb Classical Library (Cambridge, Mass.: Harvard University Press, 1961), 90d, for what may be the origin of this ideal of celestial thought: "For the divine part within us the congenial motions are the intellections and revolutions of the Universe. These each one of us should follow, rectifying the revolutions within our head, which were distorted at our birth, by learning the harmonies and revolutions of the Universe, and thereby making the part that thinks like unto the object of its thought, in accordance with its original nature."

41. This is not to say that none of the stargazers had the wit to discover a zodiac within: Michael Drayton could, for example, employ an astral conceit and compliment Marlowe as one who "had in him those brave, translunary things that your first poets had" ("To Henry Reynolds, of Poets and Poesie," line 9, as quoted by Eleanor Grace Clark, in *Ralegh and Marlowe: A Study in Elizabethan Fustian* [New York: Fordham University Press, 1941], 330).

42. *Nobilis* 75, as quoted by Duncan-Jones, in *Sir Philip Sidney*, 50.

beauty in a woman whom he calls "Stella." Sidney also is far more grounded in his consideration of ethical and political conduct, whose "ending end" of "virtuous action" is attained by reading heroic poetry rather than horoscopes, by seeking guiding lights in the "zodiac" of the poet's "wit" rather than in the prognostications of wizards.

Whereas Palingenius aligned the zodiac of the wit with "secret knowledge" and Bruno incorporated it into his seemingly magical *ars memoria*, in Sidney's use, the association of the zodiac with the occult arts is eclipsed by the conjunction of the zodiac with another encyclopedic tradition, that of the commentaries on the hexameron.[43] As is evident from the length of many of the commentaries on the first chapters of Genesis, the six days of creation suggested a framework within which authors could write about everything in the world. In these hexameral writings there can be seen a convergence of the comprehensive inclusiveness of the zodiac and God's comprehensive work of the six days. For Sidney, the most important representative of the hexameral tradition was unquestionably the *Divine Weeks* of Du Bartas, the first week of which Sidney translated.[44] For Du Bartas, the zodiac, etymologically the "circle of life," provides a heavenly model for all life below. The starry figures are "Heav'ns Principalls," the "sacred patterns" through which material creation takes place. In agreement with the hermetic maxim "As above, so below," Du Bartas asserts that

---

43. Some notable hexameral authors, such as Agostino Steuco or Jacob Boehme, dive into the depths of secret wisdom; others, such as Raleigh, embrace hermetic wisdom without departing so far from orthodox opinion (though running the risk of the accusation of atheism); most authors, however, avoid the hermetic interpretations of creation or mention them without embracing them.

44. Although Sidney's translation has been lost, it was mentioned by Fulke Greville and by Sylvester himself; though registered with the Stationers' Company by William Ponsonby, it never was printed. See Philip Sidney, *Poems of Sir Philip Sidney*, ed. William Ringler (Oxford, U.K.: Clarendon Press, 1962), 339; Guillaume Du Bartas, *The Divine Weeks and Works of Guillaume De Saluste Sieur Du Bartas*, ed. Susan Snyder (Oxford, U.K.: Clarendon Press, 1979), 1.70; and Anne Lake Prescott, *French Poets and the English Renaissance: Studies in Fame and Transformation* (New Haven, Conn.: Yale University Press, 1978), 178–79.

There's nothing precious in Sea, Earth, or Aire,
But hath in Heav'n some like resemblance faire.[45]

Sidney, however, transforms the hermetic maxim. Instead of locating real life in its plenitude in a world above, he locates it in a world within, in the "zodiac" of the poet's "wit." As indicated by this elegant locution, for Sidney the true law of correspondence is better expressed "As within, so without."

The universe that Sidney translated to the mind of the poet clearly resembled the one he found in the *Divine Weeks* of Du Bartas. Like Sidney's poet, Du Bartas's God also relies on the zodiac for his work of creation. In a passage from "The Columnes" (from the second day of the second week), after a catalogue of the signs of the zodiac in the heavens, Du Bartas narrates the creation of the heavens by God the painter. On the "tent" of the "Firmament," God "pourtray[s]" his "future Works" with starry "Figures." This "tableau" on which God paints is the veil of the heavens, and the images he paints are the stars, the preexisting essences of things.[46] Du Bartas presents an extended ekphrasis of the figures in the heavens that makes it clear that they both resemble and surpass the terrestrial life which they encompass and to which they correspond, performing a spectacular union of Platonic essentialism with Scholastic existentialism. Du Bartas makes the starry heavens the creating essences of things.

Although it may not be possible to prove that he knew *La seconde sepmaine* of Du Bartas, published in 1584, it seems very probable, as Heninger speculates, that Sidney knew the work in manuscript.[47] In

---

45. "The Columnes," 427–28, in *Divine Weeks*, 1.479.
46. See 417–20, in *Divine Weeks*, 1.478–79: "Th'Eternall *Trine-One*, spreading even the Tent / Of th'All-enlightning glorious Firmament, / Fill'd it with Figures; and in various Marks / Their pourtray'd Tables of his future Works." Heninger, in "Sidney and Milton," 72, discusses this passage in relation to Spenser's *The Shepheardes Calender*. For the French, see Guillaume Du Bartas, *The Works of Guillaume De Salluste Sieur Du Bartas: A Critical Edition with Introduction, Commentary, and Variants*, ed. Urban Tigner Holmes (Chapel Hill: University of North Carolina Press, 1940), 3.186–87, lines 407–10: "Ainsi le Trois-fois-grand tendant, ingenieux, / Du ciel esclaire-tout le rideau precieux, / Le chargea de façon, et des futurs ouvrages / Ainsi qu'en un tableau y peignit les images."
47. See Heninger, "Sidney and Milton," 60ff., for his discussion of Sidney and Du Bartas.

one passage in particular, God follows a method strikingly similar to that of Sidney's poet. In Du Bartas's scheme, "Th'All-working Word" employs an *"Idea* fore-conceaved," which is "th'eternall Plott" of creation, "the wondrous Forme of all that Forme received."

> Before th'All-working Word alone
> Made Nothing be Alls wombe and *Embryon*,
> Th'eternall Plot, th'*Idea* fore-conceaved,
> The wondrous Forme of all that Forme receaved,
> Did in the Work-mans spirit devinely lye,
> And, yer [*sic*] it was, the World was wondrously.[48]

Quite proud of the accuracy of his translation in an age when translators were not known for restraint, Sylvester retains the verbal form of Du Bartas's *mot composé "l'avant-conceu portrait"* and renders it *"Idea* fore-conceived."[49] It is also interesting to note that he sees no problem translating *"portrait"* as "idea." It is possible that his choice of "idea" was influenced by Sidney's neologism in the *Apology*, which was published eight years before Sylvester's 1603 translation of the passage. Likely, then, is that Du Bartas's *"avant-conceu portrait"* is the source of Sidney's *"Idea* or fore-conceit," a formulation that in turn influenced Sylvester's choice of *"Idea* fore-conceaved" in translating Du Bartas.[50] In any event, what is certain is that Sidney borrows an account of di-

---

48. 411–16 in *Divine Weeks*, 1.478. See Heninger, "Sidney and Milton," 60, who identifies this as a significant passage for understanding Sidney's idea of the Idea. Heninger argues that Du Bartas distinguishes between Christian creation through "th'All-working Word" and Platonic making through the *"Idea* fore-conceaved." The Christian and Platonic traditions are, however, already thoroughly interwoven in the writings of Philo and Origen. Although my analysis diverges from his, far greater than any differences is my debt to Heninger for his fine scholarship.

49."On peut . . . dire que tout ainsi / Que plustost que le Rien par une voix feconde / Fut fait et la matrice et l'embryon du monde, / L'exemplaire eternel, l'avant-conceu portrait, / Et l'admirable seau de tout ce qui s'est fait, / Logeoit divinement dans l'esprit du grand Maistre, / Et l'univers avoit essence avant son estre" (*Works*, 3.186, lines 400–406).

50. The language is picked up later by Donne. When speaking of divine creation through the Word, Donne explains that "when God would produce his *Idaea*, his *preconception* into action, that action, that production was his Dixit, his saying" (*Sermons of John Donne*, 10 vols., ed. George Potter and Evelyn Simpson [Berkeley and Los Angeles: University of California Press, 1953], 4.102, emphasis added).

vine creation for his own theory of poetic making. In his relocation of "*avant-conceu portrait*" to his own poetics, Sidney takes the tradition of representing God as an artist and inverts it, showing how the artist is like God. Following a model of divine creation that itself is represented in terms of the human art of painting, Sidney is, in a sense, closing a metaphorical loop. Du Bartas is the culmination of the tradition that translated the art of painting from the human painter to God the creator; Sidney is at the origins of the tradition that brings it back to the human realm, bestowing it, however, not on the painter but on the poet, who produces "speaking pictures."

Although the emphasis that this tradition places on the "Idea" over the "work itself" runs counter to some of the basic theoretical assumptions of modern (and postmodern) criticism—exhibiting none of the New Critics' embarrassment with intentionality, nor an ounce of the cultural materialists' anxiety over the so-called problematic privileging of the intellectual over the material—it could not be more common in Renaissance presentations of divine creation. The preexistence of the Idea, and the commonplace identification of what Sidney calls "the skill of the artificer" with that Idea, is particularly evident in a passage from Sylvester's *Little Bartas* (1621). The skill of Sylvester's artist, like that of Sidney's poet, is not in the work itself but in the Idea or conceit:

> A passing Artist is no less Complat [*sic*],
> Then in Composure, in his rare Conceit:
> For, in the Knowledge, Art's perfection lies;
> And, *Works* deferd vail not the *Work-mans* Prize.
>   The Minde's not idle, though the Hand awhile
> Vse neither Pen, Pencil, nor Gouge, nor File.
> The Minde's before the Work; and works within,
> Vpon th' *Idea*, yer the Deed begin.[51]

In this work, which Sylvester calls the "quintessence" of the *Divine Weeks*, "Art's perfection" is to be found not in the "Deed" but in

---

51. Joshua Sylvester, *Little Bartas* (London: 1621), 777.

"Knowledge." According to Sylvester, in God's work of creation, "the Minde's before the Work." It "works within, / Vpon th' *Idea*, yer the Deed begin."[52] What is clear from this formulation is that work on the "conceit" or *"Idea"* in the world of the "Minde" is understood to have both temporal and ontological priority over the material production of the work, as it clearly does in Sidney's theory of poetic making. This two-step process of creation, far from being an innovation of Du Bartas, can be traced to the very beginnings of the Christian speculation on the nature of divine creation. Taking up this tradition of a twofold creation in the next chapter, I hope to show those qualities, largely hidden to modern readers, that made it so attractive to Sidney.

52. It should be noted that Sylvester is not wholly consistent in his use of the terms *"Idea"* and "conceit." Early in the work, Sylvester's Du Bartas makes it clear that "Th' admired Author's Fancie" did *not* fix upon "some fantastick fore-conceited Plot" in the work of creation. Furthermore, he not only insists that God created *ex nihilo*, but in a marginal notation goes so far as to deny unequivocally that God created through his Ideas: "God, needing no Idea, nor premeditation, nor Patterne of his work, of nothing made all the World" (5–6). This denial is no doubt intended to distance Sylvester's Du Bartas from the Platonic account of creation from preexisting matter. The formulation of the denial, however, reveals the unavoidable question that implicitly accompanies all speculation on creation: What was God doing before he created the world?

CHAPTER 4

THE IMITATION OF CREATION

Not easily identified with any of the notions of "creativity" circulating today, Sidney's idea of human creativity more closely resembles the sometimes heady late medieval theories of divine creation. Scholars who have examined the idea of creativity in Sidney's *Apology* all agree that it is modeled on divine creation, but they do not agree on which account it mirrors. The range of nuanced models available in sixteenth-century England was great, and a survey of these often subtle theories suggests that Sidney's model—and likewise his theory of poetic creativity—is far more sophisticated than anyone has yet imagined. After surveying the standard Christian and Platonic models of creation, which those writing on creativity in the *Apology* commonly place in opposition to one another, I will turn to patristic models. Uniting rather than opposing the Christian and Platonic approaches, these patristic theories correspond quite precisely with the few mechanical details Sidney gives regarding poetic production. When recognized as Sidney's model for poetic creativity, these theories of divine creation illuminate several of Sidney's otherwise enigmatic formulations, including his description of the poet as an "artificer" whose "skill . . . standeth in that *Idea* or fore-conceit of the work, and not in the work itself" (101).

Sidney's allusions to the Christian account of creation are unmistakable. Echoes of Genesis can be heard quite clearly in the *narratio* of the *Apology*, most obviously in Sidney's justification of the poet as made by God "to His own likeness" (101). Sidney pushes the likeness quite far: whereas God created the world by sending his Spirit out on the waters and created man by breathing his Spirit into his nostrils, the poet "bringeth things forth" "with the force of a divine breath" (101). This playful pneumatology is matched by Sidney's later claim that the poet "doth not learn a conceit out of a matter, but maketh matter for a conceit," a formulation that translates the theology of creation to the theory of rhetoric, producing a witty formulation of *inventio ex nihilo* (120). Indeed, the freedom that Sidney gives the poet, who "goeth . . . freely ranging only within the zodiac of his own wit" (100), has suggested to many the freedom, affirmed by dogmatic definitions, with which the Christian God created the universe. On the basis of these and other passages, some have argued, quite sensibly, that Sidney is directly modeling his theory of poetic invention on the Christian doctrine of creation *ex nihilo*.[1]

Despite Sidney's allusions to Genesis, S. K. Heninger, the scholar who has unquestionably made the greatest contribution to understanding Sidney's idea of poetic creativity, gives the *Timaeus* precedence as a source. Heninger argues that Sidney is most influenced by the Platonic creation myth, in which the Demiurge forms the cosmos using preexisting archetypes and matter.[2] According to Heninger, Sidney deliberately chooses the term "maker" in order to evoke the Platonic cosmogony. Similarly, he cites Sidney's use of the term "Idea" to locate Sidney's poetic theory within a Platonic context. Indeed, within the context of the Mosaic account of the six days' work, it is hard to make sense of Sidney's assertion that "the skill of the artificer" is not to be found "in the work itself" but in the "*Idea* or fore-conceit of the

---

1. Abrams, in *The Mirror and the Lamp*, 273–74, argues that Sidney relies on the analogy of the poet and God in developing a theory of the poem as "heterocosm." Milton Nahm, in *The Artist as Creator: An Essay on Human Freedom* (Baltimore: Johns Hopkins University Press, 1956), 74–83, stresses the same "great analogy," but argues that the essential common feature of poetic making and divine creation is freedom. Shepherd, ed., *Apology*, argues for Sidney's debt to mannerist art theory, which relied on the analogy of the poet and God (61–66). See also Erwin Panofsky, "Artist, Scientist, Genius: Notes on the 'Renaissance-Dämmerung,'" in *The Renaissance: Six Essays* (New York: Harper, 1962), who argues for the influence of Christian doctrines of creation in the visual arts.

2. *Touches of Sweet Harmony*, 287–324; "Sidney and Milton," 57–95.

work" (101). In Genesis, God does not appear to deliberate; furthermore, when he sees what he has made, God judges not that it was a good *idea* but simply that "it was good." Insofar as Sidney stresses the ontological and epistemological superiority of the "Idea" over the material artifact, he does indeed seem to evoke the Platonic rather than the Christian originary myth.

The one point on which Heninger and those arguing for creation *ex nihilo* agree is that the Christian and the Platonic models stand in opposition to one another.[3] They seem to find ample support for the opposition in the writing of the Church Fathers, whose authority they happily enlist. Athanasius, a touchstone of orthodoxy, is often cited upholding the distinction between creation out of nothing and the Timaean workmanlike construction from preexisting patterns and material: "to think of God as composing and putting together the universe out of matter is a Greek notion; it represents him as a workman rather than as a creator."[4] And Augustine is found to enforce the same distinction between creation *ex nihilo* and the work of "builders or artisans": whereas "God is quite rightly believed to have created [*fecisse*] all things from nothing," "builders and artisans [*fabros et . . . opifices*] of any kind can build [*fabricare*] nothing unless they have something out of which to build [*fabricent*]."[5] The Schoolmen follow Augustine. Peter Lombard points out that "Moses says that the world was made by God as a creator," and he therefore warns against "the error of certain men" who made God "a sort of artisan."[6] In the Renaissance, the prohibition against confusing the work of God with that of the artist was

---

3. See, e.g., Panofsky, "Artist, Scientist, Genius," 171; Bouwsma, "The Renaissance Discovery of Human Creativity," 21; Nahm, *Artist as Creator*, 69–70; and Heninger, "Sidney and Milton," 62, who says that he recognizes "that both traditions had been assimilated into Christianity," but, for the sake of his study, chooses to "separate the Timaean cosmogony and consider it as an autonomous system."

4. *Oratio contra Arianos* 2.22, as quoted by Bouwsma, "The Renaissance Discovery of Human Creativity," 25. See J.-P. Migné, ed., *Patrologiae Cursus Completus. Series Graeca*, 161 vols. (Paris: Migné, 1857–1887), 26, col. 192. Hereafter the *Patrologiae . . . . Series Graeca* will be abbreviated as PG.

5. *De Genesi contra Manichaeos* 1.6.10, in William Jurgens, ed., *The Faith of the Early Fathers*, 3 vols. (Collegeville, Minn.: Liturgical Press, 1970), 3.37, and PL 34, col. 178.

6. As quoted by Bouwsma, "The Renaissance Discovery of Human Creativity," 25.

still taken seriously; and, indeed, as late as Coleridge the distinction could still be invoked, if not strictly enforced.[7] Expressed by Augustine in the short phrase "*Creatura non potest creare*," the orthodox distinction is best encapsulated as "God creates, man makes."[8]

Not only the Church Fathers but Sacred Scripture itself seems to uphold the distinction. In the Hebrew Scriptures, the word for the divine creative activity, "ברא [*bara*]," is reserved to God alone. And the Septuagint translators, for their part, took pains to maintain the distinctiveness of this divine activity, which is most evident in their faithful resistance to the temptation to use Plato's "δημιουργέω." Although they did not refrain from using ποιέω to translate "ברא," this was due primarily to the lack of a more fitting alternative.[9] Because of the rough equivalence of "ποιέω" and "δημιουργέω" in the *Timaeus*, the translators found a new term for the divine activity, "κτίζω." Originally used to refer to the builder of a city, "κτίστης" had come to refer to the founder of a city, one who establishes the *polis* with his decree alone, remaining aloof from the actual building of the city—the work of a δημιουργός. By transferring "κτίζω" from the founding of cities to the foundation of the world, the Septuagint translators introduced a metaphoric term to help secure the distinctiveness of the work of the six days. Considered a better translation for "ברא," "κτίζω" was enlisted to replace "ποιέω." In the New Testament, "κτίζω" is firmly established as the term for divine creation, and "ποιέω" is generally used for human activities involving making, doing, keeping, and performing.[10]

Although the distinction between creating and making does indeed

---

7. See Milton Nahm, "The Theological Background of the Theory of the Artist as Creator," *Journal of the History of Ideas* 8 (1947): 365, who argues that Coleridge's definition of poetry as a "dim analogue of creation" is a compressed version of the argument of Athanasius in *De Decretis* 3.11, Philip Schaff and Henry Wace, eds., *Nicene and Post-Nicene Fathers (Second Series)*, 14 vols. (Peabody, Mass.: Hendrickson, 1994), 4 (hereafter NPNF2).

8. As quoted by Panofsky, "Artist, Scientist, Genius," 171.

9. See Gerhard Kittel, *Theological Dictionary of the New Testament*, ed. Geoffrey Bromily (Grand Rapids, Mich.: Eerdman's, 1995), 3.1026–27, on whose account I rely in the following discussion of language in Sacred Scripture.

10. Kittel, *Theological Dictionary*, 6.464f.

play an important role in the history of Christian theology, it does not play the role critics claim for it. Whereas a number of those writing on the *Apology* cite the distinction as a restraint against humans aspiring to God-like powers, the Church Fathers were not especially interested in denying man the power of creation *ex nihilo*—for it had barely occurred to anyone to make such a claim. The challenge they faced did not come from overweening human ambition but from ancient materialist philosophies, which threatened to limit God's creative power by insisting on the eternal existence of matter. These philosophies (e.g., the Manichaeism that Augustine embraced and later rejected) asserted a metaphysical dualism, which raised various ethical as well as metaphysical problems and forced Christian apologists to respond by asserting God's ability to create *ex nihilo*. The main objective of the apologists was not to place a check on human ambition but to free God from the fetters that materialist worldviews sought to impose. They formulated the distinction not to deny creativity to human beings but to secure it for God.

If the distinction between divine creating and human making was as absolute in the thought of the Fathers as it is in the minds of some critics, one would expect the Fathers to avoid the Platonic vocabulary when speaking of creation. One would expect them, for instance, to follow the example of the Septuagint translators and avoid applying "δημιουργός" and its forms to God. The Greek Fathers do not, however, abandon use of the term. Clement of Rome does not have any qualms about calling on the authority of Plato's *Timaeus* to support apologetical arguments: indeed, in asserting the superiority of God to matter, he explicitly compares God to Plato's Demiurge.[11] For this first-century bishop of Rome, Plato was not an adversary but an authoritative ally.

---

11. In the Latin texts in which his writings are preserved, Clement refers to God as *"opifex"* and *"artifex"* (*Recognitions* 8.15, in Alexander Roberts and James Donaldson, eds., *The Ante-Nicene Fathers: The Writings of the Fathers Down to A.D. 325*, 10 vols. [Peabody, Mass.: Hendrickson, 1994], 169; PG 1, col. 1379), terms which, along with *"fabricator,"* *"aedificator,"* *"genitor,"* and *"architectus,"* Cicero, Chalcidius, Seneca, and others used to translate Plato's "δημιουργός." Hereafter *The Ante-Nicene Fathers* will be abbreviated as ANF. See Curtius, *European Literature*, 544, on how these authors, elevat-

Of course, one might imagine that, with clarification over time, this Platonic vocabulary would be replaced by more suitable ways of speaking of God's creative power. However, in the third century, God is still thought of as *"opifex," "artifex,"* and "δημιουργός." Origen expresses astonishment that intelligent men have embraced materialist philosophies that imagine a world "without an architect or overseer [*sine opifice vel provisore*]."[12] Irenaeus argues against pagans who claim that the Demiurge has an animal rather than a spiritual nature, and he identifies the Demiurge with God the Creator.[13] And Athanasius, cited as an authority upholding the distinction between Christian and Platonic accounts of creation, repeatedly and explicitly uses "δημιουργός" to refer to God. Indeed, the previously cited distinction Athanasius makes between "workman" and "creator" is not quite what it seems. Whereas the English terms suggest the Greek "δημιουργός" and "κτίστης," the terms Athanasius uses are "τεκνίτης" and "ποιητὴς," which indicate that Athanasius is distinguishing not the "workman" from the "creator" so much as the "human artisan" from the "divine maker."[14] Even Augustine could speak of God as "the great workman [*artifex magnus*]," identifying the "Wisdom of God [*Sapientia Dei*]" with the "art [*ars*]" by which he created all things.[15] Obviously, the distinction between God the "workman" and God the "creator" is not as absolute as many have claimed.

Whereas critics have claimed that Athanasius separates the two notions of God, in fact he conjoins them. Again and again, he multiplies rather than limits the names of God and his work, referring to God as "Maker and Artificer [ποητὴς καὶ δημιουργὸς]" and to creation as "the making [δημιουργίαν] of the universe and the creation [κτίσιν]

---

ing to the divine level terms previously used to describe human making, prepare the way for the long tradition in the Latin West of speaking of God as a "maker."

12. *De Principiis* 1.14, 2.14 in ANF 4.240, 269; PG 11, cols. 117, 185. The original Greek unfortunately is not extant; nevertheless, here it can be inferred that included among Origen's original terms would have been "δημιουργός."
13. *Against Heresies* 2.30–31, in ANF 1.403–7.
14. *Oratio contra Arianos* 2.22; in PG 26, col. 192.
15. *The City of God*, 2 vols., ed. R. V. G. Tasker and Ernest Barker, trans. John Healey (London: Dent, 1945), 11.21–22; *Works*, 11 vols. (Paris: Gaume, 1835–38), 6.462–63.

of all things."[16] This doubling of names is not unique to Athanasius. In arguing against the eternity of matter, Theophilus of Antioch employs the same distinction, asserting that God "made [πεποίηκε]" and "fashioned [δεδημιούργηκεν]" the world.[17] Similarly, his second-century contemporary Tatian generally refers to the world as "creation" but he does not hesitate to think of it in certain contexts as God's "workmanship [δημιουργίαν]."[18] This sort of patristic parallel processing can be traced all the way back to the first century, when Clement of Rome defended the doctrine of creation *ex nihilo*, writing that God "creates and also arranges [*creavit atque composuit*]" all things.[19] In all of these Church Fathers, the two divine activities, creating and fashioning, are complementary rather than contradictory; though distinct, they are not opposed.

The attribution of the two powers to God, to create and to fashion, was commonplace in subsequent hexameral literature. Although the work of the six days is divided differently by different authors, it was commonly understood that the first three days relate God's work of creation and the second three his work of adornment. Furthermore, the work of creation itself was often divided between God's initial creation of the formless matter, which was but "waste and void," and the subsequent formation of the matter through a series of divisions—separating light from darkness, the waters above the heavens from the waters below the heavens, the seas and the dry land. In allowing God to arrange what he had invented out of nothing, the Fathers thus did not share the concern of some of those writing on the *Apology* to keep the God of Moses and the God of Plato apart. Rather, their training in classical rhetoric made it seem quite natural to think of God operating in this way. As the Original Orator, he naturally thought first of invention and then of arrangement.

In the fourth century, Basil does not retreat from Athanasius's position. In his homilies on the work of the six days, he goes well beyond

16. See, e.g., *On the Incarnation of the Word* 1.1.2–3; NPNF2.
17. "Letter to Autolycus," 10, in ANF 2.98; PG 6, col. 1065.
18. *Address to the Greeks* 4, in ANF 2.66; PG 6, col. 808.
19. *Recognitions* 8.20, in ANF 1.170–71; PG 1, col. 1381.

the analogy to rhetoric and compares God to a humble potter. In commenting on the first words of Genesis, Basil says that Moses chose the word

"Created" [ἐποίησεν] to show that that which was made [δημιουργοῦ] was a very small part of the power of the Creator [ποιηθέν]. In the same way that the potter [τέχνης], after having made [διαπλάσας] with equal pains a great number of vessels, has not exhausted either his art or his talent; thus the Maker [δημιουργὸς] of the Universe, whose creative power [ποιητικὴν], far from being bounded by one world, could extend to the infinite, needed only the impulse of His will to bring the immensities of the visible world into being.[20]

Of course, Basil's point is to explain that Moses' choice of the verb "ποιέω" for the divine activity is appropriate since it connotes a broader power than the mere crafting of the visible world. According to Basil, it is inappropriate to call God a Demiurge not because the work of the Demiurge is beneath him, but because his powers extend further. Basil is willing to call creation God's "workmanship," and he is even willing to call God a "Workman"—but a Workman whose power is not limited to what can be seen in his workmanship. For Basil, Plato's theory is not wrong but incomplete, since it accounts for only one aspect of the creative (poetic) power of God.[21]

If it were not for the contrary testimony of those writing on the *Apology*, the interplay of the Platonic and Mosaic accounts would hardly be surprising, since it is a commonplace to note the interpenetration of the Christian and the Platonic traditions. For the Church Fathers, it was generally held that Plato probably acquired certain aspects of his wisdom from the Jewish people, either through the Hebrew Scriptures (which was the belief of Clement of Alexandria in the second century) or through conversations with those who knew them (as Augustine believed in the early fifth century).[22] In the Greek Fathers, the exegesis

20. *Hexaemeron* 1.2, in PNF2 8.53; PG 29, col. 8.
21. See Pelikan, *Christianity and Classical Culture*, 90–106, on the Cappadocian Fathers' use of the Platonic cosmology.
22. See Harry Bober, "*In Principio*: Creation before Time," in *Essays in Honor of Erwin Panofsky* (New York: New York University Press, 1961), 17.

The Imitation of Creation 89

of the first chapter of Genesis routinely employed the Platonic causal analysis of creation exemplified in the *Timaeus*. Similarly, the *Timaeus*, as it was transmitted through the Middle Ages, was a much more Christian version than Plato ever could have imagined. Chalcidius, the fourth-century translator of the *Timaeus*, was a Christian, and in his accompanying commentary he includes the theories of Origen and Philo on divine creation.[23] Indeed, when medieval and Renaissance commentators look for the historical Plato, they find a Plato already transformed by predominantly Christian Neoplatonists; and when they read Genesis, they view it through the Platonic interpretative frame, crafted by Philo and the Greek Fathers, and handed down from generation to generation.[24]

Unfortunately, the rich variety of interpretations of Genesis—still available and widely known in the Renaissance—is now appreciated only by specialists. The tradition of commenting on the first few chapters of Genesis is generally said to have its origin in the *Homilies in Hexaemeron* of St. Basil. Basil's work, completed by his brother Gregory of Nyssa in his *De hominis opificio*, established the genre; and Ambrose's imitation of Basil's commentary introduced it in the Latin West. This tradition, which reaches its climax with Milton, was still very much alive at the end of the sixteenth century. The book of Genesis served not only as a topic for poetry but often as a skeleton for studies in theology, history, or science. Commentaries on Genesis were for Renaissance readers what encyclopedias are for us today. As Arnold Williams has documented, forty of these commentaries were published in England and on the Continent between 1525 and 1633,

---

23. See Stephen Gersh, *Middle Platonism and Neo-Platonism: The Latin Tradition* (South Bend, Ind.: University of Notre Dame Press, 1986), 2.430–31.

24. Raymond Klibansky, in *The Continuity of the Platonic Tradition during the Middle Ages* (Millwood, N.Y.: Krauss, 1982), 74–77, gives many medieval examples of the convergence of Christian and Platonic accounts of creation, such as the liturgical hymns of Abelard, which borrow terms previously used to describe the Demiurge. As Klibansky notes, Ficino's commentary on the *Timaeus*, driven by an attempt to return to Plato, only gets as far back as Christian Alexandria (73). See also E. N. Tigerstedt, *The Decline and Fall of the Neo-Platonic Interpretation of Plato: An Outline and Some Observations* (Helsinki, Finland: Societas Scientiarum Fennica, 1974).

many of them containing hundreds of pages on the first few chapters of Genesis.[25] Among the authorities were the Greek Fathers, excerpts of whose writings were plentiful.[26] These commentaries provided, for better or worse, what Samuel Purchas described as "a cloud indeed of Authors, both for their numbers, and the variety of their opinions."[27] Given this variety, it would be quite surprising if there were no traces of the Platonic cosmogony to be found. Indeed, these commentaries are no more purely Christian than Chalcidius's commentary on the *Timaeus* is purely Platonic. Despite the firm pronouncement of those writing on creativity in Sidney, the myriad of commentaries on Genesis and the *Timaeus* do not simply divide themselves into two piles.

Showing a greater philological sophistication than do modern scholars, Scaliger recognized the semantic range and complexity of the terms associated with poetic making. In his *Poetics* (1561), from

---

25. Arnold Williams, *The Common Expositor: An Account of the Commentaries on Genesis, 1527–1633* (Chapel Hill: University of North Carolina Press, 1948), 9. On interpretations of Genesis from the apostolic period to the present, see also Stanley Jaki, *Genesis 1 through the Ages* (London: Thomas More Press, 1992); and Paul Vignaux, ed., *"In Principio": Interprétations des premiers versets de la Genèse* (Paris: Études Augustiniennes, 1973).

26. More widely available than has been commonly acknowledged, these patristic writings were often published in complete editions as well as compendia. Thanks to the efforts of humanists such as Erasmus, Latin translations of the collected works of Lactantius, Basil, Gregory of Nazianzus, and Athanasius were already printed in multiple editions by the mid-sixteenth century. Many individual works by these and other early Christian writers were also available in Latin translation, and some editions in the original Greek were published in this period as well. Given the extent of his travels and friendships, Sidney certainly would have known of these books and would have had opportunities to consult them. On the availability of the Greek Fathers, see Harold Weatherby, *Mirrors of Celestial Grace: Patristic Theology in Spenser's Allegory* (Toronto: University of Toronto Press, 1994), 4–9, who points out that although "no historian of Renaissance ideas would dispute the importance of patristic influence in the period, . . . very few students of English literature have taken that influence seriously into account" (4). See also William Haugaard, "Renaissance Patristic Scholarship and Theology in Sixteenth-Century England," *Sixteenth Century Journal* 10 (1979); and S. L. Greenslade, *The English Reformers and the Fathers of the Church* (Oxford, U.K.: Clarendon Press, 1960).

27. *Purchas His Pilgrimage* (1626), as quoted by Williams, *The Common Expositor*, 6.

The Imitation of Creation 91

which Sidney borrowed heavily, Scaliger argues forcefully that there was no disrespect in the tradition of calling God "ποιητής." Knowing well the dignity of the appellation, he believed that in transferring it to the human maker, he was offering the highest praise. Therefore, when he calls the poet "another god" and attributes to him the power "to create [*condere*]," he does not see a need to forsake the Platonic terminology—any more than the Greek Fathers did. On the contrary, he seeks to rehabilitate it. Fully aware that calling God "Maker" would suggest Plato's Demiurge, Scaliger defends his choice of the term for the Christian God, noting that the early Christians could call God a "Maker" without denying his creative powers or slighting him in the least. Standing on firm philological ground, he argues that there is no reason to restrict the term, as contemporary usage had done, to "candle-makers" and the like. Calling for a return to the original usage of "the learned Greeks," Scaliger applies the term both to God and to the poet.[28]

If one followed the arguments of Sidney's critics rather than the scholarship of Scaliger, Giovanni Antonio Viperano would seem to be speaking nonsense in his treatise *De poetica* (1579): "Because [the poet] creates from nothing [*ex nihilo res creat*], he is called *a maker* [ποιητής], since he who makes something from matter [*ex materia conficit*] is said to be a *craftsman* [δημιουργὸς]. So the poet brings forth [*producit*] wonderful things made out [*configendo*] of almost nothing . . . , and so he has acquired the very name applied to God."[29] Here the distinction between "craftsman" and "maker," deployed (according to critics) to defend God's creative work from confusion with human work, is used to protect the dignity of the work of the poet. The poet, just like God, is not a "craftsman" but a "maker." As if setting a seal securing the dignity of the poet, Viperano bestows on him, because of his ability to create "almost out of nothing," the title of "maker."

Similar to Viperano's identification of "maker" with "creator" is

---

28. Adams, ed., *Critical Theory*, 140.
29. *On Poetry* (Greenwood, S.C.: Attic Press, 1987), 8; *De Poetica Libri Tres*, ed. Bernhard Fabian, *Poetiken Des Cinquecento* (Munich, Germany: Wilhelm Fink, 1967), 15.

Puttenham's opposition of "making" to "imitation" and "counterfaiting."[30] Although poetry does imitate, it also is an art of making what never existed before. Puttenham opens his *Arte of English Poesie* with a strong though reverent assertion of the resemblance between human and divine making:

> A Poet is as much to say as a maker. And our English name well conformes with the Greeke word: for of ποιεῖν to make, they call a maker *Poeta*. Such as (by way of resemblance and reuerently) we may say of God: who without any trauell to his diuine imagination, made all the world of nought, nor also by any paterne or mould as the Platonicks with their Idees do phantastically suppose.[31]

Both the poet and God are makers—makers *ex nihilo*: God "made all the world of nought," and "even so the very Poet makes and contriues out of his owne braine, . . . and not by an foreine copie or example" (3). In an effort to describe the originality of the work of the human poet, Puttenham stresses the originality of the work of the divine Creator. This attempt to preserve the freedom of God and of the poet leads him to suppress the role of the divine Ideas in creation and in poetic making. For Puttenham, the maker does without not only material but even Ideas. Bringing the praise of the maker, the tradition initiated by Scaliger, to its climax, Puttenham presents a version of making that surpasses creation *ex nihilo*, for it does not even require thought. For him, "maker" has been so thoroughly assimilated into Christian vocabulary that he can unwittingly use the Platonic term in his rejection of Platonism.

Scaliger, Viperano, and Puttenham use the term much as it was used by the early Christian councils, in whose dogmatic formulations there is no well-defined opposition of divine creation and human making. "ποιέω" still retains its ability to signify divine creative activity as late as the Council of Constantinople, whose creed follows the Septuagint translation and calls God "ποιητὴν [Maker] of Heaven and Earth." Although this creed clearly shows the limitations of the dis-

---

30. *The Arte of English Poesie*, 3.
31. *The Arte of English Poesie*, 3.

tinction between making and creating, it does illustrate a different distinction. Calling God the Father the Maker not only of heaven and earth but also "πάντων ὁρατῶν τε καὶ ἀοράτων ποιητήν [of all that is visible and invisible],"[32] the council fathers assert the distinction between the invisible intellectual world and the visible world of the senses.

Unlike the supposed division between making and creating, this division between the visible and the invisible is indeed operative in the Greek hexameral literature.[33] In Basil's *Hexaemeron*, the invisible intellectual world (τα ἀόρατα καὶ νοούμενα) preexists the world of the senses (αἰσθήσει), and in it the "Creator and Demiurge [κτίστης καὶ δημιουργὸς]" "perfects" his "works."[34] More extreme than Basil's version of the separation of the two creations is that of Origen, who reasoned that because the Church provides no clear teaching on "what existed before this world," it is proper to apply reason to the question. Doing so, he begins with the omnipotence of God, and from it he deduces the eternity of the incorporeal creation. He reasons that since to be omnipotent one must have something other than oneself to rule, if God is eternal and omnipotent, some form of creation must always have existed.[35] Although Origen was extreme in his claim for the eternity of the spiritual creation, there was nothing extraordinary in his belief that the spiritual creation preceded the material one.

In a more metaphysical continuation of the *Hexaemeron* of Basil, his brother Gregory of Nyssa explains the twofold method of God. According to Gregory, the first chapter of Genesis presents only the

32. H. Denzinger, ed., *Enchiridion symbolorum: Definitionum et declarationum de rebus fidei et morum* (Barcelona, Spain: Herder, 1965), 125. The earlier version, the Nicene Creed, speaks of God the Father as "Maker of all that is seen and unseen"; it is only later, at the Council of Constantinople, that he is further defined as maker "of heaven and earth." See Tigerstedt, "Poet as Creator," 465.

33. As it is in the thought of St. Paul, who in Col 1:13–16, identifies the Son "in whom we have redemption through his blood" with the "image of the invisible God, the first begotten of every thing created," and says that "by him, and in him" "all things [were] created, which are in heaven and which are in earth, thinges visible, and invisible [τὰ ὁρατά καὶ τὰ ἀόρατα]" (Geneva version).

34. *Hexaemeron* i.5, in NPNF2 8.54 and in PG 29, col. 13.

35. *De Principiis* I, Pref. 7 and 1.3.10, in ANF 4.240–41, 249–50.

creation of the sensible (αἰσθητὸν) world and omits, with one exception, the preceding creation of the intelligible (νοητὸν) world.[36] The exception is in the account of the creation of man at 1:27, which relates his visible as well as invisible creation. According to Gregory, the first half of this verse presents the making of man in the image of God: "God created man in his own image; in the image of God he created him." This ideal man is single, immaterial, and without sex. The second half of the verse goes on, however, to relate what Gregory understands as a subsequent, less ideal creation: "Male and female he made them." In this half of the verse, man no longer is integral and God-like; instead he is multiple, divided into male and female. For Gregory there is no question that the second creation represents a deterioration of the image of God. Since Christ is identified as the image of the Father, and since in Christ "there is neither male nor female," the distinction of sex must represent a loss of the divine image.[37] Of greater interest to our purposes is Gregory's belief that the first creation provides a pattern, a "verbal picture [λόγου γραφῆς]" for the second, and that the creation of man is therefore "twofold [διπγῆ]."[38]

This tradition of a twofold creation goes all the way back to Philo, who was known in the sixteenth century both directly and indirectly. In the work of Philo, Greek metaphysics and Hebrew revelation meet.

---

36. PG 44, col. 76. On Gregory's theory of creation, see the excellent work of Harold Cherniss, *The Platonism of Gregory of Nyssa* (Berkeley and Los Angeles: University of California Press, 1930); see also John Callahan, *Greek Philosophy and the Cappodocian Cosmology* (Cambridge, Mass.: Harvard University Press, 1958), 12.31–57; and, for a more general overview, Hans Urs Von Balthasar, *Presence and Thought: An Essay on the Religious Philosophy of Gregory of Nyssa*, ed. Mark Sebanc (San Francisco: Ignatius Press, 1995).

37. *De Hominis Opificio* XVI.7 in NPNF2 5.405; and in PG 44, col. 181. Gregory is quoting Gal 3:28.

38. *De Hominis Opificio* 3.1, in NPNF2 5.390; PG 44, col. 133; and 16.8 in NPNF2 5.405; PG 44, col. 181. For Gregory, Scripture seemed to confirm that God's creation was double. He notes "that Daniel has Susanna declare that God "sees all things before they come to be" (*In Hexaemeron Liber*, PG 44, col. 72; the reference is to Dn 13:42). See Jean Rousselet, "Grégoire de Nysse, Avocat de . . . Moïse," in *"In Principio": Interprétations des premiers versets de la Genèse*, 104, who quotes this passage as well as the Psalmist's praise of God for having created all things "in wisdom," which Gregory understands to mean "in the λόγος" (Ps 103).

He quite appropriately is known by two names, Philo Judaeus and Philo Alexandrinus—or three, if one counts Donne's epithet for him, "the Jews Plato."[39] Heavily indebted to Plato's *Timaeus* and to Alexandrian philosophical culture in general, Philo's *De opificio mundi* is a commentary on the creation narratives in Genesis. Although Platonic thought had already developed into so-called Middle Platonism, and although the Hebrew Scriptures had already been translated into Greek by the Seventy, Philo's synthesis of Hellenic and Hebraic thought on creation was nevertheless a dazzling innovation, one that was to have a profound influence on the subsequent development of the Jewish and Christian traditions. Philo introduces two innovations that alter the course of the history of the idea of creation. The first is his assimilation of the Stoic λογός into Jewish and Christian accounts of creation. The second innovation, the one of interest for the present discussion, is Philo's understanding that the two creation narratives of Genesis correspond to the creation of the intelligible and the sensible worlds, respectively.[40]

In the second creation story, man "is an object of sense-perception, partaking already of such or such quality, consisting of body and soul, man or woman, by nature mortal." This material man stands in contrast to man as created in the first chapter, who "was after the [Divine] image [and] was an idea or type or seal, an object of thought [only], incorporeal, neither male nor female, by nature incorruptible."[41] The first creation serves as the pattern for the second. For Philo, "universal Nature . . . brings forth no finished product in the world of sense without using an incorporeal pattern [ἀσωμάτου παραδείγματος]" (130):

---

39. Donne, *Sermons*, 6.236.
40. On the history of the relocation of the Platonic Ideas to a divine Mind, which had already taken place by Philo's time, see Erwin Ramsdell Goodenough, *An Introduction to Philo Judaeus* (Lanham, Md.: University Press of America, 1986), 107; and Jean Potter, *Introduction on the Division of Nature* (Indianapolis, Ind.: Bobbs-Merrill, 1976), xxviii.
41. *On the Account of the World's Creation Given by Moses (De Opificio Mundi)*, ed. F. H. Colson and G. H. Whitaker (London and New York: William Heinemann and G. P. Putnam's Sons, 1929), 134: "ὁ δὲ κατα τὴν εἰκόνα ἰδέα τις ἢ γένος ἢ σφραγίς, νοητός, ἀσώματος, οὔτ᾽ ἄρρεν οὔτε, θῆλυ, ἄφθαρτος φύσει."

So when He willed to create [δημιουργῆσαι] this visible world [ὁρατὸν κόσμον] he first fully formed the intelligible [νοητόν] world, in order that he might have the use of a pattern [παραδείγματι] wholly God-like and incorporeal [ἀσωμάτῳ] in producing the material world [τὸν σωματικὸν] as a later creation, the very image of an earlier to embrace in itself objects of perception [αἰσθητὰ] of as many kinds as the other contained objects of intelligence [νοητά].[42]

Like Plato's world of Forms, this intelligible world provides the patterns for the subsequent material creation; but unlike Plato's world of Forms, Philo's ideal world is created.[43]

In explaining the nature of the intelligible world, Philo introduces what would become a lasting element of the tradition, the analogy of the architect. In a no less important analogy, he compares God to the founder of a city, thus helping establish the word for founding, "κτίζω," as the replacement for "ποιέω" and "ברא." The founder stands above both the architect and the builder because he establishes the city simply by dictate, by fiat.[44] Having explained how the autocrat "founds" the city and how the architect first sketches the city in his mind before setting his hand to the job, Philo then applies the model to God, who is both founder and architect.

We must suppose that, when He was minded to found [κτίζειν] the one great city, He conceived beforehand [ἐνενόησε πρότερον] the models [τύπους] of its parts, and that out of these He constituted and brought to completion a

---

42. *De Opificio Mundi*, 130, 16.
43. To prove that the first chapter narrates the creation of the ideal rather than the material world, Philo cites Gn 2:4–5, a passage in which Church Fathers and even Renaissance commentators, following Philo, find evidence of God's two-step method in creation: "'This is the book of the genesis of heaven and earth, when they came into being, in the day in which God made the heaven and the earth and every herb of the field before it appeared upon the earth, and all grass of the field before it sprang up.' Is [Moses] not manifestly describing the incorporeal ideas present only to the mind [ἀσωμάτους καὶ νοητὰς ἰδέας] by which, as by seals [σφραγῖδας], the finished objects that meet our senses [αἰσθητῶν] were molded? For before the earth put forth its young green shoots, young verdure was present, he tells us, in the nature of things without material shape, and before grass sprang up in the field, there was in existence an invisible grass" (*De Opificio Mundi*, 129).
44. *De Opificio Mundi*, 17–18.

world discernible only by the mind [κόσμον νοητòν], and then, with that for a pattern [παραδείγματι], the world which our senses can perceive [τὸν αἰσθητόν]. As, then, the city which was fashioned before-hand within the mind of the architect held no place in the outer world, but had been engraved in the soul of the artificer as by a seal; even so the universe that consisted of ideas [ἰδεῶν κόσμος] would have no other location than the Divine Reason [θεῖον λόγον], which was the Author of this ordered frame.[45]

Sidney's *"Idea"* in the "zodiac" of the poet's "wit" does in fact look very much like the "universe of Ideas" in the "Divine Reason"; and his distinction between the "skill of the artificer" and the "work itself" resembles Philo's distinction between the work of the "founder" and that of the "builder" of the great city. This is not to say, however, that Sidney simply modeled poetic creativity on Philo's account of creation. Philo's account, more than a model, is the point of origination for a whole tradition of approaching creation as twofold, a tradition that extends to and includes Sidney's immediate predecessor, Du Bartas. It is within the context of this theology of creation, thoroughly imbued with Platonism, that Sidney's theory of human creativity must be understood.

Modern readers, of course, are generally unaware of this idea of a twofold creation. This is due in part to the fact that Greek theories have tended to be occluded by the Latin tradition, which has different emphases. In an effort to protect God's transcendence and timelessness, Augustine insisted on an instantaneous creation and on the identification of the divine Ideas with the divine Essence. Thus, Augustine avoided the Greek tendency to think of God developing his Ideas before the material creation, and he instead theorized that God had inserted into the material creation "seminal Ideas" that germinate and develop in the course of time. In addressing problems that did not strike many of his predecessors as particularly problematic, Augustine in certain respects refined the Greek theory, circumventing some of the messy questions potentially raised by their speculations, such as whether God must have Ideas for the Ideas he creates. But as often

---

45. *De Opificio Mundi*, 19–20.

happens, the solution generated a new set of problems. In protecting the divine transcendence from the imperfection of temporal activity, Augustine raised the problem of whether the identification of the divine Ideas with the divine Essence compromises the absolute otherness of the divinity, which the Greeks preserved by placing the Ideas outside of the unknowable essence of God. Whether or not the approach of Augustine is better than those of his more Platonizing predecessors, what is certain is that his genius and authority, combined with the rise of the language barrier between East and West, has tended to keep the Greek opinions outside of the mainstream of the Western tradition and to fix Augustine's emphasis on God's timelessness as the mark of transcendence.

But even Augustine, at least in his earlier writings, employed the Platonic distinction between the two worlds. And he was as adept as his predecessors in finding scriptural support for his position: "But there is another world utterly remote from these eyes of ours, a world which the intellect of a few sound men beholds—this, Christ Himself indicates clearly enough: He does not say, 'My kingdom is not of the world'; He says, 'My kingdom is not of *this* world.'"[46] It is true that Augustine did eventually adjust this opinion, and in his retractions he expresses his regret at having formerly "proposed two worlds, the one sensible, the other intelligible." But he severely qualifies his regret, stating that Plato "did not err in saying that there is an intelligible world if we are willing to consider not the word, which in that connection is unusual in ecclesiastical usage, but the thing itself."[47] Augustine resolves the problem not by discarding the "intelligible world" but by renaming it, calling it not a world but a *"ratio,"* an "eternal and unchangeable plan." In his instantaneous act of creation, God impregnates creation with these plans, his "seminal reasons" that germinate in time.

Where the Greek Fathers felt little need to resist the Platonizing

---

46. *Divine Providence and the Problem of Evil (De Ordine)*, trans. Robert P. Russell (New York: Cosmopolitan Science & Art Service, 1942), 1.11.32.

47. *The Retractations*, trans. Mary Inez Bogan, vol. 60 of *The Fathers of the Church* (Washington, D.C.: The Catholic University of America Press, 1968), 1.3.2.

tendencies of Origen, Ambrose and Augustine consciously guarded against the charms of the Platonists. Chastening their vocabulary by avoiding names such as *"artifex"* for God, they set an example of circumspection for the Latin Fathers. But as great as their influence was, it did not prevent an underground current of Greek thought from resurfacing from time to time. The philosophical approach to creation of Scotus Eriugena in the ninth century and the Platonism of the School of Chartres in the twelfth century demonstrate the irrepressibility of the Platonizing speculation on creation. In his commentary on the *Timaeus*, Chartrian master William of Conches does not hesitate to liken God and the Demiurge: "For as a craftsman wishing to make something first arranges it in his mind and afterward, having procured material, forms it according to his Idea [*juxta mentem suam*], so the Creator, before he was to create anything, had an idea of it in his mind and thereafter performed it by his act."[48] Not coincidentally, the times when this current of Platonic thought resurfaces have been seen as Renaissances: Carolingian, Chartrian, Florentine. Whereas Augustine was unable to complete to his satisfaction a commentary on Genesis, during these periods of what would commonly be called "heightened creativity," thought about creation not only flows freely, it seems almost to pour forth in a torrent.

The tension Augustine felt, at once agreeing and disagreeing with the Platonists, has become a standard characteristic of theological speculation in the West. The tradition is at once unable to do without the Platonic philosophy and yet unwilling to let it run its course. The allure of both the theologically correct and the philosophically captivating accounts of creation was keenly felt in Renaissance England. According to Arnold Williams, the explicit application of Platonic cosmology to the interpretation of Genesis was relatively rare in sixteenth-century England. Although the commentators would indeed mention the Platonic doctrine of the world of Ideas, they generally were in agreement that "any such notion, by presuming to limit God

---

48. As quoted by Hanning, "'Ut Enim Faber . . . Sic Creator': Divine Creation as Context for Human Creativity in the Twelfth Century," 108.

to a certain method of operation, betrayed a lack of understanding of His power and wisdom and came more from the *Timaeus* than from Holy Writ."[49] Williams's opinion must, however, be qualified by the popularity of Philo, at least among the learned. Sidney certainly knew of Philo's theory. It is quite possible that he read Philo in the Latin translation of Bellier, if not in the original Greek.[50] In any event, he would have encountered significant passages from the Alexandrian commentator in the eclectic theological treatise of Philippe du Plessis Mornay, *A Woorke concerning the trewnesse of the Christian Religion*, part of which Sidney translated.[51] In England, Philo had made a very strong impression on the humanist and Platonist John Colet, who, in his *Letters to Radulphus on the Mosaic Account of Creation*, defends his belief in a created and eternal intelligible universe. Colet argues that the first day of Moses' account describes the entire creation in epitome: "God created all things at once in his own eternity."[52] According to Colet, time, which begins with the second day of Moses' account, is "a kind of unfolding of eternity, just as the heaven and the visible world are an unfolding of the earlier and invisible world."[53] Seemingly unaware that he has arrived at the position previously held by Origen, Colet defends it by saying that Philo shared his belief.

---

49. *The Common Expositor*, 44.

50. According to Duncan-Jones, *Sir Philip Sidney*, 297–98, in a death-bed letter, now lost, Sidney expressed thanks for a translation to one "Belarius," who was likely Pierre Bellier, who translated Philo into Latin (although he might instead have been Jean Beller, who translated, among other works, the *Imitation of Christ*).

51. Sidney translated the first six of Mornay's thirty-four chapters; Arthur Golding translated the remaining chapters. As Duncan-Jones, *Sir Philip Sidney*, 251–52, points out, Golding's close association with the Earl of Oxford, Sidney's great rival, would have made a collaborative effort between Sidney and Golding unlikely; and Golding's entry of the translation in the Stationers' Register hard on Sidney's death suggests a pecuniary motive. Duncan-Jones is not correct, however, in her judgment that the book as published "does not appear to retain any of Sidney's wording." Rather, as Albert Feuillerat, ed., *The Prose Works of Sir Philip Sidney*, 3.viii–ix, has shown, lexical and stylistic variations provide strong evidence that the first six books (and possibly the fourteenth and the fifteenth) were translated by Sidney.

52. *Letters to Radulphus on the Mosaic Account of Creation*, ed. J. H. Lupton (London: George Bell and Sons, 1876), 4.

53. *Letters to Radulphus*, 13.

Indeed, Colet is a good parallel case of English Neoplatonism. As Sears Jayne demonstrates, although Colet was deeply indebted to Ficino during his years at Oxford, there is a very different temper to the Neoplatonism of Colet and Ficino. Colet did not share Ficino's enthusiasm for human potential, nor did he seek enlightenment like the members of the Platonic Academy. He had, much like Sidney, a keen sense of the fallen condition of humanity. For him, Platonism remained subordinate to Christian theology; for Ficino, it was certainly more than a handmaid. Colet's understanding of bodily existence was quite opposed to that of Ficino. Whereas Colet thought of the body as a prison to the soul, Ficino held that the body is part of the soul. The snares of the world were much more evident to Colet than to Ficino. So too was the need to take action in that world: Colet placed the active over the contemplative life, something quite alien to Ficino. This is not to say that Colet did not believe in the truth of Platonism. He clearly thought that Plato had revealed truths of the mystery of creation that are only presented in a veiled form in Christian Scripture. Nevertheless, he still thought of these truths as essentially Christian, and for him Christianity retained primary authority. Despite the sincerity of Ficino's Christian belief, on the other hand, it would be hard to say that his Platonism took second place to his Christian faith. What Colet saw in Philo and Origen was a similar theological approach that used Platonic philosophy without elevating it to the status of Christian theology. This process could aptly be called the "Renaissance Re-Hellenization of Christianity."[54]

Mornay would certainly have contributed to this process. In a chapter in which he argues that all ancient authorities (with the exception of Aristotle and the Gnostics) have agreed that the world was created, it becomes clear that for this Calvinist Huguenot the orthodox Christian doctrine of creation is something very much like the teaching of the Greek Fathers. After presenting Hermes Trismegistus as an independent authority confirming the Mosaic account of creation, Mor-

---

54. See Sears Reynolds Jayne, *John Colet and Marsilio Ficino* (Oxford, U.K.: Oxford University Press, 1963), 40, whose phrase "the Hellenization of Christianity" I modify.

nay quotes some verses of Orpheus proving that he believed "that God did euerlastingly hold the world hidden, (as the Apostle sayth) in the Treasurie of his infinite wisedome: Or (as *Dennis* sayth) in the Closet of his purpose and will; and afterward brought it foorth in tyme when it pleased him."[55] For Mornay, Plato's definition of time as the image of eternity corresponds to the two stages of creation: "*Timeus of Locres* termeth Tyme the Image of eternitie, and sayth that it [time] tooke his beginning from the creating of Heaven and Earth, and that God created the very Soule of the World afore the World it selfe."[56] Finding that the wisdom of the ancients confirms the Christian teaching of creation, Mornay reveals not only his own belief in a twofold creation but also his belief that this is in fact Christian belief.

This acceptance of a double creation, though implicit, was widespread in the English Renaissance. The Platonic cosmology that made the commentators on Genesis uneasy had in effect already captured the imaginations of many, including some of the greatest writers. Thomas Browne's allegiance to hermeticism, with its inveterate dualism, makes a double creation a foregone conclusion. He asserts his belief "that this visible world is but a picture of the invisible, wherein as in a pourtract, things are not truly, but in equivocall shapes; and as they counterfeit some more reall substance in that invisible fabrick."[57] This is virtually identical to divine creation in Sylvester's Du Bartas. It naturally follows for Browne that creatures exist before their creation—as Ideas in the mind of God. Going well beyond anything Augustine would grant, Browne in effect arrives at the Greek doctrine of a double creation: "I was not onely before my self, but Adam, that is, in the Idea of God," and more simply, "The World was before the Creation."[58]

Although Browne's paradoxical formulations are unmatched, his

---

55. *A Woorke Concerning the Trewnesse of the Christian Religion*, trans. Philip Sidney and Arthur Golding (Delmar, N.Y.: Scholars' Facsimiles & Reprints, 1976), 131–32. The translation is that of Golding.
56. *The Trewnesse of the Christian Religion*, 133.
57. *Religio Medici*, 1.12.
58. *Religio Medici*, 1.45, 59.

Christian Neoplatonism was not. Those who knew where their ideas of the Idea came from could display their Platonism for effect. Spenser makes a show of his, calling God a "workmaister" who created the world by placing before his eyes a "goodly Paterne."[59] In an elegant expression that does not emphasize the Platonic heritage, Milton speaks of the world as "answering [God's] great Idea."[60] But he also can conflate Christian and Platonic heavenly existence by having Raphael raise the possibility that the Earth

> Be but the shadow of Heav'n, and things therein
> Each to other like more than on Earth is thought?[61]

These evocations of the Platonic cosmology are much flashier than the standard Scholastic doctrine, which can be seen in the *Confutation of Atheism* of John Dove, who says that "God had eternally the verie shape and Idea of the world which he conceaued in his minde."[62] But even in Dove's formulation, it should be noted, there is a lack of Scholastic precision that betrays a Platonic turn of mind. In equating "Idea" with "shape," which is used to translate the Latin *"species"* or *"forma"* and the Greek "εἶδος," Dove draws the Idea down toward the human mind, if not all the way to the workshop of the craftsman.

Although Donne is as clear as Spenser in his belief that "God proceeds by example, by pattern," he is careful to distinguish his God from Plato's Demiurge, and he adds that "God had no external pattern in the Creation, for there was nothing extant." Adhering to Augustinian doctrine and staying clear of unfiltered Platonism, Donne instead holds that "God had from all Eternity an internal pattern, an *Idæa*, a pre-conception, a form in himself, according to which he produc'd every Creature."[63] Nevertheless, in the same sentence in which

---

59. *Hymne in Honour of Beautie*, 29–32, in *The Yale Edition of the Shorter Poems of Edmund Spenser*, ed. William A. Oram (New Haven, Conn.: Yale University Press, 1989).
60. *Paradise Lost*, 7.557. See Ulreich, "'The Poets Only Deliver': Sidney's Conception of Mimesis," 150, who discusses these lines in the context of his argument that Sidney unites in his own poetic theory Platonic and Aristotelian ideas of *mimesis*.
61. *Paradise Lost*, 5.574–76.
62. As quoted by Williams, *The Common Expositor*, 44.
63. *Sermons*, 4.98. Elsewhere, Donne says the same thing: "God had conceived in

Donne explicitly denies the possibility of a double creation, with a "though" and a "yet" he grants the Ideas in the mind of God a quasi-independent ontological status: "for though there were no world, that was elder brother to this world before, yet God in his owne minde and purpose had produced, and lodged certaine Idea's, and formes, and patterns of every piece of this world, and made them according to those pre-conceived formes, and Idea's."[64] Expressing the same tension Augustine felt toward the idea of a preexisting world of Ideas, Donne's formulation denies that the Ideas were created, but still speaks of their being "produced" and "lodged."

It may seem that Donne, whose identification of the Idea as a "pre-conception" clearly echoes Sidney, wants to have his Ideas both ways: "produced" and uncreated. His formulation, however, simply reflects the logical identification of the divine Ideas with the Λόγος. Translated into Latin as both *ratio* and *oratio*, this term was borrowed from the Stoics and put to use by Christians trying to explain the Trinity. Like the Ideas, the Λόγος is the content of the divine Mind; and like the Ideas, it provides the pattern by which all things are made. But unlike the Ideas, in Christian theology there is no ambiguity about the origin of the Λόγος: eternally begotten by the Father knowing himself, the Word like the Father is uncreated. And when the many Ideas are resolved into this one Λόγος, they too are understood to be just what Donne understood them to be, produced but not created. The technical term Trinitarian theology uses for this production is "generation."[65]

Available to Sidney, of course, were numerous accounts of the gen-

---

himselfe, from all eternity, certaine Idea's, certaine patterns of all things, which he would create. But these Idea's, these conceptions produced not a creature, not a worme, not a weed; but then, *Dixit, & facta sunt*, God spoke, and all things were made" (8.120). See also 9.73–74.

64. *Sermons*, 9.276.

65. See *ST* Ia, qq. 27–38. Eternally knowing himself, God generates the Word; eternally loving himself, God generates the Spirit. God's knowledge and love of himself are so perfect that they are themselves God. This Trinity, God the Father, Word, and Spirit, is such a perfect unity that it is not three Gods but rather one God knowing and loving himself.

eration of the Λόγος, from Philo's *De opificio mundi* and the prologue of the Gospel of John and the *Corpus Hermeticum* to Du Bartas's *Divine Weeks*. Incorporating many sources, Mornay presents an account of the generation of the Λόγος that is consonant with Scholastic doctrine, if not style.[66] One feature that distinguishes Mornay's thought as characteristic of the Renaissance is his emphasis on self-knowledge. For Mornay, it is obvious that what God knows in his Word is himself, since "the chiefest wisedome is to knowe ones selfe, whereof [God] could not fayle." Mornay cannot speak of this divine and Delphic self-knowledge through which the Word of God is generated without bringing in the figure of the mirror, calling the Second Person of the Trinity the "reflexion" of God, his "perfect image" as in a "Looking-glasse."[67] This "reflexion" is at once the "perfect image" of God and the pattern for creation. It is generated, and through it creation takes place. This scheme—a complex mirror trick—avoids the problems involved with a double creation, but it nevertheless preserves a twofold understanding of creation: the generation of the Word prior to creation, and then the creation of the world through the Word.

Mornay, and therefore Sidney his translator, specifically address the problem of naming the "perfect image" of the understanding of God, and they note that "the second person for divers respects is betokened by divers names." Mornay notes that "Son" and "Word" recommend themselves because both are "conceived" by the Father, and he refers to the Word at times as the *"Concept"* or the *"Conception"* of the Father.[68] Following Mornay, Sidney introduces the word "Conceyt." In a passage in which Sidney translates Mornay's translation of Philo, Philo's "λόγος" becomes Mornay's *"la Parole ou le Concept,"* which in turn Sidney translates as "Word or Conceyt": "'For what other place could conteyne the operations of God, yea or even the simplest of his conceived patternes? Therefore to speake plainly, The World in under-

---

66. See Heninger, "Sidney and Milton," and *Touches of Sweet Harmony,* 293, who formulates the strongest argument for Sidney's reliance on a model of creation through the divine λόγος.
67. *Prose Works,* 3.265.
68. *Prose Works,* 3.265, 73.

standing [*le Monde intelligible*], is the Word or Conceyt [*c'est la Parole ou le Concept*] of God that made it.'"⁶⁹ Attributing a "Conceit" to God sounded as strange in Sidney's time as it does today. In the dedicatory epistle, dated 13 May 1587, Golding says that he and Sidney "form[ed] and deriv[ed] . . . fit names and tearmes" with the intention that they be "alwaies conceivable and easie to be understoode." He acknowledges, however, that the choice of terms is "not altogether most usual."⁷⁰ Certainly, neither before nor after this translation has it been usual to refer, as Sidney does, to the persons of the Holy Trinity as "In beings."⁷¹ Nor has history approved Sidney's "forming and deriving" of "Conceyt" as a name befitting the Second Person of the Trinity. But what is clear is that just as Sidney was willing to place the "Idea" in the mind of the poet, he also did not balk at locating "conceit" in the mind of the Creator, a conceit in which self-knowledge and creative activity converge.

Mornay's emphasis on self-knowledge in his survey of various theories of creation through the λόγος extends to a broader emphasis on the inwardness of the creative act. He relies on the Stoic distinction between the "inward word [λόγος ἐνδιάθετος]" and the "outward word [λόγος προφορικός]," which corresponds to the distinction between the idea and the spoken word.⁷² For Mornay, all of nature is characterized by "breeding," and "the excellenter that the life is, the more inward [*intime*] to it is that which procéedeth or is bred thereof" (266). More "inward" still than the generation of animal offspring in their "Dames bellies" is that of "sensitiue life [*la vie sensitiue*]," which "conceyveth [*conçoit*] an imagination which hoordeth up it selfe in the memorie [*qui se thesaurize en la memoire*]." Reason is more inward yet, "For it hath his reflexion backe to it selfe; and wee commonly terme the doings or actions thereof by the name of Conceptions or Con-

---

69. *Prose Works*, 3.290; Philippe De Mornay, *De la veritaté de la religion christienne: Contre las Athées, Epicuriens, Payens, Iuifs, Mahumedistes, & autres Infideles* (Anvers: Christofle Plantin, 1582).
70. *The Trewnesse of the Christian Religion*, fol. 4v.
71. *Prose Works*, 3.262.
72. *Prose Works*, 3.267.

ceyts [*conceptions*], after which maner the learned sort doe call their bookes their Children."[73] Whereas Plato said that one gives birth to Ideas (λόγοι) in the presence of beauty, Mornay makes the most inward self-knowledge rather than beauty the occasion of "Conceptions or Conceyts." Whereas Plato speaks of ecstasy and ascent, a movement outward and upward, Mornay speaks instead of a movement inward, not to the World of Forms but into the mind. This emphasis on the inward generation of the mental conception was not unique to Mornay—but neither was it original with Descartes. Both were part of a much larger cultural movement, inspired by various strands of Neoplatonic philosophy, toward a discovery of inward worlds. Following Ficino and Augustine, Sidney believes that the way upward is inward: to know the Ideas, one knows the vestiges of those Ideas imprinted on the soul. He also believes that the paradigm for this inward journey is the inward movement of God.

According to Mornay, the model for inwardness is that of God, whose conceptions are most inward of all. Mornay likens the creator to a craftsman, an *artifex*, who "conceives" his own patterns:

> For as the craftsman maketh his worke by the patterne which he had erst conceyued in his mynde [*par la forme qu'il en a cōceuë premier en son entendement*], which patterne is his inward word [*qui est sa parole interieure*]: so God made the world and all that is therein, by that sayd Spéech of his as by his inward skill or arte [*par ceste parole comme par son art interieur*].[74]

Calling freely on Platonic and Stoic elements in his Trinitarian exposition of creation, Mornay calls the "conceyued" "pattern" the craftsman's "inward word," and likens this to God's "Spéech." Particularly interesting for the light it sheds on the *Apology* is Sidney's translation of God's "*art interieur*" as "inward skill or arte," introducing the term "skill," which figures in his explanation of poetic making (101). The "skill" of the poet stands in his "*Idea* or fore-conceit" just as the "skill" or "art" of God stands in his "Speech" or "*parole*."

While Mornay is writing about God's creation through the Λόγος,

---

73. *Prose Works*, 3:266.
74. *Prose Works*, 265.

he is simultaneously thinking about human making; similarly, as Sidney is writing about poetic making, he is thinking about divine creation. And like many before him, from Philo and the Eastern Fathers to Mornay and Du Bartas, he thinks of it as a twofold process. Having located Sidney within this tradition, I now will examine how he extends it. In the following two chapters I will explore what Sidney's understanding of divine creation reveals about his analogous theory of poetic creativity.

CHAPTER 5

FROM CREATION TO REGENERATION

Notable by its absence in Sidney's approach to poetic creativity is any great concern for the subjective experience of the poet, a concern that overshadows Neoplatonic and romantic speculation on creativity. Although creation is an explanation of origins, Sidney does not become fascinated with the originating mind of the poetic genius, nor does he have any interest in the melancholic brooding or the inner turmoil of the poet-artist. Neither does he embrace any of the ubiquitous theories of poetic inspiration—which make much of the rapture or divine frenzy of the poet—nor does he shroud the creative activity in an atmosphere of mystery. Though a Neoplatonist, Sidney thus stands apart from more faithful adherents to the doctrines of the Florentine Academy, such as George Chapman, who follows Ficino closely, describing the *Divinus furor* by which the true poet "is elevated above the nature of man and translated into deity [*supra hominis naturam erigitur, & in Deum transit*]," and depicting the creative process as a nocturnal illumination

> Where Gloweworme like doth shine
> In nights of sorrow, this hid soule of mine:
> And how her genuine formes struggle for birth,
> Under the clawes of this foule Panther earth.[1]

This standard Neoplatonic approach, which places the artist under the influence of Saturn and identifies creativity with obscurity, can be

---

1. The dedicatory epistles to his translations of the *Odyssey* and *Achilles' Shield* in Tayler, ed., *Literary Criticism*, 45, 33.

seen in the earlier brooding of Dürer's *Melencolia I* and the later spiritual crisis of Wordsworth's *Prelude*. In contrast with these Platonic theories, which direct attention to the psychological processes of the poet, Sidney's poetics show far greater interest in the psychology of the reader. He is interested primarily in the *effect* of poetry rather than its *cause*, and this teleological approach, Aristotelian and rhetorical ("pragmatic," to use Meyer Abrams's term), runs counter to postromantic attitudes toward the author as a creative genius.

The degree to which this emphasis on the audience does not seem essential to poetic creativity is precisely the degree to which Sidney's idea of poetic creativity is not our idea. Whereas we tend to focus almost exclusively on the origin of the poem, Sidney believes that the mystery of creativity is seen most clearly in what the poem originates in the lives of readers. To understand Sidney's theory of poetic creativity, one must attend to Sidney's formulations of the "end and working" of the poem, which is more closely related to the poet's initial "liberty of conceit" than is commonly appreciated (99).[2] Like the poet's freedom, the "end and working" of the poem has something divine about it. Because the "right" poets use "delight to move men to take that goodness in hand . . . and teach, to make them know that goodness whereunto they are moved," they achieve "the noblest scope to which ever any learning was directed" (103). The nobility of moving an audience to "take . . . goodness in hand" is such that the work of the poet, "being rightly applied, deserveth not to be scourged out of the Church of God" (99). Unlike the money changers, poets do not deserve to be driven from the Temple: though not sacred, the work of the poet is not profane either. The assertion that the end of poetry is not profane is one of the central tenets of humanist poetics. Endeavoring to justify poetry vis-à-vis theology, Boccaccio and Petrarch argued that neither the subject matter nor the effect of poetry was opposed to theology. Accordingly, they did not emphasize the creative origin of the poem but rather its not ungodly effect.[3] Poetry's emula-

---

2. See Deneef, "Rereading Sidney's Apology," who does notice the relation.
3. The effort to reconcile pagan (profane) wisdom with Christian revelation is best

tion of theology, deeply embedded in the humanist poetic tradition that Sidney inherited and advanced, emphasizes above all else the good moral effect of the poem. In arguing that poetry, just as with theology, can lead an audience to God, Sidney follows the method of his humanist predecessors and begins not with the beginning but with the end of poetry.

Justifying the poet not by what he receives but by what he delivers, Sidney puts forth one of his most striking and most explicit assertions of poetic creativity, his claim that the poet "bringeth things forth" "with the force of divine breath" (101). Arguing by allusion, Sidney claims for the poet the power of God, who created by sending his Spirit—his "divine breath"—out over the waters and "bring[ing] things forth" through the power of his Word.[4] In referring to the

---

exemplified in Boccaccio's *De genealogia deorum* 14 and Petrarch's defense of poetry in his "Coronation Oration." Whereas Boccaccio reveals the Christian truth hidden in pagan mythology, Petrarch structures his oration as a sermon, while filling it with quotations not from the Bible but from Virgil and other classical sources. To prove that neither the subject matter nor the effect of poetry was immoral, humanists typically compared poetry to theology. In his *Life of Dante*, Boccaccio first gives a qualified recommendation of poetry: "I say that theology and poetry can be considered as almost one and the same thing when their subject is the same." But dropping the condition and citing Aristotle's opinion that the poets were the first theologians (*Metaphysics* 3.4), he delivers a more striking formulation: "Indeed I go further, and assert that theology is simply the poetry of God. . . . It is clear, then, that not only is poetry theology, but also that theology is poetry" (Adams, ed., *Critical Theory*, 126–27). Petrarch repeats Boccaccio's argument, dropping all qualification of his praise: "Poetry is in no sense opposed to theology. I might almost say that theology is a poetry which proceeds from God" (*Le Familiari* 10.4, as quoted by Curtius, *European Literature*, 226). See also "From *Theologia Poetica* to *Theologia Platonica*," in Trinkaus, "*In Our Image and Likeness*," 1.683–721. For a translation as well as a discussion of Petrarch's "Coronation Oration," see E. H. Wilkins, *Life and Works of Petrarch* (Cambridge, Mass.: Harvard University Press, 1955).

4. This notion of creation by ventilation had already found imaginative expression. In Charles Bovelle's *Liber de intellectu* (Paris, 1510), God is pictured as a regal glassblower, bringing things forth through the force of his divine breath. Extending the medieval tradition of *deus artifex*, this picture of God brings him one large step toward human nature. For a reproduction of this picture, see S. K. Heninger Jr., *The Cosmographical Glass: Renaissance Diagrams of the Universe* (San Marino, Calif.: Huntington Library, 1977), 16. But Sidney takes an additional and a larger step, reversing the terms of the metaphor. Whereas the tradition he received personified God, Sidney puts the poet in the role of God and deifies the person of the poet.

poet's "breath," Sidney is of course making a further pneumatic allusion—to the convention of poetic inspiration. In the two decades that preceded his composition of the *Apology*, there had been a renewed interest in poetic inspiration, in part as a reaction against the rise of Aristotelian poetics. The Pléiade poets tended to assert extravagant theories of poetic inspiration, claiming that the rapt poet can see the Ideas in the mind of God. So too those in the academy at the court of Navarre, such as Du Bartas and Mornay, attributed the poet's power to a poetic frenzy.[5] Sidney of course does not subscribe to this Platonic theory of poetry as inspired through a divine furor. For Sidney, the poet does not need to experience ecstasy in order to discover the divine truth of things: he needs only to look within. For Sidney, the poet does not receive divine inspiration, he gives it. He is not moved; rather, he moves others. Such a bold claim makes it clear that Sidney was not put off by the extravagance of the Platonic theory of inspiration. Indeed, he could hardly be more extravagant when he claims that the poet breaths forth a "golden" world "far surpassing [Nature's] doings," and when he claims to deliver "no small argument to the incredulous of that first accursed fall of Adam" (101). Adumbrating Milton's "great argument," designed to "justify the ways of God to man," Sidney's "no small argument" aims high, persuading unbelievers, "the incredulous," to believe. Like *Paradise Lost*, the *Apology* is intended as a complex instrument of divine grace, through which audiences observe the justice of God's ways and discover their own justification.

Although poetry had long been thought to produce virtuous action in readers, the origin of good acts remained a deep mystery for Christians, a mystery not much clarified by the disputes over grace and justification that were raging as Sidney wrote the *Apology*. Minturno and

---

5. For a discussion of the common features of theories of poetic inspiration, see Aguzzi-Barbagli, "Humanism and Poetics," 121–22. On the relation of French poetics to Sidney, see E. H. Gombrich, "*Icones Symbolicae*: The Visual Image in Neo-Platonic Thought," *Journal of the Warburg Institute* 11 (1948): xx; Grahame Castor, *Pléiade Poetics* (Cambridge, U.K.: Cambridge University Press, 1964), 31–33; and Soens, ed., *Defense*, xxii–xxiii, whose discussion of Ronsard, Du Bellay, and Pontus de Tyard is excellent.

Scaliger had already developed rhetorical poetics, in which poetry has the power to persuade audiences to embrace the "very soul of virtue," and Sidney does not hesitate to borrow freely from them.[6] But the Ciceronian rhetorical theory that Sidney's predecessors translate into poetic theory cannot adequately account for the power of poetry to provide "no small argument to the incredulous of that first accursed fall of Adam," which is the power to move the reader from incredulity to belief. This is an accomplishment beyond the hopes not only of Cicero's ideal orator but also of his successor, the persuasive poet of the cinquecento theorists. Bestowing on the audience a fiction that convinces them at once of the Fall and of the possibility of a better world, Sidney's poet provides a vehicle of faith. It is in achieving this godly effect that the art of Sidney's poet rivals the art of God.

With a wit that combines levity and seriousness, Sidney explains the good effect of poetry by exploiting the traditional connection between creation and regeneration, a connection that would have been obvious to many of his contemporaries. John Donne, for example, explains (simply following St. Paul) that "the Spirit of God wrought upon the waters in the Creation, because he meant to doe so after, in the regeneration of man."[7] The relation here is the traditional typological understanding of creation as a foreshadowing of the recreation in grace. It allows Sir John Davies to speak in *Nosce teipsum* of God having "fashioned twice this soul of ours": "But thou which didst man's soul of nothing make, / . . . . . / To make it new the form of man didst take."[8] Although most have become accustomed to think-

---

6. On Minturno's translation of Ciceronian rhetoric into a theory of poetry in his influential *De poeta* (1559), see Weinberg, *Literary Criticism*, 743, who shows how Cicero's praise for oratory as the highest art becomes Minturno's praise for poetry, and how Cicero's claims for the preeminent power of the orator becomes Minturno's argument for the power of the poet. For the relevant passage in Scaliger's *Poetice* (1561), see Adams, ed., *Critical Theory*, 139.

7. *Sermons*, 11.104, as quoted by Terry G. Sherwood, in *Fulfilling the Circle: A Study of John Donne's Thought* (Toronto: University of Toronto Press, 1984), 7. Sherwood notes the same relation in *Sermons*, 2.243, 4.102, and 9.98. He also points out that for Donne regeneration has, as it must, six stages (*Sermons*, 2.243).

8. Lines 61 and 66, in *The Poems of Sir John Davies*, ed. Robert Krueger (Oxford, U.K.: Clarendon Press, 1975).

ing of divine creation as a unique and isolated event (and, by contrast, of human creativity as nearly ubiquitous), many throughout history have recognized an invocation of the original Creation whenever God makes a new beginning. As early as the Pentateuch itself, the new start God makes with Noah after the Flood looks back to the opening creation narrative, as does Israel's passage through the Red Sea. And the two testaments are united in part by the parallel between God's gift of his Spirit at the Creation of the world and Jesus' gift of his Holy Spirit to the apostles at Pentecost. Given Sidney's clear emphasis on moving the will of the reader, his pneumatic allusion points to a specific kind of inspiration: the spiritual regeneration that St. Paul speaks of, by which the fallen world becomes a "new creation" and the fallen human person becomes a "new creature."[9] Bestowing on the "artificer" a skill more beneficent than has generally been supposed, Sidney conceives a theory of poetic creativity that is really a theory of spiritual regeneration.

From the beginning, Christian theories of creation have been intrinsically united to theories of salvation. The fundamental Platonic distinction between the visible and the invisible worlds, for example, drove Christian speculation not only about the origin but also about the destiny of creation. Essential to all of the models that Sidney drew on—creation through the Λόγος, the *Idea*, or the zodiac—is the establishment of a relation between the ideal and the real. The obvious relation is that the ideal, invisible world is a pattern that God uses in making the real, visible world. However, when examined within the larger theological systems of which these theories of creation are only parts, it becomes clear that the relation between the real and the ideal does not end with creation. When with the Fall the original conformity of the real to the ideal is lost, the ideal becomes not only what has been lost but also what is to be restored through the Redemption. Just as Creation is understood to establish the real according to the specifi-

---

9. E.g., "Therefore if anie man (be) in CHRIST, (let him be) a newe creature" (2 Cor 5:17, Geneva version); "For we are his workmanship created in Christ Iesus vnto good workes" (Eph 2:10); "And be renewed in the spirit of your minde, And put on the new man, which after God is created in righteousnes, and true holines" (Eph 4:23–24).

From Creation to Regeneration 115

cations of the ideal, Christian salvation history is understood to reestablish the original relation between the real and the ideal that was lost with the Fall.

Although this redemption is often understood in terms of liberation from bondage, a ransom that frees captive humankind, it is also and arguably more properly understood in terms of a new creation, a "re-generation." In their speculations on spiritual regeneration, theologians have traditionally resorted to Platonic metaphysics and centered their speculation on the figure of the original pattern or "image" in which humankind was created and through which they will be restored. In the double creation, with the Λόγος or the intelligible world providing an invisible "image" of the visible world as it should be, one should understand not only the way creation took place, but the way redemption will be carried out. Just as the visible world came to be through the divine Word, so too it will be redeemed through, by, or in (one may choose a favorite preposition to indicate participation) the same Word. In the introductory section of his influential *On the Incarnation of the Word*, Athanasius presents just such a theory of creation and salvation through the Word. Offering something far more interesting than the supposedly authoritative distinction between "creating" and "making," Athanasius gives what is, in effect, the hermeneutic key to the work, asserting the similarity between creation and regeneration:

> It is, then, proper for us to begin the treatment of this subject [the Redemption] by speaking of the creation [κτίσεως] of the universe, and of God its Artificer [δημιουργοῦ θεοῦ], that so it may be duly perceived that the renewal of creation [τὴν ταύτης ἀνακαίνισιν] has been the work [δημιουργήσαντος] of the self-same Word [Λόγου] that made [γεγενῆσθαι] it at the beginning. For it will appear not inconsonant for the Father to have wrought its salvation in Him by Whose means He made [ἐδημιούργησεν] it.[10]

Both the creation and the renewal of the world are "the work [δημιουργήσαντος] of the self-same Word [Λόγου]." Clearly Athana-

---

10. *On the Incarnation of the Word* 1.4, in NPNF2 4.36; *De Incarnatione Verbi*, ed. E. P. Meijering (Amsterdam: Gieben, 1989), 35.

sius has no qualms about using the Platonic vocabulary. On the contrary, in an attempt to undermine subordinationist heresies, Athanasius explicitly identifies God "the Father of Christ" with the Demiurge.[11] But he carries on this polemic merely with his left hand. His primary intention is to establish the necessary role of the Son, Word, Demiurge, or whatever else the Second Person of the Trinity may be called, in the salvation of the world.

For Athanasius, creativity suggested not only a plenitude of power or genius—as it does now—but also an overflowing of goodness—an aspect of creativity too often overlooked. This goodness is seen not only in the work of creating the universe out of nothing; it is seen preeminently in God's bestowing on the material creation a share, a participation, in the immaterial creation. To speak of this goodness, Athanasius turns to the *locus classicus* for the goodness of the creator, which is the *Timaeus*. There Plato gives the reason for the activity of the Demiurge: "He was good, and in him that is good no envy ariseth ever concerning anything"; and this goodness is such that he, "being devoid of envy[,] desired that all should be, so far as possible, like unto Himself."[12] Philo quotes and paraphrases this passage from the *Timaeus* in order to explain that because "the Father and Maker of all" "grudged not a share in his own excellent nature," he provided a model by which the changeable matter could turn and become conformed "to all that is characteristic of the more excellent model [πᾶν ὅσον τῆς κρείττονος ἰδέας]."[13] Here Philo transforms the divine goodness

---

11. *On the Incarnation of the Word* 1.4, in NPNF2 4.36; *De Incarnatione Verbi* 35.
12. *Timaeus* 29E.
13. *De Opificio Mundi*, 21–22. For Plato's notion of the imitation of the Ideas and the fashioning of oneself in their likeness, see *Republic* VI (500C–D). Of course, absent in Plato are essential elements of the Pauline doctrine. God and providence do not enter into his conception, nor does the figure of the mirror. What Plato does offer, however, is the analogy of the individual and society: in contemplating the Ideas, the person discovers not only a pattern to which he can attach himself with admiration but also patterns for public life. This union of the knowledge of the Ideas and the political life, taken up by Cicero, is central to Sidney's thinking. Plato also addresses the notion of the assimiliation of oneself to the Ideas at *Timaeus* 90A–C; *Theaetetus* 176B–C; and *Phaedrus* 249C. See also John M. Rist, *Eros and Psyche: Studies in Plato, Plotinus, and Origen*

From Creation to Regeneration 117

of the Demiurge, which bestows order and harmony on chaotic matter, into the divine goodness that plans the elevation of material creation to the status of the immaterial Ideas. When it is his turn, Athanasius too quotes the *Timaeus* and says, "For God is good, or rather is essentially the source of goodness: nor could one that is good be niggardly of anything: whence, grudging existence to none, He has made all things out of nothing by His own Word, Jesus Christ our Lord." Athanasius argues that God did not stop with the bare creation of human beings, but "made them after His own image, giving them a portion even of the power of His own Word; so that having as it were a kind of reflexion of the Word, and being made rational, they might be able to abide ever in blessedness, living the true life which belongs to the saints in paradise."[14] Drawing out what is implicit in Plato and Philo, Athanasius makes explicit the salvific power of the model or image. The model is that through which creation was worked, and it is by participation in that model that creation finds its blessedness. The goodness of God the creator is seen in the gift of his image to human beings—and in the restoration of that image when it was lost.

This recognition that the masterplan of God is not simply a plan for creation but also a plan for redemption is evident in numerous analogues. Renaissance historiography relied heavily on the idea of providence, that history is a story written by God. It was commonly understood that God's Idea for the world is not simply a plan for the beginning of history but for the whole of history. Accordingly, consideration of the divine Ideas has traditionally been intertwined with theories of divine providence and foreknowledge. Instructing Boethius, Lady Philosophy defines providence as "the divine reason [*ratio*] itself, established in the highest ruler of all things, the reason which disposes [*disponit*] all things that exist."[15] Similarly, Bernardus Silvestris calls his personification of Noûs not only "Noys" but also "Providence." And

---

(Toronto: University of Toronto Press, 1964), 17–18, 164; and Culber Rutenber, *Doctrine of the Imitation of God in Plato* (New York: King's Crown Press, 1946), 4–17.

14. *On the Incarnation of the Word* 3.3, in NPNF2 4.37–38.

15. *The Consolation of Philosophy* IV.6, in Boethius, *The Theological Tractates*, trans. S. J. Tester, Loeb Classical Library (Cambridge, Mass.: Harvard University Press, 1973).

Aquinas follows Boethius and understands providence as analogous to the divine Ideas: in each is found the goodness of created things. When creatures conform to God's Idea of them, they fulfill the good of their substance; when they conform to God's providence, they fulfill the good of their end.[16]

This providential view, of course, is the norm rather than the exception in this period when the historian's work was thought to begin with an account of creation. In the writings of Raleigh and Browne, providence works in history according to a preconceived "design."[17] In their view, history is made, though not by men but by God. "Design"—as in the "Eternal designe" of which the Cambridge Platonist John Smith speaks—was a popular metaphor for God's providential disposition of history.[18] It points beyond the initial creation to the whole course of the world from genesis to apocalypse. In this Christianized version of what is fundamentally a Hebraic view of history, the central event is, of course, the Redemption. Just as the Creation is an expression of God's goodness at the beginning of time, the Redemption is the expression of his goodness in the fullness of time. This view of history as salvation history allows Thomas Browne to find virtually present in the "Idea" of God not only his own existence but also his fall and redemption. Even though he can say with conviction that he was born in sin, "Eve miscarried of mee before she conceiv'd of Cain," he also can affirm his salvation from all eternity: "That which is the cause of my election, I hold to be the cause of my

---

16. *ST* Ia, q. 22, a. 1: "In created things good is found not only as regards their substance, but also as regards their order towards an end, which . . . is the divine goodness [itself]. This good of order existing in things created, is itself created by God. Since, however, God is the cause of things by His intellect, and thus it behoves that the type [*rationem*] of every effect should pre-exist in Him, . . . it is necessary that the type of the order of things towards their end [*ratio ordinis rerum in finem*] should pre-exist in the divine mind: and the type of things ordered towards an end is, properly speaking, providence."

17. Here I am following C. A. Patrides, *The Grand Design of God: The Literary Form of the Christian View of History* (London: Routledge, 1972). See 74–78 for a synopsis of sixteenth and seventeenth-century chronicles relying on the notion of divine design.

18. *The Cambridge Platonists*, ed. C. A. Patrides (Cambridge, Mass.: Harvard University Press, 1970), 190, as quoted by Patrides, *Grand Design*, 70.

salvation, which was the mercy and beneplacit of God, before I was, or the foundation of the world." According to this providential view, not only his personal history but also the history of the world is the design of God, in which "the world was before the Creation, and at an end before it had a beginning."[19]

As strange as it may now seem to think of the whole course of history as a design enclosed in an Idea in the mind of God from all eternity, it was, in Sidney's time, a habit of thought.[20] Jonathan Edwards's comment on his *History of the Work of Redemption* shows that he does not think of the Redemption as the central feature of God's "grand design," but as the "design" itself: "The affair of Christian theology, as the whole of it, in each part, stands in reference to the great work of redemption by Jesus Christ; which I suppose to be of all others the grand design of God, and the summum and ultimum of all the divine operations and decrees."[21] In Edwards's formulation, the "redemption by Jesus Christ" corresponds to the conceit of God's work. As the "summum and ultimum of all divine operations," this "great work" is more than an isolated event; it is the head or principle that unites all the parts and gives them their true meaning. Just as God created all things through his "grand design," he restores all things through the same "grand design."[22]

19. *Religio Medici*, 1.59.
20. See Craft, *Labyrinth of Desire*, 19–20, who notes that according to Luther and Calvin, God's creative activity, although a single act, is also a "process that began with the first *fiat* and continues until 'creation' is no more." He concludes then that "by calling the poet a maker made in the image of the Heavenly Maker, Sidney indicates that human invention attains validity because it imitates (in the earthly kingdom) this godly action."
21. Letter to the Trustees of the College at Princeton, 19 October 1757, in *The Works of President Edwards* (New York: B. Franklin, 1968), 1.50, as quoted by Patrides, *Grand Design*, 119.
22. It is perhaps worth noting Marvell's use of "design" as an analogous term in his poem "On Paradise Lost." The term refers primarily to the ambitious plan of Milton's "slender book," but it also refers to that book's "Theme sublime," which is the "vast Design" equally of God and Milton. Just as the "vast Design" of God can be seen to "unfold" in Milton's "slender Book," so too Milton's "Verse" bears the sure imprint of the One who has disposed all things *in mensura, et numero, et pondere* (Wis 11:21): "Thy Verse created like thy Theme sublime, / In Number, Weight, and Measure, needs not Rime" (Milton, *Complete Poems*, 209–10).

The divinity of design became a tenet of mannerist art theory during Sidney's time. Looking for clues as to the workings of the mind of the artist, Federico Zuccaro had searched St. Thomas's *Summa theologiae*, which he quotes at length, and from which he derives his notion of the *"disegno interno."*[23] Although he draws primarily on Thomas's treatise on the divine Ideas, he could have found what he wanted just as easily in Thomas's treatise on providence. His treatment of the divine Ideas as "the internal Design" adds to the Thomistic doctrine an emphasis on the inwardness of the creative process and also on the extension of creation to all of time. In the "internal Design," God sees past, present, and future "with a single glance." This "internal design," which Zuccaro also refers to as a "concept [*concetto*]," has its origin in God himself, and it "is of the same substance as He."[24] And as with God, so with his image, man. God, "having created man in His image and likeness" and having given him faculties making him "almost a second God," has

wished to grant him the ability to form in himself an inner intellectual Design [*un Disegno interno intellettivo*]; so that by means of it he could know all the

---

23. Zuccaro is probably best known for the many portraits attributed to him in England, only two of which in all likelihood are authentic (one is of Queen Elizabeth, the other of Leicester). Near the end of his life he published *L'Idea de' pittori, scultori ed architetti* (1607), a work that marks, according to Panofsky, the climax of the Aristotelian-Scholastic movement in speculative art theory (85). As Shepherd points out, although the works of Zuccaro postdate the *Apology,* Zuccaro was in the early stages of developing a systematic approach to the idea of the Idea while Sidney was writing his *Apology* (64–66, 158). Sidney may well have learned something from Zuccaro, who was fourteen years his elder. Although it is unclear whether the two coincided, they would at least have known of each other, for they shared a patron in Leicester, whose portrait Zuccaro painted in 1575, the same year Sidney returned from the Continent and took up residence with Leicester. On Sidney and Zuccaro, see also Craig, "A Hybrid Growth: Sidney's Theory of Poetry in An Apology for Poetry," 66, and Robinson, *The Shape of Things Known*, 105. On Sidney and mannerist art theory in England, see Lucy Gent, *Picture and Poetry 1560–1620: Relations between Literature and the Visual Arts in the English Renaissance* (Leamington Spa, Warwickshire, U.K.: James Hall, 1981); Mirollo, *Mannerism and Renaissance Poetry;* Summers, *The Judgement of Sense;* and Clark Hulse, *The Rule of Art: Literature and Painting in the Renaissance* (Chicago: University of Chicago Press, 1990), who supplement Panofsky's *Idea*.

24. *L'Idea de'pittori, scultori et architetti* (Milan, 1607), I.6, pp. 46ff., as quoted and translated by Panofsky, *Idea,* 87.

creatures and could form in himself a new world, ... and so that with this Design, almost imitating God and vying with Nature [*quasi imitando Dio ed emulando la Natura*], he could produce an infinite number of artificial things resembling natural ones, and by means of painting and sculpture make new Paradises visible on Earth.[25]

For Zuccaro, it is by this internal design that human beings both know the world and form a new world within themselves, a world by which they subsequently can produce what looks very much like Sidney's "golden" world: "new Paradises visible on Earth." As Panofsky explains, at the end of the treatise Zuccaro "interprets the term '*disegno interno*' as an etymological symbol of man's similarity to God." "*Disegno*" is, according to Zuccaro, the "*segno di dio in noi* [the sign of God in us]."[26] And this design is the "second sun of the cosmos," the "second creating Nature," and the "second life-giving and life-sustaining world spirit."[27] Here Vasari's modest "design" has been divinized by his student Zuccaro, and it has become that through which the artist carries out the poetic work, realizes the image of God within himself, and produces a Paradise on Earth. Within this soteriological context it is not surprising that Sidney's "Idea or fore-conceit" should be a pattern not only of creation but of redemption.

The process by which the artist came to share in the renewing work of God spanned many centuries and several "renaissances." Despite Athanasius's early explanation of the theological connection between creation and redemption, understanding both as the "work of the self-same Word," the further development of this close relation between the theology of creation and soteriology was greatly moder-

---

25. *L'Idea* I.6, pp. 46ff., as quoted by Panofsky, *Idea*, 88. Zuccaro goes on to say how the internal design in man differs from that in God: "But in forming this internal Design man is very different from God: God has one single Design, most perfect in substance, containing all things, which is not different from Him, because all that which is in God is God; man, however, forms within himself various designs corresponding to the different things he conceives. Therefore his Design is an accident, and moreover it has a lower origin, namely in the senses." On Zuccaro's *disegno interno*, see also Summers, *The Judgement of Sense*, 283–308.
26. *L'Idea* II.16, p. 196, as quoted and translated by Panofsky, *Idea*, 88.
27. *L'Idea* II.15, p. 185, as quoted and translated by Panofsky, *Idea*, 88.

ated in the Latin West by Augustine's emphatic distinction—developed in response to heresies like Pelagianism—between nature and grace.[28] However, in those revivals of Platonic thought that historians label "renaissances," creation and salvation, nature and grace can be seen to draw closer together. In the Carolingian Renaissance, the *De divisione naturae* (862–66) of John Scotus Eriugena brings creation and regeneration closer than they had ever been before. Though hardly a hallmark of orthodoxy as was Athanasius, Scotus Eriugena was, like his predecessor, very influential. Incorporating the circular movement that Plotinus says leads from the One into nature and back to the One, Scotus Eriugena understands the Christian doctrines of creation and regeneration as a parts of a single movement from God back to God. While highlighting God's role as origin (the uncreated nature who creates) and end of creation (the uncreated nature who does not create), he also bestows on all created nature a dynamic participation in the divine nature. He distinguishes between the created nature that in turn creates, *natura naturans*, and the nature that it engenders, which does not have the power to create, *natura naturata*, giving the distinction, which dates to Plato, a new prominence. Bringing together Christian creation, Neoplatonic emanation, and the Platonic theory of the two worlds, Scotus Eriugena gives the invisible *natura naturans* the power to create.

The next renaissance, that of the twelfth century, was also characterized by a renewed interest in nature, evident in a new dedication to the natural sciences and to the mechanical and technological arts. This new interest led to, among other things, the popular personification of nature. Although there is great variety in the presentation of the goddess Natura, in the ode of Alain de Lille her role as "Child of God and Mother of things" and "Rule of our world" quite clearly gives her the power of *natura naturans*.[29] For Bernardus Silvestris, "elementing nature . . . is in fact the firmament, and those stars which tra-

28. NPNF2 4.36.

29. *De planctu Naturae [The Complaint of Nature]*, as quoted by Marie-Dominique Chenu, *Nature, Man, and Society in the Twelfth Century; Essays on New Theological Perspectives in the Latin West* (Chicago: University of Chicago Press, 1968), 19.

verse the circle of the Zodiac, for it is these that arouse the elements to their natural activity."[30] Following Bernardus's belief that in the "starry ciphers" "ages to come might be beheld in advance," Alain adorns Natura with a crown whose jewels represent the firmament, with the signs of the zodiac and the planets.[31] The continuity of this personification is evident in the numerous examples from the later renaissance, such as Robert Flood's striking depiction of Nature, one foot on earth, one on the sea, milk from her breast nourishing the earth below, her head thrust into the celestial sphere.[32]

Alongside the medieval discovery of nature's creative powers, there was a bursting forth of speculation on the analogy of man and nature, which is especially evident in the other great poem personifying nature, Bernardus's *De mundi universitate*. Dividing the work into two parts, the first on the macrocosm and the second on man as microcosm, Bernardus develops the distinction on which Scotus Eriugena relied and which became ubiquitous in the thought of the masters of the twelfth century.[33] Although it is true that nature had long before been personified by Aristotle (e.g., "Nature does nothing in vain") and that man had been seen as a microcosm already in the *Timaeus* (30d), in the twelfth century the doctrines exfoliate, and they are applied with an exuberance matched only in the hermetic writings.[34] Bringing together the fascination with nature and the fascination with seeing man as a reflection of nature, these masters of Chartres recognize that the mind of man has a power like Natura.[35] Glorifying nature and

---

30. *Cosmographia* 1.4, p. 88.

31. *Cosmographia* 1.3, p. 76; see George Economou, *The Goddess Natura in Medieval Literature* (Cambridge, Mass.: Harvard University Press, 1972), 75.

32. For a reproduction of the image, see Evans, ed., *The Riverside Shakespeare*, plate 17.

33. On the burst of interest in man as microcosm in the twelfth century, see Chenu, *Nature, Man, and Society*, 28–33.

34. On the history of the personification of nature, see Economou, *The Goddess Natura in Medieval Literature*, 175, n22, who offers the quotation from *De caelo* 291.b13.a24 along with other examples.

35. This habit of thought survived the Aristotelian tide that rose in the next century, and Aquinas takes it for granted. Answering the question whether man had mastery over all other creatures in Eden, he begins: "Man in a certain sense contains all

man, they give nature a share in the power of creation and come as close to a theory of human creativity as possible without actually arriving.

Sidney, however, does arrive. He goes further and identifies the starry zodiac not with the head of Nature but with the "wit" of the poet. Whereas the masters of Chartres had made Nature into *vicaria dei*, which Chaucer would later render "the vicaire of thalmighty lorde," Sidney extends this vicarious power of creation to the poet.[36] Likening the mind of man to *natura naturans*, Sidney "balance[s] the highest point of man's wit with the efficacy of Nature" (101). Indeed, Sidney's careful distinction throughout the *Apology* between "poesy" and "poetry," that is, between the "skill of the artificer" and "the work itself," is a perfect reflection of the division between *natura naturans* and *natura naturata*.[37]

Just as Bernardus, Alain, and their contemporaries had discovered in nature a creative power resembling that of God, so too Sidney and his contemporaries discovered in the artist a creative power like that of nature. Shakespeare's image of grafting in the *Winter's Tale* illustrates how art not only "shares / With great creating nature" but also "does mend nature" and "make conceive a bark of baser kind / By bud of nobler race."[38] Like Sidney's image of the poet delivering a "golden" world, Shakespeare's imagery invests art with a meliorative power. However, the difference between the two is instructive. Whereas Shakespeare ultimately resolves art into nature—"nature is made better by no mean / But nature makes that mean"—Sidney has the poet go "hand in hand with Nature," uniting the two in a partnership, though one in which the poet nevertheless has the upper hand, since Nature's "world is brazen" and that delivered by the poets is "golden"

---

things; and so according as he is master of what is within himself, in the same way he can have mastership over other things" (*ST* I, q. 96, a. 2). See Chenu, *Nature, Man, and Society*, 33.

36. *Parliament of Fowles*, 379, in *The Riverside Chaucer*, 3rd ed., ed. Larry Dean Benson and F. N. Robinson (Boston: Houghton Mifflin, 1987).

37. On *natura naturans* in Sidney, see Ulreich, "'The Poets Only Deliver.'"

38. 4.4.87–88, 94–95.

(100). In the *Winter's Tale*, art is part of nature—nature's way of perfecting itself.[39] In the *Apology*, by contrast, art is above nature. It is, in the strict etymological sense, supernatural.

Sidney's "golden" world is the world of nature restored by art. The epithet unmistakably evokes the Golden Age of pagan mythology, that original era that was followed by the Silver, Bronze, and Iron Ages. Standard in Sidney's time, and indeed since patristic times, was the identification of the classical Golden Age with the Christian Eden.[40] Both were ages of an innocence that was lost in later times. In Sidney's Christianized adaptation of the classical myth, the "brazen" world that Nature delivers is clearly a fallen world. And poetry somehow has the power to restore the lost "golden world"—and not just imaginatively but also "substantially." Through the identification of origin and end of creation, much appreciated during the medieval Platonic revivals, what was lost is also that which must be found. Though expelled from Eden, mankind is destined for Paradise. Seeing that in our beginning is our end—that the alpha is the omega—Sidney claims that the poet can restore fallen ("brazen") creation to its original goodness, delivering a "golden" world that is a once and future paradise. Milton makes the same identification, describing the "New Heav'n and Earth" that will spring from the ashes of the old world as "golden days."[41] In delivering a fictional "golden" world, Sidney's poet reveals another version of the new heaven and new earth. Going

---

39. On Aristotle's discussion of nature and art, in *Physics* ii.1,193a32–36; ii.2,194a21 see Edward Tayler, *Nature and Art in Renaissance Literature* (New York: Columbia University Press, 1964), 135.

40. Having translated Ovid's *Metamorphoses*, with its description of the Golden Age, Arthur Golding offers the standard allegorization in his dedicatory epistle: "Moreover by the golden age what other thing is ment, / Than Adams tyme in Paradyse, who beeing innocent / Did lead a blist and happy lyfe untill that thurrough sin / He fell from God? From which tyme foorth all sorrow did begin" ("Epistle," 469–72, in *Shakespeare's Ovid, Being Arthur Golding's Translation of the "Metamorphoses,"* ed. W. H. D. Rouse, trans. Arthur Golding [Carbondale: Southern Illinois University Press, 1961]). For the description of the Golden Age, see 1.103–28. On the patristic identification of Eden and the Golden Age, see Jean Delumeau, *History of Paradise* (New York: Continuum, 1995), 6–15.

41. *Paradise Lost*, 3.337.

"hand-in-hand" with nature, the art of the poet presents a fictional remedy for the Fall; and to the extent that that fiction is not purely imaginary, it does a work analogous to that of grace: it regenerates fallen nature.

The belief that art has a power like grace has antecedents. In his *Didascalicon*, a medieval guide to the arts, Hugh of St. Victor attributes to the arts the power "to restore within us the divine likeness." Possessing the knowledge of the arts, one possesses Wisdom, which Hugh defines (quoting Boethius) as "a living Mind and the sole primordial Idea or Pattern of things." When we posses Wisdom, "there begins to shine forth again in us what has forever existed in the divine Idea or Pattern."[42] The arts—Hugh has in mind philosophy, the queen of the arts—thus perform an *opus restaurationis*, bringing us back to our original pattern, the "primordial" reality. The resemblance to Sidney, though unmistakeable, is nevertheless limited. Sidney is less Platonic and more biblical than Hugh, and he is also more realistic about the recalcitrance of fallen human nature. Although the image of the "infected will"—which keeps people from reaching unto the "perfection" that their "erected wit" can glimpse—may seem appealingly ambiguous to modern ears, for Sidney and his audience its tenor was quite unambiguous. Infection and deformity (with all of its etymological significance) were the commonplace metaphors for the effect of original sin.[43] Infected with sin, the image of God in the soul is de-

---

42. Hugh of St. Victor, *Didascalicon: A Medieval Guide to the Arts*, ed. Jerome Taylor (New York: Columbia University Press, 1961), 2.1.

43. See, e.g., Jean Calvin, *A Commentarie of John Caluine, Upon the First Booke of Moses Called Genesis*, ed. Thomas Tymme (London: John Harison and George Bishop, 1578), 40: "Now although certeine obscure lineaments and markes of that image remaine in us: yet notwithstanding, they are so corrupted & lame, that we may truly say that it is blotted out. For beside the deformitie, whiche appeareth in euerie parte of the soule, this mischiefe sheweth foorth it selfe, that there is no parte which is not infected with the pollution of sinne." John Woolton, in *A Newe Anatomie of Whole Man, as Well of His Body, as of His Soule: Declaring the Condition and Constitution of the Same, in His First Creation, Corruption, Regeneration, and Glorification* (London: Thomas Purfoote, 1576), 15r, uses the same metaphor, along with some other of his favorites: "For being infected with the poyson of sinne, he coulde not reteyne any longer the image of iustice, wisedome and lyfe, which was stamped in him."

formed. And the difficulty of moving the reader is the difficulty of turning the will—of converting it—to the good. It is a task of epic proportions: "To be moved to do [the good] which we know, or to be moved with desire to know, *hoc opus, hic labor est*" (113). As the Virgilian tag elegantly asserts, moving the reader is no less a feat than returning from the underworld. For Sidney—as for Augustine and Calvin—to move the "infected will" was a labor that found figurative expression in the image of raising the dead back to life. And the golden bough that enables the return is grace. With the power to "erect" the "wit" of the reader and reveal the "infected" state of his "will," the poet prepares the way for the action of grace. But more precisely, the poet's work is the channel of grace. Or more precisely yet, it is a secondary cause of that which grace effects: conversion.

Pushing the likeness of art and grace toward identity, Sidney does not gloss over their differences. Rather, he introduces a Scholastic distinction of primary and secondary causality. Without abandoning the claim that Nathan's fable "made David . . . as in a glass to see his own filthiness," Sidney qualifies it with a parenthetical insertion, saying that he speaks "of the second and instrumental cause" (115). His point is that David was moved to contrition by grace and by the parable as the instrument of that grace. Like Sacred Scripture, prayer, sacraments, or sacred liturgy, Nathan and the parable are used by God as an instrument for imparting grace.[44] Although Nathan was a prophet, Sidney is not thinking of his prophetic powers in this passage, which is meant to illustrate the work of "right poets." And Sidney's inclusion of "second[ary]" in addition to "instrumental" makes it clear that for Sidney Nathan's tale is not a special "instrument" of God but instead an example of a secondary cause that God uses in his ordinary provi-

---

44. Speaking of Sidney's claim that poetry plays a role in curing the "infected will," Soens, ed., *Defense*, 63, points out that "the regenerative power which Sidney here attributes to poetry is similar to the power which commentators on the Bible had attributed to the poetry of the Bible, the Psalms in particular." Prescott, in "King David as a 'Right Poet': Sidney and the Psalmist," goes further and argues that David is Sidney's model for the "right poet" and that the psalms are a model for Sidney's theory of poetry.

dence. Despite Sidney's division between theological, philosophical, and "right" poets, for Sidney "feigned" "discourse" can have the same power as prophesy. Unlike the prophet, who is an extraordinary instrument of grace, the poet is a very ordinary instrument—but an instrument nonetheless. What is revolutionary about Sidney's claim is that ordinary human activity, carried out freely and on one's own initiative, becomes recognized as a channel for grace. Participating in God's work of regeneration, the poet, by means of his "golden" world, moves the reader's will to embrace the good. This gives the poet a God-like power, or, better, it allows him to share in God's actual power.

This sense that human beings somehow participate in divine activity has an important antecedent in the Platonic revival of the twelfth century. A threefold division between the work of God, the work of nature, and the work of the human artisan—already made standard in Chalcidius's commentary on the *Timaeus*—provided twelfth-century commentators on the *Timaeus* a framework for exploring the analogy between the three. Distinguishing rather than dividing, they hold that God, nature, and human art are all three aspects or agents in the single work of the divine governance of the world.[45] This is evident in the thought of Gilbert de la Porrée, who gives a very elegant presentation of God acting through the human artisan in such a way that the work is at once the work of the artisan and the work of God.[46] As Chenu

---

45. *Nature, Man, and Society,* 40–41.
46. *Nature, Man, and Society,* 40, quotes *Notae super Johannem* (MS London Lambeth Palace 360, fol. 32r b): "It is asked whether artificial things—footgear, cheese, and like products, which we say are works of man and not of God—have been made by God.—Indeed, all things have been made by God as their author; but certain things are called God's works just as they are, namely those which he makes by himself and neither after some resemblance in nature nor through the intermediary service of someone else, as he makes heaven and earth. Others are called works of nature, and these are created by God after some natural resemblance, as a seed from other seeds, a horse from other horses, and similar things from their similars. Others which he makes through the intermediary service of man are called works of men. God, therefore, is the sole author of all things; but there are different ways of making, both as to authority and as to intermediary service, such that on the one hand man is said to be the author, and on the other hand, God. In a similar manner we customarily say that some

notes, this new recognition—that nature and art are at once instruments that God uses in his government of creation as well as realities independent of God and worthy of attention in their own right—led to great scientific and technological advances in the twelfth century.[47] Incorporated by St. Thomas into his own synthesis, where it is especially evident in his treatise on divine government, this new appreciation of secondary causality is, as Chenu holds, a "doctrinal development." Certainly, giving the creature a participation in the work of the Creator struck many as too lofty a claim for the human condition, and it was certainly part of the reason for the condemnations of Aquinas, who was accused of (among other things) naturalism, that is, of following a naturalistic philosophy that compromises the absolute power of God. Although this conservative Augustinian criticism of Aristotle's benign understanding of nature continued into the Renaissance and was amplified by Reformation thinkers, it was not able to root out the tendency to divinize nature. As if by its own logical progression, the theology of instrumental participation made inevitable the eventual divinization of human art—which is, as Aristotle explained, an imitation of nature. If nature has a share in God's creative and regenerative power, so too, if the premise is taken to its logical conclusion, the human artist must have a share in those powers. And just as the Augustinian authorities in the High Middle Ages were ready to strike against the comparison of God and nature—defending the absolute transcendence of the Creator over creation—so too, as Sidney understood, many of his contemporaries could not help but consider the comparison of the poet to what Shakespeare would call "great creating nature" "too saucy."

Whereas certain elements in the Platonic revival of the twelfth century anticipate Sidney's idea of human creativity, Sidney's presentation itself is an anticipation of later romantic theories of the creative imagination. The hope for renewal evident in the *Apology* clearly ex-

---

rich man has built many buildings which in fact a carpenter has built, but the one has built them only by his authority and command, the other by his service."

47. *Nature, Man, and Society*, 42–44. See also Lewis Mumford, *Technics and Civilization* (New York: Harcourt Brace & World, 1963).

tends into the romantic period, where poetry again is thought to play an important role in regeneration. The obstacles to that renewal are, however, formulated in more subjective terms. For the romantic poets, what needs to be restored, essentially, is perception. Where Sidney sees a fallen world restored to a prelapsarian state through creativity, Shelley sees a world of "impressions blunted by reiteration" where creativity is what allows one to *experience* the universe "anew."[48] For both Coleridge and Wordsworth, the discovery of poetic creativity is bound up with their personal development, and the narration of that development follows the old pattern of crisis and conversion. For Coleridge, his discovery of the active power of the imagination came through his intellectual conversion, through his extricating himself from the skepticism of Hume and Hartley and embracing the idealism of Kant and Schelling. In the *Prelude*, Wordsworth relates the personal crisis out of which he discovers his vocation as a poet and the true power of the mind. The central books of the poem, in which Wordsworth relates his crisis and recovery, are entitled "Imagination, How Impaired and Restored"; and as Abrams has explained at length, it is a story of loss and restoration that is a secularized version of biblical and Platonic accounts.[49] Wordsworth's discovery of his vocation as poet and of the divine power of the human mind represents a great change in his perception of reality, and in such cases as his, perception is reality.

As Marvell had done in "The Garden," Wordsworth links creativity with a conversion in consciousness. In "Tintern Abbey," he gives his famous formulation in which the senses not only "perceive" "all the mighty world" but also "half create" it. Wordsworth speaks of the "tranquil restoration" he experiences when he passes into his "purer mind" and sees there "beauteous forms" of things he had seen long ago. In this "blessed mood," "laid asleep / In body," we "become a living soul" and "see into the life of things."[50] What Wordsworth under-

48. *A Defence of Poetry*, in Shelley, *Poetry and Prose*, 505–6.
49. *Natural Supernaturalism: Tradition and Revolution in Romantic Literature* (New York: Norton, 1971), 119.
50. "Tintern Abbey," 22–49, in *Selected Poems and Prefaces*, 108–9.

stands by creativity differs considerably from the modern commonplace understanding, which too readily identifies creativity with artistic productivity. For Wordsworth, creativity is a state of enhanced artistic ability only in a secondary manner. In its essence, it is a state of restored perception, in which one penetrates through the "unintelligible world," with its "heavy and . . . weary weight," and "see[s] into the life of things."

This creative power by which the mind escapes its own deadened sensibility is that faculty described by Coleridge under the name of the "secondary imagination." The secondary imagination takes the objects it finds, which "are essentially fixed and dead," and brings them to life, "recreat[ing]" them or, if this is not possible, "idealiz[ing]" and "unify[ing]" them.[51] Elsewhere, Coleridge makes the philosophical lineage of his thought more explicit. Those things that "are essentially fixed and dead" are *natura naturata;* and the mind that "recreates" them, restoring their original "ideal" "unity" or integrity, has the power of *natura naturans*. In his brief treatise *On Poesy or Art*, he sets forth a theory of imitation that bears an unmistakeable resemblance to that of Sidney:

> If the artist copies the mere nature, the *natura naturata*, what idle rivalry! If he proceeds only from a given form, which is supposed to answer to the notion of beauty, what an emptiness, what an unreality there always is in his productions, as in Cipriani's pictures! Believe me, you must master the essence, the *natura naturans*, which presupposes a bond between nature in the higher sense and the soul of man.[52]

---

51. *Biographia Literaria*, 2 vols., ed. James Engell and W. Jackson Bate (Princeton, N.J.: Princeton University Press, 1983), 1.304.

52. *Biographia Literaria*, 2.257–58. The passage continues: "The wisdom in nature is distinguished from that in man by the co-instantaneity of the plan and the execution; the thought and the product are one, or are given at once; but there is no reflex act, and hence there is no moral responsibility. In man there is reflexion, freedom, and choice; he is, therefore, the head of the visible creation. In the objects of nature are presented, as in a mirror, all the possible elements, steps, and processes of intellect antecedent to consciousness, and therefore to the full development of the intelligential act; and man's mind is the very focus of all the rays of intellect which are scattered throughout the images of nature. Now so to place these images, totalized, and fitted to the limits of the human mind, as to elicit from, and to superinduce upon, the forms

This "bond between nature in the higher sense and the soul of man" is a more philosophical presentation of the "hand in hand" union Sidney speaks of in the *Apology*. Thinking of the same distinction between *natura naturans* and *natura naturata*, Sidney speaks of the sensible world not only as the "brazen world" but also as a "second nature." It is Coleridge's "nature in the higher sense," Shakespeare's "great creating nature," with whom Sidney's poet goes "hand in hand."

Completely at one with Coleridge's belief that creativity presupposes such a bond between *"natura naturans"* and the "soul of man," Wordsworth speaks of creativity as issuing when "the discerning intellect of Man" is "wedded to this goodly universe." Echoing Marvell on the creative mind, Wordsworth makes its product "paradise."

> Paradise, and groves
> Elysian, Fortunate Fields—like those of old
> Sought in the Atlantic Main—why should they be
> A history only of departed things,
> Or a mere fiction of what never was?
> For the discerning intellect of Man,
> When wedded to this goodly universe
> In love and holy passion, shall find these
> A simple produce of the common day.[53]

Not a mere fiction or history—not the insubstantial "castles in the air" of which Sidney speaks—the product of the creative mind is the real world transformed. This "paradise" is neither a now-"departed" Edenic world nor a heaven that is yet to come. Neither is it the endlessly deferred end point of a secularist utopia, nor is it an extraordinary mystical experience. It is, rather, "the simple produce of the common day." Like Sidney's "golden" world and Marvell's garden of the mind, Wordsworth's "paradise" promises that beatitude can be an everyday experience.

---

themselves the moral reflexions to which they approximate, to make the external internal, the internal external, to make nature thought, and thought nature,—this is the mystery of genius in the Fine Arts. Dare I add that the genius must act on the feeling, that body is but a striving to become mind,—that it is mind in its essence."

53. Prospectus to *The Recluse*, 47–55, in *Selected Poems and Prefaces*, 46.

This clearly is not the old epistemology, in which the mind is a passive mirror of the world. In this new creative epistemology, however, the old *adaequatio rei ad mentem* is not abandoned but instead discovered for the first time. Not only is the "Mind" a mirror of the "World," the "World" is the mirror of the "Mind." When one discovers how they are "fitted" one to the other, one discovers that each images the creative activity of the other, and that in doing so knower and known become one.

> How exquisitely the individual Mind
> (And the progressive powers perhaps no less
> Of the whole species) to the external World
> Is fitted:—and how exquisitely, too—
> Theme this but little heard of among men—
> The external World is fitted to the Mind;
> And the creation (by no lower name
> Can it be called) which they with blended might
> Accomplish:—this is our high argument.[54]

Striking is the care Wordsworth uses in attributing creation to the "blended might" of the "Mind" wedded to the "World." Showing the same reverence that led Sidney to avoid the term and Puttenham to handle it so gingerly, Wordsworth inserts a parenthetical justification for his use of so lofty a name. Doing so within the Miltonic statement of his "high argument," Wordsworth subtly indicates that it will be in showing the power of the "creation" accomplished by the "external World" and the "individual Mind" "with blended might" that he will justify the ways of nature, if not of God, to man.

In evoking Milton's "great argument," Wordsworth establishes an analogy between the problem of knowledge and the problem of sin. Transforming Milton's theodicy into his own creative epistemology, he brings his audience to a correct understanding of the relationship between the Mind and the World. However, in doing so, he does not leave behind Milton's argument any more than Virgil's Aeneas leaves

---

54. Prospectus to *The Recluse*, 63–71, in *Selected Poems and Prefaces*, 46.

behind Achilles or Odysseus. In reinterpreting Milton's argument, Wordsworth preserves it and makes it his own. As Meyer Abrams has shown, the "wedded" union of the "Mind" and the "universe" is the type of the apocalyptic marriage of the lamb and the New Jerusalem. The problem, as formulated by Wordsworth, is secular rather than biblical; but the secular is understood in relation to the biblical. So even though the shift seems to be one of subject matter—from the problem of sin to the problem of consciousness—in fact, it is more like a shift in focus, with the subject matter the same. The subject remains alienation, but it is treated within a natural rather than a biblical framework. In both cases, the problem is the alienation of human beings from the ultimate principle of being, from nature, from one another, and from themselves. The arguments of both authors are designed to address this alienation. For Milton, the remedy lies in the discovery of the providential pattern of the *felix culpa;* for Wordsworth, it is found in the personal discovery of creativity. By evoking Milton, Wordsworth is showing that in answering the problem of consciousness he is also responding to the problem of evil.

Before Milton's "great argument" and Wordsworth's "high argument," Sidney held the power of poetry to present its audience "no small argument." Thinking not only of epics but of any poetry that presents heroic examples, such as Xenophon's *Cyropaidaia*, Sidney believed that poetry can reveal to the audience the true nature of alienation while presenting the remedy for restoring lost integrity. Like Milton, Sidney frames the problem in religious terms, saying that poetry offers "no small argument to the incredulous of that first accursed fall of Adam" (101). Addressing the "incredulous," the poem confronts the problem of the lack of belief, of atheism, understood in its Elizabethan sense. Presenting heroic examples, poetry convinces audiences that their condition is not natural but fallen, and it makes a strong case for a more upright kind of life. Like that of Wordsworth, the solution Sidney provides is not obviously religious. The noble patterns that the poem provides audiences are examples of virtue as lived, for the most part, by pagan heroes. But the creative imitation of ancient examples is no more a departure from Christian ideals than is

Wordsworth's presentation of the creative imagination.[55] Just as Wordsworth brings Christian regeneration into the problem of subject and object in order to resolve it, so too Sidney relies on Christian regeneration to resolve the problem of noble conduct in a postchivalric culture. Solving the contemporary crisis in nobility, the imitation of Cyrus resolves the more basic problem of fallen human nature in the process.

In calling attention to the kinship of Sidney and the romantic poets, I do not wish to minimize their differences, which are, to say the least, significant. Whereas Wordsworth finds the ideal forms in nature itself, in the world of landscapes and humble rural life, Sidney looks to the lives of epic heroes. For Coleridge, "Nature in the higher sense" is a spirit found in nature, a *Natur-geist*, what Wordsworth would call "a living Presence of the earth," not Sidney's "zodiac," distilled from nature and removed to the "wit" of the poet.[56] In general, the romantics will think of "mind" where Sidney is more likely to use "soul"; and conversion, for them, essentially results in a new consciousness, whereas for Sidney it issues in ethical and political action. Perhaps the greatest difference is simply the extent to which Wordsworth, Coleridge, and their contemporaries are able to develop their thought, investigating areas on which Sidney is silent, such as the psychological experience of creativity and aesthetic perception.

But underlying these differences is a fundamental continuity. The similarity amid difference is evident in the biblical allusions of the opening and closing of the *Prelude*. Whereas Wordsworth begins the Prospectus with the beauty and divinity of the "World," he concludes the *Prelude* speaking of the beauty and divinity of the "mind of Man":

> Prophets of Nature, we to them will speak
> A lasting inspiration, sanctified
> By reason, blest by faith: what we have loved

---

55. I borrow the phrase "creative imitation" from Thomas Greene, *The Light in Troy: Imitation and Discovery in Renaissance Poetry* (New Haven, Conn.: Yale University Press, 1982).

56. Prospectus to *The Recluse*, in *Selected Poems and Prefaces*, 41.

> Others will love, and we will teach them how,
> Instruct them how the mind of Man becomes
> A thousand times more beautiful than the earth
> On which he dwells, above this Frame of things
> (Which 'mid all revolutions in the hopes
> And fears of Men doth still remain unchanged)
> In beauty exalted, as it is itself
> Of quality and fabric more divine.[57]

Wordsworth thinks of himself as a poet-prophet, whose vocation "(should Providence such grace . . . vouchsafe)" is to be one of the "joint laborers in the Work" of the "deliverance" of the people who repeatedly fall back into "idolatry" and "servitude."[58] Although Sidney does not adopt the prophetic mode, his evangelical spirit in carrying out his "unelected vocation" is no less fervent and arguably more hopeful than that of his successor (95). Not only did Sidney believe that the stellar beauty in the mind of the poet could lead audiences to discover the beauty of their own minds, he also believed, as Wordsworth no longer could, that political action could be an instrument in the great work of spiritual regeneration. And he died from wounds he sustained while fighting for that end. More effective than the "lasting inspiration" bestowed by Wordsworth's poet-prophet, the fictional worlds brought forth by Sidney's poet-hero, with the "force of a divine breath," have the power to change not only the minds of men but also men themselves and, through them, all of creation (101).

57. *The Prelude*, 14.444–454.
58. *The Prelude*, 14. 434–442.

CHAPTER 6

THE IMITATION OF CYRUS

If Sidney does in fact conceive of the poet's work as analogous to the divine work of creation and regeneration, it is surprising that he seems to abandon his theological paradigm when he proceeds from the *narratio* to the "more ordinary opening" of his next section, the *confirmatio*. Notably absent are not only lexical parallels of the kind detailed in the preceding chapters, but also the much more obvious biblical allusions such as those to the fall of Adam and the Spirit-like breath of the poet. Grounding his argument on more generally accessible philosophical principles, in the *confirmatio* Sidney defends poetry by showing that it can bring about the "knowledge of a man's self, in the ethic and politic consideration, with the end of well-doing and not of well-knowing only" (104). Although this argument does not employ the theological vocabulary of the *narratio*, its emphasis on self-knowledge whose "ending end" is "virtuous action" is hardly at odds with the original approach. Not only does the *confirmatio* preserve the earlier emphasis on the moral efficacy of poetry, its climax is a discussion of "heroical" poetry which, it turns out, happens to be the same kind that Sidney uses in the climax of the *narratio*. Indeed, as C. S. Lewis and others have pointed out, Sidney does not abandon his original argument but merely alters the terms. When one recognizes that Sidney's concession of a "more ordinary opening" is strategic, it becomes clear that his illustration of the power of poetry to effect "knowledge of a man's self . . . with the end of well-doing" is in fact an articulation of the power of poetry present, though only implicit is in the presentation of "a Cyrus to make many Cyruses" in the *narratio*.[1]

The *confirmatio* is divided into two parts, and each shows the power of fiction for "winning . . . the mind from wickedness to virtue" through self-knowledge (113). In the memorable first part, on the "works" of poetry, Sidney presents the competition between philosophy, history, and poetry, which the poet wins by providing both the philosopher's "precept" and the historian's "example" in his "perfect picture" (106–7). Sidney concludes this passage with two historical examples of the power of fiction. The first is the "tale of the belly" that Menenius Agrippa used to quell a rebellion against the Roman Senate. Telling the people the story of "a time when all the parts of the body made a mutinous conspiracy against the belly, which they thought devoured the fruits of each other's labour," Agrippa showed how in "punishing the belly, they plagued themselves" (115). Sidney explains that the people, seeing themselves in the story, underwent a "sudden . . . alteration" and were moved to "perfect reconcilement." Equally marvelous is Sidney's other example, that of Nathan telling David the tale of "a man whose beloved lamb was ungratefully taken from his bosom." David, who in sinning with Bathsheba "had so far forsaken God as to confirm adultery with murder," eventually saw himself in Nathan's story. Performing the "tenderest office of a friend," Nathan had provided David with "a glass to see his own filthiness" (115). For Sidney, these exemplary tales of Menenius Agrippa and Nathan are akin to other moral tales designed to lead audiences to greater self-knowledge, such as the fables of Aesop, "whose pretty allegories, stealing under the formal tales of beasts, make many, more beastly than beasts, begin to hear the sound of virtue from these dumb speakers," and the parables of Christ, especially that of the prodigal son, for which Sidney has an obvious affection (109).

When Sidney moves to the second half of his *confirmatio*, from the "works" of poetry to its "parts," he extends his argument for the pow-

1. On the relation of Sidney's "more ordinary opening" to the argument of the *narratio*, and on the identification of "divine" and "right" poets, see Chapter 2.

er of poetry to bring about self-knowledge and virtue. In his survey of the "parts" or kinds of poetry, what underlies the differences in the genres is their common ability to bring the audience to self-recognition and, through this recognition, to moral reform. Some of the kinds—such as comedy, which makes an audience laugh at defects it recognizes as its own—more obviously reveal their ability to work reform through self-knowledge. But Sidney's survey reaches its climax with "heroical" poetry, which he says is "not only a kind, but the best and most accomplished kind of Poetry" (119). Although it would seem to follow that the powers Sidney attributes to poetry should be most perfectly manifest in this most perfect genre, it is far from obvious how heroical poetry reveals readers to themselves. Indeed, it reveals a heroical character who is decidedly different—decidedly *better*—than the reader. Subtly, however, the hero does in fact show readers not the selves they *are*, but instead the worthier self they *should be*. The "lofty image" of the hero is a model for imitation, effective because it at once "inflameth the mind with the desire to be worthy" and "informs with counsel how to be worthy" (119). Although Sidney does not hold Cyrus up as the pattern for the reader in the *confirmatio*, he offers the equally heroic example of Aeneas: "Only let Aeneas be worn in the tablet of your memory . . . and I think, in a mind not prejudiced with a prejudicating humour, he will be found in excellency fruitful" (119–20). Just as Xenophon's Cyrus is a "Cyrus to make many Cyruses," Aeneas is "fruitful" and will multiply himself in his readers, provided they are willing.

With the example of Aeneas, Sidney brings his readers back to the argument of the *narratio*. And having returned, they are in a better position to understand what they previously saw. In his "Cyrus . . . to make many Cyruses," Sidney presents a device that bestows at once self-knowledge and a moral ideal. Seeing in Cyrus "what perfection is" with their "erected wit," readers experience the poignant realization that their "infected will keepeth [them] from reaching unto it." Providing "no small argument to the incredulous of that first accursed fall of Adam," the "golden" figure of Cyrus makes apparent to Sidney's Christian readers both perfection and their "brazen" state. Just as sickness and health are two sides of one concept—one understands health as "not-sickness" and sickness as "not-health"—so too are the "brazen" and "golden" worlds. Seeing the "golden" world, readers recognize their own as defective. Similarly, in beholding the poet's Idea of Cyrus, they see both their true form and their "de-formity."

Underlying the presentation of Cyrus is Sidney's belief in the two-sidedness of the human condition. While sharing the optimism of Renaissance Neoplatonists, Sidney also shared the Reformers' keen sense of human infirmity. He was well aware that those who contemplate the heavens are prone to falling in ditches (104). As early as Savanarola, the characteristic Renaissance expressions of the dignity and God-like potential of human nature had been modified in light of the critique of overweening ambition for knowledge and power. This skeptical movement in Renaissance culture, which Hiram Haydn calls the "Counter-Renaissance," finds its characteristic expression in the Agrippa of the *De incertitudine*. In the great literary authors, both strains, the optimistic and the skeptical, are often subtly interwoven.[2] Milton expresses a commitment to Christian humanism in the face of scientific revolution when he has Raphael reprove Adam for his curiosity about the motions of the heavens and encourage him to seek, instead of a higher knowledge, the self-knowledge that will make him "lowly wise." Before Milton and much more on the side of skepticism, Montaigne addresses Neoplatonic excesses without abandoning the fundamentally optimistic belief in the dignity of man, providing a reminder in his last essay, *Of Experience*, that what makes man like God is not his ability to transcend his human condition but his willingness to embrace that human condition, with all of its limitations and infirmities. Similarly opposed to those who would attempt to transcend human nature, Shakespeare argues in *The Tempest*, a work also intended as a final word of sorts, that the likeness of human beings to God lies not in knowledge or power, symbolically represented as magic, but in the ability to renounce that power in favor of the "rarer virtue"

---

2. See Sukanta Chaudhuri, *Infirm Glory: Shakespeare and the Renaissance Image of Man* (Oxford, U.K.: Clarendon Press, 1981).

of mercy. Just as these authors attend to the play of light and dark in the human condition, so too Sidney's optimistic theory of poetry receives nuance in the dark observations and expressions of disappointment that surface from time to time in the *Apology*. Sidney is not naïve about the general infection of the human will, and he has little doubt that most in his audience will fail to "understand" let alone "grant" his encomiastic arguments for the dignity of the poet (101). His optimistic theory of poetry is offset by the historical survey of poetry in England that he provides in his less encouraging *digressio*. In the end, these problems qualify Sidney's optimism, though they do not negate it.[3]

For Sidney as for Spenser, Shakespeare, and Milton, although the fallen condition of humanity is keenly felt, so too is the remedy offered by Christianity. All of these authors share a vision of the need as well as the possibility for human regeneration. Whereas the Christian significance of the epic wanderings of the Redcrosse Knight and Adam and Eve are obvious, the works of Shakespeare appear as naturalistic as Christian in their reflection of the human condition. In this, they are more closely akin to Sidney's *Apology*, whose Christian vision is not to be found on the surface but in the depth of the work. In *The Tempest*, Shakespeare presents a stylized version of a long-standing ambivalence toward magic, toward the human condition, and, ultimately, toward human nature itself. To Miranda's exclamation, "O brave new world, / That has such people in 't!," Prospero, regarding the same men but having fuller experience of them, responds sardonically, "'Tis new to thee" (5.1.183–84). Miranda's admiring expectation is countered by Prospero's ironic recollection of his own disappointing experiences. Although Prospero has the last word, Miranda's argument stands. Despite his knowing realism, she still finds humanity wonderful. Whereas Pico finds man marvelous for his potential and Prospero finds him pathetic for his utter failure to reach any such potential, Miranda finds him marvelous as he is. What is most marvelous, of course, is her own innocence, which allows her to behold

---

3. See Chaudhuri, *Infirm Glory*, 52–56.

flawed humanity and see its original goodness. Although the audience knows the evil of Antonio, it finds hope in the innocent vision of the younger generation. Alongside the sad reality of human degeneration, the audience sees the possibility of regeneration.

Nowhere is the contrast between the two sides of nature more evident than in Hamlet's disquisition on creation. Hamlet begins with his assessment of the world, and says that the "goodly frame the earth" seems to him "a sterile promontory." Turning from the macrocosm to the microcosm, he sees the same bifold condition in man, who is at once the "beauty of the world" and the "quintessence of dust."[4] Though the pronouncement of a melancholy spirit, Hamlet's feeling is not, to use the modern sense, merely subjective. Through Hamlet Shakespeare holds a mirror up to nature and reveals the two poles between which the human drama was thought to be enacted. This bifold vision of the world was not of course only an idea for an age. The recognition that man is "like a god" and yet the "quintessence of dust" dates at least to Genesis, which has, after all, two accounts of creation, one in which human beings are the image of God and one in which they are made from the dust of the earth. It is this same story in which Sidney finds both creativity and the "first accursed fall of Adam."

Faced with the recognition of the general "infection" of human nature brought about by that "first accursed fall of Adam" and by the many sins subsequently heaped upon that first one—sins like those of Antonio—Sidney and Shakespeare respond with very similar devices. Sidney formulates a theory of poetic creativity that is really a theory of poetic regeneration. Shakespeare presents a drama in which the Old Dispensation of power and revenge yields to the New Dispensation of regenerative love and forgiveness. The love that conquers all is the love of the younger generation that expresses itself in mutual submission, like the love between Christ and the Church. Whereas Shakespeare gives great importance to love, marriage, and community in restoring the image of God in human beings, Sidney emphasizes the power of a heroic ideal to transform humankind into what it was

4. *Hamlet*, 2.2.298–308.

meant to be. At the center of this theory is a "Cyrus to make many Cyruses," who mediates between the "brazen" and the "golden" worlds by offering a pattern of redemption. And for Sidney, it is the poet who bestows this Cyrus on the world. Regenerating the brazen world in his mind and re-creating the world in its original perfection, the poet gives perfection a "local habitation and a name" and moves readers to embrace that perfection he shows them.

Cyrus has the power to reveal the ideal from which readers have departed and, through this revelation, to move them to amend their lives. This same power is evident in what Thomas Browne later describes as "the Ideated Man":

Could we intimately apprehend the Ideated Man, and as he stood in the intellect of God upon the first exertion by Creation, we might more narrowly comprehend our present Degeneration, and how widely we are fallen from the pure Exemplar and Idea of our Nature: for after this corruptive Elongation from a primitive and pure Creation, we are almost lost in Degeneration; and *Adam* hath not only fallen from his Creator, but we our selves from *Adam*, our Tycho and primary Generator.[5]

With the vision of one's true self, the "pure Exemplar and Idea of our Nature," comes the realization of how far one is from that true self. In Cyrus, we see Browne's "Ideated Man"; and by contrast, we see that "we are almost lost in Degeneration." Sir John Harington speaks of the same power to reveal the two-sidedness of the human condition in his defense of *Orlando Furioso*. Harington picks up on the tradition of understanding the epic hero as a perfect exemplar of human conduct and extends it by arguing that the hero also acts as a mirror in which the audience recognizes its own errors.[6] Claiming that Ariosto's work has the same power as the *Aeneid* to make the reader virtuous, Harington credits Virgil's epic with Dante's "coming to himself" in the dark wood: "That excellent Italian Poet *Dant* professeth plainly that when

---

5. *Christian Morals*, 1.28, in Browne, *Religio Medici*, 214.
6. For the tradition of conflating the Platonic doctrine of Ideas with the interpretation of epic heroes in Italian criticism from Robertelli to Tasso, see Hathaway, *Age of Criticism*, 151, 45–46.

he wandred out of the right way, meaning thereby when he liued fondly and looslie, *Virgill* was the first that made him looke into himselfe and reclaime himselfe from that same daungerous and lewd course."⁷ Elaborating on what he no doubt discovered to be an essential feature in Sidney's theory, Harington praises pagan heroic poetry as an instrument of moral—and even Christian—conversion. Sidney would have the reader, like Harington's Dante, "looke into himselfe and reclaime himselfe" through the reading of Virgil or, in the example of the *narratio*, through the reading of Xenophon.

Although Cyrus leads readers to the painful recognition of the fallen state of humanity, it is important to emphasize that he also gives them cause for optimism. Whereas the tales of Menenius Agrippa and Nathan—and even Browne's "Ideated Man" and Harington's Virgil—are very effective at pricking the consciences of their audiences, they do little to provide encouragement or positive guidance. The heroic example of Cyrus, on the other hand, not only provides "no small argument" for the fallen state of humanity, it also provides an attractive pattern for amending one's life. Similarly, Sidney's proof in the *confirmatio* that poetry is the "architectonic" art, though no mean argument, pales in comparison to what Sidney offers in the *narratio*. Although poetry, as the architectonic art, brings us to our "ending end," which is "the knowledge of a man's self, in the ethic and politic consideration, with the end of well-doing and not well-knowing only," it really has little to say about what exactly that self is beyond the fact that it will be engaged in the active life (104).⁸ In the *narratio*, however, Sidney gives a very specific example of what that self should look like. Self-knowledge is still necessary—the audience must know "how" and "why" "that maker made him"—but there is no question about what the audience will find when it knows itself. It will know itself as other Cyruses. And the same could be said about the "ending end," which is

---

7. Hardison, ed., *English Literary Criticism*, 214.

8. See Doherty, *The Mistress-Knowledge*, who calls attention to Sidney's feminine personification of poetry in this section and gives it a foundational role in what she sees, along with Lewalski and Weiner, as the Protestant poetics of the seventeenth century.

left unspecified in the *confirmatio* but is concretely figured forth in the *narratio*. Not only able to see the end, the audience is able to approach it through the image of Cyrus. Here the architectonic art is not only an ethical and a political art, but a soteriological art, able to redeem the "brazen" world and restore it to its original "golden" state.

While dwelling in the distant "golden" world of the poem, Cyrus also bridges the divide. The Cyrus presented by Xenophon "is not wholly imaginative"; he has, rather, the power "to make many Cyruses" in the real world, if readers "will learn aright why and how that maker made him." For readers who "learn aright" the intention and method, the "why and how," the benevolent "end and working" of the maker—that is, for those who will grasp the author's *"Idea"*—Cyrus becomes the means for imitative readers to make their "brazen" world more "golden." In revealing the "brazen" world to itself, Cyrus does not leave it confused in its own shamefulness; rather, he offers, in himself, the possibility for being reconciled to the "golden" world. In the living imitation of Cyrus, readers know Cyrus and then become what they know.

This transformation or re-creation of the "brazen" world is accomplished through imitation—the imitation of an ideal image. Taking the often mind-numbing practice of artistic imitation, so embedded in his culture, Sidney unites it to moral imitation and produces an elegant version of imitation that unites life and art, and brings artistic imitation to life. Although there is no question that Sidney would have readers arrive at the Idea of the author, he would not have them rest contented in the discovery of that knowledge. For Sidney, the proper end of poetry is "well-doing and not . . . well-knowing only" (104). Having made the author's Idea their own, readers must then body forth that Idea in their own lives and become what they have read. To use the modern cliché, it is in Xenophon's heroic Idea of Cyrus that readers "find themselves." The image of Cyrus is so moving that readers are moved—like David having heard Nathan's tale—as if by a sudden recognition, as if they had found something that had been lost. And this discovery of their better self issues in spontaneous imitation, not calculated self-fashioning. The new self is, as Pope would say, "discover'd, not devis'd." Sidney has no intention of forcing his readers into slavish imitation, like the imitation of Cicero to which Sidney himself was subjected at Shrewsbury and Oxford.[9] Rather, he would have the reader practice inventive imitation—so inventive that it issues not in a poem or oration, as did the imitation enforced by schoolmasters, but in living, heroic action. In imitating Cyrus, what the reader imitates is not only a model of virtue, but something very close to what later would be called an "individual." It is, paradoxically, through imitation that the reader learns to be an individual.[10]

Sidney's interest in avoiding deadening imitation also appears later in the *Apology*, in the brief but often-remarked passage in which Sidney recommends that the reader "use the narration but as an imaginative ground-plot of a profitable invention" (124). As Shepherd points out, this formula follows Plutarch, who advises the listener who would profit from a lecture to "make his memory a guide to invention: looking on the discourse of others only as a kind of first principle or seed."[11] The "ground-plot" is the place in the memory where material is stored, material out of which listeners will later draw their own inventions. According to Plutarch, one should listen with an eye to one's own later invention, not in order to be able to repeat the speech verbatim. This note of freedom is certainly a "more ordinary" version of the liberty seen in the poet who goes "freely ranging only within the zodiac of his own wit." But this plain-style explanation ultimately points back, as do most of his "more ordinary" arguments, to the orig-

9. See *Prose Works*, 3.132, where Sidney warns his brother Robert against the mind-numbing imitation of Cicero, a pedagogical practice which, he says, directs the student's attention toward words and away from things.

10. On the Renaissance invention of the now-embattled idea of the individual, see especially Edward Tayler, "The First Individual," in *Soundings of Things Done: Essays in Early Modern Literature in Honor of S. K. Heninger, Jr.*, ed. Peter Medine (Newark: University of Delaware Press, 1997).

11. From the conclusion of *On Listening to Lectures*, as quoted by Shepherd, ed., *Apology*, 201. On the nature of the "ground-plot," see Robinson, *The Shape of Things Known*, 122–28, who considers the "ground-plot" a "Confused Conceypte" in the mind of the poet which preceeds the actual discovery of the "*Idea* or fore-conceit" (127); and Heninger, *Touches of Sweet Harmony*, 295–96, who emphasizes the role of the "ground-plot" in leading the reader to the Idea in the mind of the poet.

inal golden theory. When the poet "figures forth" an Idea he already has in his starry mental firmament, if readers will store away the lights they see shining through the narration in the dark "ground-plot" of their minds, this mental ground-plot, the seat of future invention, will come to be seen as a zodiac within which they can freely range in the noble art of ethical self-invention.

For Sidney, the Idea of Cyrus has a crucial function in—and indeed unites—self-knowledge, moral action, and poetic making. Its ability to carry out these several ends at once highlights the Aristotelian and Scholastic heritage of the Idea as Sidney uses it. Like Sidney's Idea, Aristotle's *eidos* has a twofold function. It is both the end point of the abstractive process of knowing and the starting point of the technical process of making something. Whereas Aristotle uses the term to explain the workings of the human mind, the medieval theologians use it to understand the Ideas, which, as they received them, had been translated from Plato's world of forms to the divine Mind. Aquinas borrows Aristotle's *eidos*, which becomes *forma* in Latin, in order to show that in the divine Mind it is by one and the same Idea that God knows and makes all creatures. If creation is examined under the aspect of having been made, the Idea is the "exemplar or pattern" God used in creation; if creation is considered as something that God knows, the Idea is understood to be the intelligible "form" of creation. But for both functions in reality there is but one Idea.[12] Furthermore, Aquinas identifies the Ideas through which creatures are made and known with God himself. God creates all things and knows all things simply by knowing himself. God thus knows his own essence "not only as it is in itself, but as it can be participated in by creatures according to some degree of likeness." In his own essence he finds "the particular type and idea" of each and every creature.[13] It is through just this kind of self-knowledge—knowing what is in "the zodiac of his own wit"—that the poet makes Cyrus. The poet makes Cyrus by

---

12. *ST* Ia, q. 15, a. 1. Aquinas relies on, and quotes, Aristotle's *Metaphysics* 7, which Sidney clearly also read.
13. *ST* Ia, q. 15, a. 2.

knowing the Idea of Cyrus in himself; and the poet would know those who imitate Cyrus through the same Idea. More important, however, than the identification of self-knowledge and knowledge of the Idea in the poet is their identification in the reader. In successful readers, it is in the Idea that they both know themselves and make their actions into those of a hero. The instant in which readers interpret the literary Cyrus correctly is the very instant in which they see into the mind of the maker and understand "why and how that maker made him" (101); and it is also the very same instant in which they recognize themselves. Out of this self-recognition issues something analogous to a new world and a poem: a new self.

It should not be surprising that the twofold function of the Idea—as the pattern by which a thing is made and the form by which it is known—is reflected in an analogous twofold function in the λόγος, namely, that between the λόγος ἐνδιάθετος and the λόγος προφορικός, the inward and the outward word. Originally derived by the Stoics to distinguish in the human realm between the Idea and the uttered word, it was applied to the divine λόγος by Origen and was adopted by the Greek Fathers. This distinction, though alien to modern readers, would have been familiar to Sidney. Mornay refers to "a dubble Speech; the one in the mynd, which they call the inward Speech, which wee conceyve afore we utter it; and the other the sounding image thereof, which is uttered by our mouth and is termed the Speech of the Voyce." In Sidney's translation, Mornay compares the "inward word" of the Craftsman to the "inward skill or arte" of God: "For, as the Craftsman maketh his worke by the patterne which he had erst conceyved in his mynde, which patterne is his inward word: so God made the World and all that is therein, by that sayd Speech of his as by his inward skill or arte."[14]

In the "Epistle Dedicatorie" to his commentary on the first fourteen books of Genesis, Alexander Ross explains the distinction: "As the internall word was, *Principium essendi*, the beginning of the creatures; so the externall is *Principium cognoscendi*, the beginning of knowl-

---

14. Sidney, *Prose Works*, 3.267–68.

edge."[15] For Ross, the "internall word" performs the first function of the Idea as described by Aristotle and Aquinas: it is the exemplar or pattern of what is to be made. The "externall word" also performs the second function, serving as that by which something is understood. But God's external word is also more than the Idea of the thing; it is, rather, the Idea *and* the thing—the Idea embodied. In terms of Sidney's theory, the Idea or "inward word" in the mind of Xenophon is the *principium essendi* of the fictional Cyrus. The literary Cyrus is that Idea bodied forth, the "external word" of Xenophon, which becomes the *principium cognoscendi* for readers. And if readers understand what they read, and if they move beyond "well-knowing" to the proper end of poetry, "well-doing," Cyrus will become their *principium essendi* and their lives will be the *principium cognoscendi* for others. The λόγος ἐνδιάθετος will be the life of their mind, and their outward lives will be the λόγος προφορικός, the external word, the word incarnate. By grasping the Idea of Cyrus, readers not only understand what is in the mind of the maker, they have the power to become makers as well, forging living works of ethical action.

In imitating Cyrus, readers show themselves to be fully "informed"—in the technical as well as the ordinary sense—by Xenophon's Idea of Cyrus. For informed readers, the Idea of Cyrus is not just "imaginative," nor does it effect merely accidental changes; rather, it works "substantially," touching the very essence of the reader. For informed readers, not only is the "wit" "erected," but the "will" has been cured of its "infection." It is "as high a perfection as our degenerate souls, made worse by their clayey lodgings, can be capable of"; and indeed readers come "to know, and by knowledge to lift up the mind from the dungeon of the body to the enjoying [of their] own divine essence" (104). Released from "the dungeon of the body" by the Idea of Cyrus, readers achieve a self-knowledge that is the enjoyment of their "own divine essence." Those who read the life of Cyrus are what they know, and in knowing Cyrus, they know their essential, ideal, and, it would even appear, "divine" selves.

15. *An exposition of the fourteene first chapters of Genesis, by way of question and answere* (London, 1626), A4v.

This kind of self-knowledge and regeneration are closely related in the Christian Socratism of Sidney's time. That one proceeds to the intelligible world through self-knowledge and that one is most oneself in the mind of God, or Noûs, were central Neoplatonic tenets. They were, however, already incorporated into Christian teaching long before Plotinus, and they can be found in several crystallized formulations of St. Paul. In the famous thirteenth chapter of the First Letter to the Corinthians, St. Paul compares knowledge in this life with knowledge in heaven. Knowledge in this life is partial ("Now I knowe in part") and enigmatic ("as in a glass, darkly"). The perfect knowledge in heaven is, by contrast, "face to face." With the glass of the mirror gone, God is perceived directly, and the human face reflects the divine likeness brilliantly. All things are known in God, especially oneself; and this knowledge is not shadowy but substantial. It is knowledge of the essences of things in the mind of God ("but then shal I know *euen as I am knowen*"). Thus, looking at God face to face, one sees one's essential self and knows that self with the creative knowledge of God.

God's knowledge of himself is the Word, and in Christ, the Word Incarnate, Christians should find themselves. Following Augustine, Calvin thinks of Christ as the "mirror" for Christians, calling Christ "the clearest mirror of free election,"[16] and in his *Antidote* to the Council of Trent telling anxious believers that they can know their election by looking at it "in Christ, as though in a mirror."[17] Looking in the

16. *Institutes* 3.22.1, as quoted by Jaroslav Pelikan, in *Reformation of Church and Dogma (1300–1700)* (Chicago: University of Chicago Press, 1984), 231. On the relation between Augustine's doctrine of the *imago dei* and Sidney's theory, see Kathy Eden, *Poetic and Legal Fiction in the Aristotelian Tradition* (Princeton, N.J.: Princeton University Press, 1986), 122ff., 71–75, who shows that it is Augustine who earlier had united artistic imitation and ethical action, preparing the way for what can be seen in Sidney: "With his program of reform, Augustine rehabilitates the image and imitation of his earlier works and realigns them with ethical action. In doing so, he prepares the way for the later association of the *imitatio Christi* as an ethical program, with Aristotle's artistic program of imitation in the *Poetics*" (140).

17. As quoted by Pelikan, in *Reformation of Church and Dogma* (Chicago: University of Chicago Press, 1984), 231, who also gives Heinrich Bullinger's formulation of the idea for the Second Helvetic Confession: "Let Christ therefore be the mirror in which we contemplate our predestination" (230).

mirror of Christ, the "forknowen" will see themselves and they will see Christ; and being predestined, they will see not two images but one. Another, and perhaps the most interesting, formulation in which human knowledge is grounded in the assured foundation of the productive knowledge of the Maker is found in Romans 8, a chapter especially dear to Protestant Reformers. In the twenty-ninth verse, St. Paul speaks of how God "forknows" the "image of his sonne." This "image of his sonne" is the pattern to which the elect will eventually be conformed: "For whom he hath forknowen, he hath also predestinated to be made conformable to the image of his sonne: that he might be the first-borne in many brethren."[18] Here Christ, as "image," is a pattern for imitation, the model for the Christian's perfection, and it is by being conformed to the image that one will be known by God as a "sonne."

The way people know themselves by knowing—and by being conformed to—God's Idea of them is analogous to the way readers of the *Cyropaideia* know themselves by knowing and imitating the "*Idea* or fore-conceit" in the mind of the Xenophon. Just as imitators of Cyrus see themselves in Xenophon's Cyrus, so too Christians see themselves in Christ. And just as the readers of Xenophon can become "many Cyruses," so too the readers of the Gospel can become "many brethren" of Christ, "the first-borne in many brethren." Of course, the Idea in the mind of the poet may seem a far less "originall" pattern than the Idea in the mind of God from all eternity. For the poet's Idea is not known by or applied to readers before they encounter the literary work, whereas God's plan is applied from the beginning. But the difference is not as great as it might first appear. Since the Fall, and the "de-formity" it has worked in human nature, God's "image of his sonne" is far from universally known or embraced. Indeed, it was lost

---

18. Rheims Bible (1582); in the Geneva translation, "For those which he knewe before, he also predestinate to be made like to the image of his Sonne, that he might be the first borne among manie brethren." See also Eph 4:13 and 1 Cor 15:49. St. Paul often relies on the mirror trope to express the relation of God and human beings, who were made in God's "image." See, e.g., 2 Cor 3:18 (Geneva), "But we all beholde as in a myrrour the glorie of the Lord with open face, and are changed into the same image, from glorie to glorie, euen of the Sprite of the Lord."

by each person before birth—as Thomas Browne puts it, *"Eve miscarried of mee before she conceiv'd of Cain."*¹⁹ Thus, the image of Christ, like that of Cyrus, must be, as St. Paul says, "put on." Until they are put on, both images might as well be "castles in the air"; once applied, however, both can work "substantially," reforming human beings according to the original pattern in the mind of the maker (101).

The devotion to the imitation of Christ became widespread in the fourteenth and fifteenth centuries, and the book by that name attributed to Thomas à Kempis was still quite popular in England even in the late sixteenth century. It was translated into English and printed in various editions, by Protestants as well as by Catholics.²⁰ Of course, the Idea of Christ as the type of the Christian is easily found in Scripture and throughout the Christian tradition.²¹ But when polemics over predestination were raging, the contemplation of Christ and of his sufferings was given special emphasis since it was seen to have the salutary effect of displacing anxious speculation over one's ultimate destiny.²² Another beneficial effect of this devotion was that it tended to ease factional disputes, since all parties could agree that "the sum of the Christian religion is the imitation of him whom we worship" and that "the entire Christian life consists in following Christ."²³

Undeveloped in this pious devotion to the imitation of Christ, however, are the metaphysical underpinnings of Pauline epistemology, in which one knows oneself as known. It seems that over time, however, reflection on the imitation of Christ led to the rediscovery of the underlying mechanisms of identification of subject and object. The incorporation of a metaphysics of participation brought to the Renaissance imitation of Christ a speculative component absent in its more

19. *Religio Medici*, 1.59.
20. R. Whitford's translation was printed ten times in various editions between 1531 and 1585; E. H[ake]'s translation was published in 1567 and 1568; T. Rogers's translation was printed sixteen times between 1580 and 1640.
21. See, e.g., *ST* Ia, q. 1, a. 10, in which Thomas explains how "in the New Law, whatever our Head has done is a type of what we ought to do."
22. Pelikan, *Reformation of Church and Dogma*, 36–37; see Thomas À Kempis, *The Imitation of Christ in Four Books: Translated from the Latin*, trans. Joseph Tylenda (New York: Vintage Books, 1998), 3.58, 2.1.
23. As quoted by Pelikan, in *Reformation of Church and Dogma*, 36.

humble medieval antecedent. A striking example of this convergence of devotion and metaphysical speculation is the famous self-portrait of Albrecht Dürer in 1500, in which the artist adopts, as Panofsky points out, a pose that evokes contemporary representations of Christ.[24] It is at once a self-portrait and a painting of Christ. Looking at the portrait, Dürer would have seen Christ, whom he imitated, and in Christ he would have seen himself. In the mirror of the portrait, the subject-object opposition is resolved; knower and known are both present, and knowledge of external objects is not distinct from self-knowledge. Although it might be tempting to see Dürer as a secularist—he was, after all, the first to sign and date his works as a rule—he was in fact, to use Panofsky's characterization, a "pious and humble artist."[25] Rather than an extravagant exaltation of the artist, his identification with the Christ he presented was a statement of faith, grounded in medieval devotional practice.

If Sidney's presentation of "a Cyrus to make many Cyruses" also recalls the imitation of Christ, it nevertheless differs significantly from Dürer's use of the tradition. Wheras Dürer the artist identifies with the image he presents, Sidney would have readers identify with the image the poet gives them. A more obvious and more important difference, however, is that Sidney proposes not the imitation of Christ but the imitation of Cyrus. Sidney's author of choice was not Thomas à Kempis but Xenophon. Although Cyrus resembles Christ in the way he serves as a pattern through which knowing readers are transformed, the imitation of Cyrus is not reducible to a cipher for the imitation of Christ.

Cyrus may, however, have more to do with Christ than is readily apparent. Indeed, Cyrus had a significance for Sidney and other Renaissance readers that today passes largely unseen. Although Thomas Browne is in no sense typical, his *Garden of Cyrus* shows the mystical interpretation of Cyrus that was, if not typical, at least possible. Ac-

---

24. *Idea*, 43. See Joseph Koerner, *The Moment of Self-Portraiture in German Renaissance Art* (Chicago: University of Chicago Press, 1993), for a recent attempt to revise Panofsky's interpretation.
25. *Idea*, 43.

cording to Browne, the Gardens of Babylon that Cyrus tended were located on the site previously occupied by the Garden of Eden. "Disposing his trees like his armies in regular ordination," Cyrus the political leader is presented by Browne as the prototype of the gardener and the antitype of Adam.[26]

The popular understanding of Cyrus, it should be remembered, like that of Browne, owed as much to the Bible as it did to Xenophon. In the biblical account, Cyrus's role is that of a political deliverer. He liberates Israel from its seventy years of bondage in Babylon. Notably, 2 Chronicles ends and Ezra begins with the inspired proclamation of Cyrus, in which he declares that God has given him all the kingdoms of the earth and commanded him to restore the Temple. Although the biblical account omits mention of the quincuncial ordination of the ancients, in his presentation of Cyrus Isaiah bestows on him some striking epithets. Not only does God call Cyrus "my shepherd" and "the man of my counsel," but he sets Cyrus apart as his "anointed."[27] The significance of this final title was the subject of some debate, especially among Calvinists. Although it is fitting that Cyrus receive the title in virtue of his mission as deliverer or messiah, he was not even a Jew. The suggestion of the typological connection of Cyrus not only to David but to Christ was considered problematic—"too saucy" a comparison. The awkward but standard interpretation of the epithet was that Cyrus, though "anointed," is not to be counted among the elect.[28]

---

26. *The Garden of Cyrus*, chap. 1, in *Religio Medici and Other Works*, 131.

27. 44:28, 46:11, 45:1. For a learned discussion of how these titles are given to Cyrus in a way that places him alongside the likes of David, see the classicist John Kitto, *Daily Bible Illustrations: Being Original Readings for a Year, on Subjects from Sacred History, Biography, Geography, Antiquities, and Theology* (New York: Robert Carter & Brothers, 1860), 2.102–24.

28. The note in the Geneva edition to "anointed" betrays this uneasiness: "Because Cyrus shuld execute ye office of a deliuerer, God called him his anointed for a time, but after another sort then he called Dauid." In their attempt to distance Cyrus from his title, the Geneva commentators are following Calvin, who, in his commentary on Isaiah, explains that God called Cyrus "his annointed" "not with a perpetuall stile, but during the time he held the office of a deliuerer, and in respect he sustained the person of God, both to reuenge the cause of the Church, and to redeeme the same out of the

An alternative response to the messianic elements in the description of Cyrus was to hold that Cyrus was converted to the faith of Israel. It was commonly understood, as Raleigh explains, that Cyrus probably "receiued the knowledge of the true God from *Daniel*, when he gouerned *Sufa* in *Persia*."[29] Daniel's instruction of Cyrus was a popular topic of the period, as can be seen in Rembrandt's painting of Daniel informing Cyrus—to the dismay of the priests of the Persian religion—that bronze gods do not eat or drink. According to Raleigh, it also was believed that, in addition to being instructed by Daniel, "Cyrus himselfe had read the prophecie of *Esay*." It is interesting to imagine how Cyrus would have responded to discovering himself in the Hebrew Scriptures. In reading Isaiah, Cyrus would have seen himself "expressely named, and by God (for the deliuerie of his people) praeordained."[30] That Cyrus then knew exactly "why and how" that Maker made him is uncertain; it is clear, however, that he responded well and carried out what was preordained for him. In doing so, the historical Cyrus would have provided the first example of the moral imitation of a literary Cyrus.

It is hard to imagine that Sidney would not have entertained the general notion of Cyrus as a political leader in the service of God's chosen people. For Sidney, religion and politics were tightly bound in an idealistic configuration—one that did not sit well with the more pragmatic Elizabeth and Burghley. Writing from the Netherlands not long before his death, Sidney refers to Elizabeth as "but a means whom God useth," and he claims to be "faithfully persuaded that if she shold withdraw her self other springes woold ryse to help this action. For me thinkes I see the great work indeed in hand, against the abusers of the world."[31] For Sidney, religious considerations served a

---

Assyrians hands: which office indeed, properly appertained to Iesus Christ" (Jean Calvin, *A Commentary Vpon the Prophecie of Isaiah*, trans. C. Cotton [London: Felix Kyngston, 1609], 3.397). It should be noted that Lutheran and Catholic commentators had no less difficulty glossing the passage.
  29. *History of the World* (London: Walter Burre, 1614), 3.3.6.
  30. *History of the World*, 3.3.6.
  31. *Prose Works*, 3.166. See Fred J. Levy, "Philip Sidney Reconsidered," *English Liter-*

larger purpose than providing justification for what was politically expedient. He wanted to make religious commitments, specifically the commitment to European Protestantism, a driving force of political policy. Indeed, he did place loyalty to this cause above royal favor, and it was the displeasure of the queen that provided him the unwanted leisure to write the *Apology*.

Of course, poetry as well as religion was bound up with politics. For Scaliger (as for Aristotle), poetry stands alongside oratory and legislation as an art indispensable for healthy political life.[32] If Sidney would have the audience wish itself a Cyrus, that Cyrus with which it identifies is in turn identified with the object of another art, the art of empire. In the formulation of Cicero, which Sidney quotes more than once, Cyrus is not merely the image of an ideal ruler; he is *"effigiem justi imperii,* 'the portraiture of a just empire'" (103). This identification of the just emperor with a just empire follows the construction that identifies the horseman with a horse and the poet with a poem. The implication for Sidney's readers is that if they imitate Cyrus they will identify not only with the ruler but with the empire, and in becoming "many Cyruses" they—and their queen—will also become "the portraiture of a just empire." The outcome of this identification through imitation would be to turn England, and through England all of Europe, into a "golden" world. Sidney certainly would have liked for his queen to be more like Cyrus and for his countrymen to be more like "many Cyruses." Perhaps the *Apology*—like *Gorbeduc*, one of the few English works Sidney holds up for admiration—was written with the queen in mind. Certainly Sidney himself wanted to practice the imitation of Cyrus, and it was only his enforced rustication that prevented him from engaging himself fully in "the great work . . . against the abusers of the world." In the long run, however, it undoubtedly was fortunate that Sidney "slipped" into what he called his "unelected vocation" (95).

---

ary Renaissance 2 (1972): 7. On the close connection between virtue and religion in Sidney's thought, see Worden, *The Sound of Virtue,* 23–37.

32. Weinberg, *Literary Criticism,* 748.

CHAPTER 7

CREATIVITY AND THE ORIGINS OF MODERNITY

Although the idea of human creativity reaches its full flourishing in the romantic period, it is the Renaissance that bears witness to its birth. With the birth of creativity situated in this earlier period, the necessary context for understanding the development of the theory is not the subsequent shift in epistemology that Meyer Abrams so persuasively illustrates; it is rather the shift in anthropology that preceded, and indeed enabled, the later change in epistemology. In this anthropological awakening, human beings largely replaced God as the fixed point on which the intellectual and moral universe was thought to turn. Despite the limitations of the often-told story of the "Renaissance discovery of man," it is indisputable that something equivalent to a Copernican Revolution took place during the period. It was a fundamental reorientation in which the larger questions of meaning tended to be answered in terms of human rather than divine realities. In the face of life's troubles, for example, human beings increasingly took upon themselves, for better or worse, the burden for finding meaning and happiness in life, the burden for their own salvation. It was in the context of this shift, of this secularization of religious categories of thought and modes of behavior, that the creature became a creator.

If one believes, with many philosophers of history, that modernity is built on the ruins of a previously dominant Christian culture, Sidney's humanistic claims seem to be part of the reconfiguration of the

God-centered universe of the previous age. Sidney's conception of the poet as a creator looks like one step along the road to the secular world of modernity. According to this line of thought, the question of the nature of human creativity is one specific aspect of the larger and much-vexed question of the transition to modernity. Focusing on this connection between creativity and the birth of modernity, William Bouwsma examines the metaphoric nature of "human creativity" and argues that metaphor, and specifically the metaphor of human creativity, is a mechanism by which the culture comes to attribute what was previously considered divine power to human beings.[1] In a simple and powerful narrative of the historical development of a metaphor, he traces the broad contours of the history of the idea of human creativity. The narrative has three stages: first, that human beings can create is denied; then, the claim is made, but understood hyperbolically; finally, the term is used more widely and with less precision, and human beings come to believe that they do in fact create.[2] Quickly forgetting that creativity was borrowed from God, people came to regard it as a quality proper to human beings—which clearly is the case today, when not only artists but everyone from fashion designers to tax planners are thought to be creative. According to this theory, creativity was predicated of human beings first metaphorically and then properly; once "man creates" was no longer denied, it rapidly went from being a far-fetched metaphor to a simple fact, so that now human creativity is, like the legs of a table or the light of reason, a dead metaphor.

This narrative is, on its face, persuasive—especially for audiences who already understand the power of language to shape consciousness. That the transfer of power has been successful is obvious from present usage, where even though many would still say that God creates, few really think of him as "creative." No doubt his immutability and his omniscience have become a liability, implying for the modern mind a lack of the spontaneity now associated with creativity. But de-

---

[1]. "The Renaissance Discovery of Human Creativity." See also the earlier but related studies of Panofsky, "Artist, Scientist, Genius"; Nahm, *Artist as Creator;* and Tigerstedt, "Poet as Creator."

[2]. "The Renaissance Discovery of Human Creativity," 19ff.

spite the obvious explanatory power of Bouwsma's theory of metaphoric transfer, certain questions arise under closer examination. If the metaphor of human creativity was originally denied and then thought of only as hyperbolic or far-fetched, why did it catch on? And why was it later considered just and proper—indeed, no longer metaphoric?

To answer such questions Bouwsma falls back on the same accounts of secularization with which he implicitly started. There are basically two major versions of this secularization thesis. The first, set forth by Karl Löwith, assumes that the application of creativity to man is essentially "illegitimate," that human creativity is nothing more than a secularized version of what had previously been considered a sacred reality.[3] Indebted to the analysis of Carl Schmitt, who maintained that the romantic subject is God writ small, Löwith argues that modern culture relies on secularized categories of Christian theology (e.g., salvation history is transformed into the history of technological progress). According to this scenario, it would have been the giddiness of playing God that made the metaphor of human creativity attractive; and, presumably, once the novelty of the experience wore off, the previously extraordinary prospect of human creativity, though it remained a false consciousness, became ordinary. The second explanation, offered by Hans Blumenberg in *The Legitimacy of the Modern Age*, is a response to that of Löwith.[4] As the title of his work indicates, Blumenberg argues for the legitimacy of modern categories

    3. *Meaning in History* (Chicago: University of Chicago Press, 1949).
    4. *The Legitimacy of the Modern Age*, ed. Robert M. Wallace (Cambridge, Mass.: Harvard University Press, 1983). In line with Blumenberg's more hopeful attitude to the future is the Marxist utopian Ernst Bloch, *The Principle of Hope*, trans. Neville Plaice, Stephen Plaice, and Paul Knight (Cambridge, Mass.: MIT Press, 1986). Working on more solid ground and avoiding the ideological bogs of the philosophy of history, Ernst Kantorowicz offers a number of very useful studies on the topic: *The King's Two Bodies: A Study in Medieval Political Theology* (Princeton, N.J.: Princeton University Press, 1957); "The Sovereignty of the Artist: A Note on Legal Maxims and Renaissance Theories of Art," in *De artibus opuscula XL: Essays in Honor of Erwin Panofsky*, ed. Millard Meiss (New York: New York University Press, 1961), 261–79; "'Deus Per Naturam, Deus Per Gratiam': A Note on Medieval Political Theology," *Harvard Theological Review* 45 (1952); and "Mysteries of State: An Absolutist Concept and Its Late Medieval Origins," *Harvard Theological Review* 48 (1955). For a recent study of Blumenberg in English, see

of thought. He believes, for example, that scientific progress is not just secularized eschatology but rather a reality. Similarly, he believes that the application of creativity to human beings is essentially legitimate. Rather than a vestige of medieval theology, human creativity is the result of the liberation of a category that medieval theology had previously (and illegitimately) reserved for itself. That is to say, the assertion of human creativity is in fact a legitimate "reoccupation" of a position once occupied by theological content, an act of human self-assertion in which humanity reclaims an authentically human reality that medieval Christianity had reserved to God alone.[5] According to this way of thinking, it is the prospect of reasserting one's rights as a human being that led to the first use of the metaphor and that later allowed people to think of creativity not as something borrowed but as something rightly their own. If Löwith is right, insofar as we believe in human creativity, we are trapped in a false consciousness, thinking that we have a power that we do not have and that (according to Löwith) does not even exist. If, on the other hand, Blumenberg is correct, we must embrace the discovery of human creativity as part of the legitimate "self-articulation of modern consciousness."[6] Siding with Blumenberg, Bouwsma sees the *Apology* as an example of Renaissance self-assertion and of the cultural articulation of new answers to old questions. More important than the side Bouwsma takes, however, is that his discussion clearly shows how the *Apology*, and the present interpretation of it, is implicated in this larger philosophical debate.

Elizabeth Brient, *The Immanence of the Infinite: Hans Blumenberg and the Threshold to Modernity* (Washington, D.C.: The Catholic University of America Press, 2001).

5. According to Blumenberg's theory of "reoccupation," "What mainly occurred in the process that is interpreted as secularization, at least (so far) in all but a few recognizable and specific instances, should be described not as the *transposition* of authentically theological contents into secularized alienation from their origin but rather as the *reoccupation* of answer positions that had become vacant and whose corresponding questions could not be eliminated" (65). This idea of "reoccupation" gives Blumenberg's thesis greater flexibility; but it arguably diminishes its explanatory value proportionately. The same can be said for Blumenberg's other key word, "self-assertion," an analytical category whose usefulness is as limited as its applicability is universal. If self-assertion marks modernity, there have been modern men about as long as there has been history.

6. *Legitimacy*, 107. See also 532–33 for his discussion of creativity.

Although obviously opposed to one another, the accounts of Löwith and Blumenberg are similar in at least one essential respect: both sides of the legitimization dispute see an opposition between divine and human creativity, such that a gain for one represents a loss to the other. Underlying this is an even more fundamental similarity: both assume that Christian revelation is untrue, and that Christianity is an ideology that elevates God to the detriment of humanity, and, as a result, pits the glory of God and human dignity against each other. Indeed, these theorists of secularization, themselves both committedly secularist, ironically resemble the Puritan opponents of poetry, who also conceived of dignity as a zero-sum game played by God and humanity. Whereas Löwith and Blumenberg believe that human dignity is compromised by the existence of sacred categories that can be lorded over humanity, Sidney's Puritan opponents were convinced that a claim for human worth was an offense against the all-worthy God. Like their godly predecessors, these secularist theorists do not consider the possibility that human and divine dignity may in fact vary directly rather than inversely. Nor do they admit that the appreciation of divine and human realities—and likewise their denigration—may wax and wane together.

The *Apology*, which fits in neither the godly nor the secularist camp, gives the lie to these theories of secularization. Hopelessly inadequate for interpreting the *Apology*, these theories are unable to accommodate a thinker like Sidney, whose interest in human creativity did not preclude an interest in and indeed a reverence toward the divine work of creation. Whatever may have been the case for his contemporaries or for those who followed him, Sidney did not think that embracing secular realities implied a relaxation of theological commitments. In literature, Sidney's keen interest in classical works, such as Xenophon's *Cyropaedia*, hardly led to a cooling of his interest in Christian subject matter. His abiding interest in divinity is seen in the works he chose to translate, which range from Sacred Scripture (the psalms, which he translated with his sister) to the sacred poetry of Du Bartas to the theological and apologetical work of Mornay. Just as Sidney, the would-be statesman, brought his religious and political commitments together by working for the solidification of a Protestant League, so too he, as an apologist for poetry, tried to bring about a harmony between poetry and what he considered the true religion. His theory of poetic making was not an attempt to reclaim transcendent powers that had previously been held off limits by religious leaders. Neither a secularist nor, as some have argued, a Protestant poetics, Sidney's was a Christian poetics. Modern and yet evangelical in character, Sidney's poetics was designed to move poets and their readers to be reformed by embracing the power available to Christians of all times simply for the taking: the transforming power of grace.

Contrary to what the theorists of secularization would expect to see, Sidney's interest in poetic creativity did not supplant but instead grew out of a belief in divine creativity. A close examination of Sidney's language shows that his belief in divine creativity does not contract to make room for the poet, but instead expands so that the poet can be a participant in it, going "hand in hand" with Nature, who by Sidney's time had already been made a collaborator in God's creative plans. As he reaches the climax of his first and best argument for the dignity of the poet and his work, Sidney is well aware that his godly critics will think his balancing of human ingenuity with the creative power of nature too bold, or illegitimate—"too saucy a comparison." And he counters them with an argument provided by Scripture itself. Sidney's justification of the poet is based on the understanding, authorized in the first chapter of Genesis but often forgotten since the Fall, that human beings are "the image and likeness" of God. Exercising a freedom like that of God, the "maker" fulfills the plan of the "heavenly Maker," who made the poet to his own "likeness." For Sidney, the glory of the poet-maker is, rightly understood, a reason for giving yet greater glory to God.

Theories that are useful for describing the dynamics of broad cultural shifts are often very clumsy instruments for analyzing the thought of a single (and especially a singular) human agent, such as Sidney. Whereas theoretical generalizations are unavoidably reductive, human persons, at their best, resist being pinned down. Sidney's claim that the augmented power of the poet increases the glory of

God must necessarily complicate the major theories of secularization and metaphoric transfer, including that of Bouwsma. As applied to the *Apology*, his theory of the movement from denial to hyperbolic assertion to simple belief in human creativity is presented as a chronological narrative covering three sequential stages of a cultural shift. However, if the *Apology* is examined in its own right, denial, hyperbolic assertion, and belief seem to apply not to sequential historical stages but to contemporaneous elements in Sidney's audience. Sidney explicitly recognizes that his arguments will not gain wide acceptance, that they "will by few be understood, and by fewer granted" (101). He also seems to know that some readers will take his implicit assertion of poetic creativity as hyperbolic, for he anticipates that some readers will find his argument "too saucy." Of course, Sidney does believe some will understand his theory, but he recognizes that this fit audience will be few. That Sidney clearly adverts to the three possibilities—that his argument will be either denied, considered "too saucy," or believed—indicates that the three may not be sequential stages in a cultural shift so much as contemporaneous attitudes that are always present, though perhaps in different proportions at different times.

This synchronic scenario, in which the episodes of a historical master narrative are, as it were, dissolved like compounds in a solution, is not meant to deny the explanatory value of historical narratives; quite the contrary, it is intended to revise or at least to complicate the often-told story in order to make it more accurate and meaningful. Despite their erudition, the accounts of Bouwsma, Blumenberg, and Löwith essentially remain versions of the old story of the liberation of humanity from the yoke of medieval religious structures. Though demonstrating an impressive command of great stretches of intellectual history, they fail to address the problems of periodization that necessarily accompany such theories. Rather than questioning the validity of necessarily reductive compartmentalization, expressed in popular formulations referring to a transition from an "Age of Faith" to an "Age of Reason," or from a "God-centered" to a "man-centered" universe, they basically rely on the same Promethean historical paradigm. Their accounts thus amount to the same story, told with greater sophistication.

Although historiography cannot altogether avoid these kinds of paradigmatic narratives that marry description and evaluation, modern historians should be expected to recognize them when they see them and, above all, when they use them. The value of focusing such broad questions of cultural transformation on a single artifact such as the *Apology* is that the work, in its particularity, resists generalizations and, in resisting them, tests and corrects them. Indeed, the *Apology* resists the mythical-historical narratives of the theorists of modernity, which can accommodate Sidney's claim for human creativity only by distorting it. Although Sidney is arguing for the God-like effectiveness of the poet, the claim is not, as many of his godly opponents would have it, an impious usurpation of divine power, an encroachment on the transcendent territories of the divine. And even though Sidney's claim for the freedom of the poet is unmistakable, it is not, as many theories of modernity would propose, a noble rescue mission to liberate a humanity held captive by the religious ideology of feudal society. The myth of Prometheus, though certainly applicable to strains of early-modern culture, does little to explain what Sidney is doing in the *Apology*. It is helpful, rather, in showing what Sidney is not doing.

The myth of Prometheus, which incorporates both a myth of subjugation and a myth of deliverance, resembles the Christian pattern of a fall into bondage and a deliverance from sin. This Christian master narrative of fall and redemption, like the myth of Prometheus, can be detected in accounts of the origins of modernity. Of course, important differences separate the Christian and pagan stories, and those differences correspond to differences in the accounts of the passage to modernity. Although both accept the notion of a shift from a God-centered to a human-centered culture, each offers opposite evaluations of this shift. Whereas the Promethean accounts emphasize what some believe to be the more widespread belief in the freedom and dignity of the individual in the Renaissance—evident in, for example, Pico's *Oration*—the accounts in which modernity is seen as a falling off give greater attention to matters such as the more prevalent and poignant expressions of alienation and disorientation in the new era. These accounts focus on what has been lost, whether it be a sense of transcendence or of community, or a shared belief in the unity of truth or in the nature and end of the human person. For Marxist and certain Catholic interpreters of modernity, united in their dissatisfaction with the ethos of liberalism, the medieval world is often viewed as a kind of golden age, and modernity as a sort of expulsion from Eden. These narratives of decline and fall, like their Promethean counterparts, range from those that do not recognize the mythical patterns on which they rely to those that boldly proclaim them.[7]

Sidney himself turns to the pattern of the fall when he surveys the state of literature in England in his day. The point of the digression is to "inquire why England (the mother of excellent minds) should be grown so hard a stepmother to poets." The hardening has left England ungenerative, and Sidney can think of only a handful of English works "that have poetical sinews in them." Although formerly poets had "flourished" in England, even in times of war, now the "very

7. Those who tell some version of the story of the loss of transcendence are too many to be named. Like the neo-Thomists a generation before him, Louis Dupré, *The Passage to Modernity: An Essay in the Hermeneutics of Nature and Culture* (New Haven, Conn.: Yale University Press, 1993), blames the rise of nominalism and voluntarism for the collapse of the medieval ontotheological synthesis. Alasdair Macintyre, *After Virtue: A Study in Moral Theory* (South Bend, Ind.: University of Notre Dame Press, 1981), in a manner that is far from unreflective, offers a history of the "decline and fall" of the classical (Aristotelian) view of human nature, a narrative in which a previous, though generally unrecognized, "catastrophe" has resulted in the loss not of the language but of the "comprehension, both theoretical and practical, of morality" (2–3). Seeing Aristotle not as the solution but as part of the problem, Eric Voegelin, in *Order and History* (Baton Rouge: Louisiana State University Press, 1956), describes the problems of the modern age as deriving from a process already at work in antiquity of the immanantization of the *eschaton*. Locating the sources of modernity even further back in history is the more recent work of Marcel Gauchet, *The Disenchantment of the World: A Political History of Religion* (Princeton, N.J.: Princeton University Press, 1997), who develops Weber's claim of the linkage between Protestantism and capitalism into a much broader argument that the development of world religions brings about the end of religion. For a history of the transition from the medieval to the modern that resists the temptation to posit some specific point of rupture, whether Ockham's nominalism, Luther's Protestantism, Machiavelli's political pragmatism, Bacon's scientific method, or Descartes's dualism, see Heiko Oberman, *The Harvest of Medieval Theology: Gabriel Biel and Late Medieval Nominalism* (Grand Rapids, Mich.: Eerdmans, 1967).

earth lamenteth" the "hard welcome" poets receive there, "and therefore decketh [the] soil with fewer laurels than it was accustomed" (131). Quoting Virgil's question to the muse as to the cause for Aeneas's suffering, "*Musa, mihi causas memora, quo numine laeso?* [Tell me, o Muse, the cause, whether thwarted in will . . . ?]," Sidney suggests that poetry in England is suffering as Aeneas had suffered, because a goddess—Poesy personified rather than Juno—has been offended.[8] As the survey progresses, however, it is clear that although the goddess Poesy is no doubt unhappy with English poetry, its disfigurement is self-inflicted. To restore poetry in England, Sidney would have the current "company of paper-blurrers" "seek to know what they do, and how they do; and especially look themselves in an unflattering glass of reason" (132). The *Apology* as a whole, and the survey in miniature, is just such a mirror, intended to cure poesy in England by bringing it to self-knowledge.

This pattern of fall and redemption, evident in Sidney's digression on literary history, is also at the heart of his account of what poetry is. In his theoretical treatment of poetry in the *narratio*, the fall does more than provide a mythical pattern for ordering messy historical data. It is present explicitly and literally in Sidney's assertion that poetry, in presenting an image of the way the world could be, provides "no small argument to the incredulous of that the first accursed fall of Adam" (101). This "fall" is *the* Fall, a unique historical event, though one whose effects are felt at all moments of subsequent history. Providing an image of a "golden" world, poetry convinces its audience that its world has fallen from that "golden" state and is instead "brazen." But the "golden" world, which "only the poets deliver," is not merely a past age, it is a superhistorical world that the "brazen" world needs in every age. With their "erected wit" audiences can perceive the ideal world, but because of their "infected will" they cannot attain it. The resulting tension between the fallen and the ideal or redeemed world is not only the state of England in Sidney's time, it is the state of humankind at all times in its history since the Fall.

8. *Apology* 131; Virgil, *Aeneid*, trans. H. Rushton Fairclough (Cambridge, Mass.: Harvard University Press, 1978), 1.7.

Likening the condition of literature in England to the poignantly postlapsarian condition of humanity, Sidney relies on the same mythical paradigm as those who see modernity as a falling off from a better age. But Sidney proves himself either more naïve or more insightful than these cultural historians. Although Sidney's treatment of the Fall as a historical reality rather than a historical paradigm today seems quaint, Sidney in fact shows a keen self-awareness—rare at all times—in realizing that he is making a claim not only about the shape of history but about the nature of reality. Not falling into the trap of historicism, he knows that neither the cause nor the remedy of evil can be explained adequately simply in terms of a historical shift. He recognizes that the problem is not only historical but metaphysical. In the *narratio*, where he gives his full and lofty vision of poetry, he does not use the Fall as a mythical pattern, he presents it as both a historical and an existential reality, one that has affected not only literature but humankind. This fuller vision of the human condition is a key for understanding both the *Apology* and the cultural shift in which the *Apology* participates. Credited by Sidney and his contemporaries, this worldview, simpler yet more sophisticated than the modern historical viewpoint, can accommodate the two-sidedness of the human condition. Instead of separating the golden and the brazen aspects of our experience of reality into distinct historical periods, it accepts the complexity that exists within a single period. In place of a reductive narrative depicting modernity as a fall or a liberation, it insists that defeat and victory are part of the texture of every historical period, and indeed of every human life. It insists that one of the most important settings for the battles that alter the course of history is the human soul, where the struggle between good and evil never ends.

If the warfare in the human soul is perennial, the character of the conflict most certainly changes. As new ideology is introduced, the very nature of the struggle can seem to change. With the likes of Bacon, Descartes, and Hobbes the terms of engagement are permanently changed. Marked by an emphasis on human rather than divine agency, the intellectual systems that they construct change the ways human beings think about how they think. For present purposes, the critical feature common to all three is their treatment of thought itself as foundational. Believing that a single revolutionary work can establish a completely new point of intellectual origination, these thinkers articulate what has long been acknowedged as a radical shift in the history of thought. Modernity has ever since been captivated by the idea of originality. Their ideas of originality, necessarily bound up with modern ideas of creativity, can serve as a foil for distinguishing more clearly the key features of Sidney's very different understanding of creativity, originality, and the relation between the two.

The radical foundationalist approach to originality is perhaps most evident in the example of Descartes. The connection between originality and creativity in his thought, though not explicit, is unmistakable. With a frequency that rules out coincidence, he structures his works in six parts. Although the reason for the divisions seems insignificant in some cases—"If this discourse seems too long to be read at a sitting you may divide it into six parts"—in a number of instances the six-part structure has a significance that is clear and distinct.[9] The *Principia Philosophiae*, though published in only four parts (by Elzevir of Amsterdam in 1644), was intended to have six sections in total, including "a fifth part on living things, i.e. animals and plants, and a sixth part on man."[10] Although the correspondence to God's work of the six days may seem coincidental, the hexameral structure of the *Meditations* leaves no doubt that Descartes intends to order his new system of philosophy according to God's work in creating the world. Not only are the *Meditations* six in number, but Descartes makes it clear that they take place over the course of six "days." Just as the sixth part of the *Principia* focuses on man, the work of the sixth day, so too the sixth day of the *Meditations* introduces the topic of human nature. And on the first day of the *Meditations* Descartes concludes with his striking expression of fear that he "shall have to toil not in the light, but amid the inextricable darkness of the problems" he has raised.[11]

9. *Discourse on Method*, in *The Philosophical Writings of Descartes*, 2 vols., ed. John Cottingham (Cambridge, U.K.: Cambridge University Press, 1988), 1.111.
10. *Philosophical Writings*, 1.279.
11. *Philosophical Writings*, 1.15.

Descartes begins just as God does, by distinguishing light and darkness. But whereas God originated creation with his "Fiat lux," Descartes begins his *Meditations* by supposing that all that we think exists may not really exist, and that light—and all the rest of the work of the six days—may be nothing more than a dream that we mistakenly take for reality. Plunging the visible world into darkness, in six days Descartes produces a new creation. Whereas God lays the foundations of all creation in six days, Descartes works out "the foundations of First Philosophy in its entirety" in six meditations.[12] And just as Descartes imitates the method of God, so too readers are to imitate the method of Descartes. Recapitulating his six days' work, they begin with doubt and generate certainty. Out of nothing more than the methodical operation of the mind, readers lay the certain foundations for the operation of their own minds.

Arriving at certain knowledge through meditation was, of course, the object of meditation before Descartes. As well as the hexameron, the *Meditations* are modeled on Ignatian meditation.[13] As with Descartes's *Meditations*, the Ignatian retreat takes place over a series of days and proposes different topics for meditation for each "week" of the retreat. The object for each week is a fundamental change of life, a conversion. The foundational character is reinforced by Ignatius's indication that the retreat is only to be made once in a person's life. The ascetical aspect is reflected in Descartes, who intends for the reading of his *Meditations* to be difficult enough that "few" will be "able and willing to meditate seriously with [him]."[14] But those readers who are successful will have "certain and evident knowledge of the truth." This reconfiguration of the arrival at the truth through Ignatian meditation is notably different from an analogous reconfiguration Louis Martz has identified in many seventeenth-century poems. When Donne or Herbert or Crashaw imitate Ignatian meditation, the resolu-

12. *Philosophical Writings*, 1.8.
13. See Amélie Oksenberg Rorty, "The Structure of Descartes' Meditations," in *Essays on Descartes' Meditations*, ed. Amélie Oksenberg Rorty (Berkeley and Los Angeles: University of California Press, 1986).
14. *Philosophical Writings*, 8.

tion of the poem is, as one would expect, Christian conversion. In the case of Descartes, however, the outcome is the conversion to Cartesian philosophy.

Effectively separating the experience of conversion from the reality of renewal, Descartes goes through the Ignatian program of conversion but does not yield up his own powers of understanding and will. The old method led to the discovery of a transcendent ground for consciousness, a discovery that was at once a rediscovery of oneself, a new consciousness. Admiring the power of this method, Descartes makes not what is discovered but the power of making discoveries the ground of consciousness. Descartes thus turns a method aimed at conversion into a method aimed at confirmation. No longer oriented toward beauty, truth, and goodness, the mind has a new *telos*, certainty, which is nothing but a state of mind. Completed once and for all, Descartes's meditations yield to the scientific method, where success is finding out, time and again, that one was right all along.

It is difficult to know how to take such claims as Descartes's comparison of philosophy to the six days of creation. For students of literature, the extravagance of the implicit comparison of the philosopher to God the Creator may suggest the "conceit." The comparison might seem to be the logical but extreme consequence of one clear and distinct Idea: the resemblance between the work of God and the operation of the human mind. However, Descartes does not make the comparison in order to draw it out into an extended conceit. In comparing the philosopher to God, he wishes for the philosopher to replace God. In his new view of humanity, he does nothing to preserve the analogy with God. On the contrary, he is breaking with that antiquated tradition and starting something totally new. He echoes God's work of the six days in order to leave it behind, to make a start equally radical.

With Descartes the mind is established, alongside God, as the foundational reality, an independent entity operating outside the mechanistic material universe. By the time of Locke, however, the study of mental process had taken precedence over the inquiry into the ways of God, and epistemology had replaced metaphysics as the foundational science. The new foundationalist epistemology is perhaps but one of the myriad manifestations of the Copernican Revolution in the relation between human beings and God. In the seventeenth century, the investigation of nature became unhinged from the quest to penetrate the divine Mind. The measure of all scientific knowledge ceased to be the mysterious mind of God and became instead the mind of man. No longer was growth in knowledge associated with the purification of the soul or penetrating the Ideas of the divine Mind. Instead, the advancement of learning depended on clarifying the mirror of the human mind. Insofar as the quest to eliminate the idols of the human mind was separated from and at least in practice given priority over the quest for spiritual enlightenment, human beings increasingly thought of themselves as minds rather than as souls. The new identity necessarily resulted in a realignment of the relation not only between knower and known but also between God and human beings (no longer human "souls"), and between human beings and themselves. This is not to say that the anthropological shift was monolithic or complete. Like the Copernican Revolution, epistemological and anthropological revolution was not at once universally accepted. Indeed, just as many, four centuries after Galileo, continue to think of human beings as the center of the created universe, so too many continue to believe, generally implicitly but in some instances explicitly, that God is the ultimate origin and end of all knowledge. But these exceptions, attesting to the reality of human freedom even amid a sea of cultural determinants, nevertheless tend to prove that in the time of Descartes a radical reorientation took place in the traditional cultural forms on which people rely for thinking about themselves and the world.

Like Descartes, Hobbes conceives of his philosophical work in terms of the six days; and he is quite precise in drawing the parallel between philosophy and God's hexameral work. In the preface to his collected works, Hobbes recommends that the would-be philosopher "imitate the creation":

If you will be a philosopher in good earnest, let your reason move upon the deep of your own cogitations and experience; those things that lie in confusion must be set asunder, distinguished, and every one stamped with its own name set in order; that is to say, your method must resemble that of the creation. The order of the creation was, light, distinction of day and night, the firmament, the luminaries, sensible creatures, man; and after the creation, the commandment. Therefore the order of contemplation will be, reason, definition, space, the stars, sensible quality, man; and after man is grown up, subjection to command.[15]

Finding in God's work of the six days a method for ordering his own contemplations, the philosopher understands that reason reflecting upon experience is like the Holy Spirit brooding upon the waters. As creation proceeded from confusion to cosmos, the philosopher's contemplations move from confusion to mental microcosm. With philosophy, we imitate creation and produce the image of creation within us. For Hobbes as for Descartes, philosophy is a new and internal work of creation, one that resembles the original creation even to the point of asserting its own originality. By imitating God's original method, they produce not imitations but what they and history have credited as original systems of thought.

The other great foundationalist program is, of course, Bacon's "Great Instauration." The title page of the *Instauratio Magna* shows the Pillars of Hercules, through which the reader will pass, launching out into unchartered seas, with the turn of the page. Bacon embarked on his "Great Instauration" in the hope that the "commerce between the mind of man and the nature of things" might "be restored to its perfect and original condition, or if that may not be, yet reduced to a better condition than that in which it now is."[16] Incessantly concerned with giving knowledge the foundation it had up to that time lacked, Bacon believed that it was vain to try to graft new knowledge on old when what is required is a "total reconstruction of sciences, arts, and all human knowledge, raised upon the proper foundations."[17] Accord-

---

15. "The Author's Epistle to the Reader," in Thomas Hobbes, *The English Works of Thomas Hobbes of Malmesbury*, ed. Sir William Molesworth (London: Scientia Aalen, 1962), 1.xiii. Hobbes also speaks of philosophy as an unborn child whose development recapitulates creation: "Philosophy, therefore, the child of the world and your own mind, is within yourself; perhaps not fashioned yet, but like the world its father, as it was in the beginning, a thing confused" (1.xiii).
16. Proemium of the *Instauratio Magna*, in *Works*, 4.7.
17. *Works*, 4.8.

ing to his six-part plan for the *Instauratio*, the first part was to be a "summary, or universal description of such science and learning as mankind is, up to this time, in possession of."[18] The second part, the *Novum Organum*, exposes the faults in all previous learning and provides the true foundations for a science that could, from that time forward, make methodical progress. Of course Bacon's debt to his predecessors is now commonly recognized. But what is surprising is that, with his devastating analysis of the idols of the mind and the distempers of learning, he was not more critical of his own claim. Calling his work the "new" *Organum*, Bacon evokes Aristotle's *Organum* even as he is trying to supplant it. This is, of course, the method of the "New" Testament as well as the secondary epics in the Homeric tradition, whose originality is the product of a retrospective gaze on an original, a predecessor who thus becomes present throughout the new work. It is worth recalling that "novus" in Latin is not opposed to "old" but to the "first," "primus." And a claim for novelty thus paradoxically suggests that the claimant is, rather than the originator, the last in a series. But the last are first, in terms of the fullness of knowledge; and in his *New Atlantis* Bacon has no doubt that the House of Solomon, alternatively called the "College of the Six Days Works," is the *summum* and *ultimum* in its kind.

It should hardly be surprising that the enthusiasm for making fresh starts reached a new register in the Renaissance—a period that defined itself as a break from the immediate past of the "Middle Ages." What should be surprising, rather, is that, given history's many lessons in the dangers of false hopes, the enthusiasm endures. Promises of transformation have been made and broken with a frequency that cannot but suggest a compulsion. Too often, as in the case of Oedipus, the desire to flee the past has had unfortunate results, and modern advances unwittingly have turned out to be the cause rather than the cure for problems of the times. Many have attempted to diagnose the malaise of modernity; indeed, one characteristic of modernity, at least in its maturity, is its obsession with its own illness. The cause of

---

18. "Plan of the Work," in *Works*, 4.22.

the illness is, paradoxically, modernity's incessant effort to cure itself by starting anew. This is evident, I believe, in the programs of both Löwith and Blumenberg. In an effort to restore (what he calls) the "pagan" understanding of history as cyclical, Löwith would accomplish with his book what the Roman Empire could not accomplish with the sword: the extirpation of the Christian worldview. One might wonder whether the end, the eradication of the cult of progress, justifies the means—not to mention whether his goal is not tainted by the same utopian longing for progress that he so forcefully rejects. In a similar way, one might find it odd that Blumenberg's argument for the legitimacy of progress is an argument for programs no more progressive than those of Bacon and Descartes—which are indeed quite old now.

The cult of progress, though it has historically intersected with evangelical reform movements from time to time, is also independent of religion and evangelism. Indeed, it is a modern version of secularist ideology, an ideology that in former times more usually found expression in imperial aspirations. As in former times, religion and empire tend to become intertwined. Both, of course, proffer originary myths. And they can find mutual support and comfort when their self-justifications coincide. In the modern period, the cult of progress is often aligned with Christian evangelism. But, as in all times, it is driven by more basic motivations found within human nature itself. As well as greed, pride, and the whole company of vicious inclinations that have always set up camp in human souls, there are other, not necessarily ignoble, desires that drive the effort to progress, including the simple desire for material well-being and cultural development. It is, after all, because people see the good that science can do that they, through an often unreflective process of extrapolation, believe and hope in its power to do things yet unseen. What makes the cult of progress an ideology is not this hope in the future (which is not without basis), but rather the belief in the myth of its origins, the belief that it rests on its own foundation and is therefore autonomous. Wishing to provide for a myth of origins, Bacon, Descartes, and Hobbes each used the pattern of God's work of the six days.

Alongside and in contrast to this self-assertive originality, there exists another approach to originality, an approach that identifies a new foundation with the discovery of the rock from which one was hewn. This older notion of originality also posits a break from the past. However, the rupture, a discontinuity or crisis either historical or personal, is not the effect but the cause, the occasion of the discovery. And what is discovered is not an origin of our own invention. It is rather the origin from which we strayed, the home to which we long to return. In this older version, what modernity understands as the experience of novelty is instead the shock of recognition. There is a continuity in this tradition from *anagnorisis* in Aristotle to *anamnesis* in Wordsworth, from homecoming in Homer to epiphany in Joyce. This sudden penetration to the essence of a thing, to that which makes it what it is, has the force of the rediscovery of a lost original. Fittingly, this older approach to originality was characteristic of the period that thought of itself as a time of renewal, of a return to the culture of classical antiquity. Alongside those who emphasized the radical originality of their systems of thought there were those who, though also convinced that the preceding age was one of darkness, nevertheless believed that the way forward was the way back, and thought of their period as one of rebirth. Indeed, this Janus-like orientation was characteristic of the period, at least characteristic enough that, following Vasari, generations have called it a "Renaissance"—which, it goes without saying, is something quite different from a "Naissance."

This pattern of return and renewal, as old as the cycle of the seasons, can suggest constancy rather than originality, as in Ecclesiastes' "The sun also ariseth, and the sun goeth down, and hasteth to his place where he arose.... The thing that hath been, it *is that* which shall be; and that which is done *is* that which shall be done: and *there is* no new *thing* under the sun."[19] But the transition from winter to spring, as the bare trees bud and brown turns to green, also suggests renewal, rebirth. It suggests a more modest originality than the radical originality of Bacon or Descartes. Instead of aiming beyond the Pillars

19. 1:5, 9, Authorized Version.

of Hercules, it makes one's destination no further away than one's own point of origin. As Eliot puts it,

> And the end of our exploring
> Will be to arrive where we started
> And know the place for the first time.[20]

This recognition of origins leads, in Eliot's poem and in the Christian Neoplatonic tradition as a whole, back to the garden. In the beginning of Christian history is its end, the garden. History runs from Eden to heaven, from Paradise to Paradise. This process of returning to one's origin and there finding one's end is, in Christian terms, conversion. And it is out of conversion that creativity is discovered.

As should be evident from previous chapters, the association of conversion and creativity clearly occupies a central place in the *Apology*. Drawing on the theology of regeneration, Sidney sees in poetry the power to lead readers back to their true selves through self-knowledge. Returning to the true Idea of themselves, readers discover the potential for a more heroic life—like that of Cyrus. This is admittedly a different kind of originality than that to which we are accustomed. Rather than the creative originality of the artistic genius, it is the restoration of the integrity originally present at Creation. It marks the beginning not of a work of art but of something even more attractive: a noble life.

This kind of restorative creativity is evident in Marvell's "The Garden." Standing in opposition to the assertive creativity of Bacon, Descartes, and Hobbes, Marvell, like Sidney, thinks of human creativity in terms of conversion and regeneration. In Marvell, the twin powers of creation and annihilation, formerly reserved to God alone, have become powers of the human mind. Whereas Sidney stops short of saying that the "wit" of the poet "creates," Marvell does not hesitate to use the term for the mind's production of "other Worlds," heterocosms.

---

20. "Little Gidding," in *The Complete Poems and Plays, 1909–1950* (New York: Harcourt Brace and Co., 1952), 145.

For Marvell, human creativity begins when the mind "withdraws" into itself, making of itself a *hortus conclusus*, an enclosed garden.[21]

> Mean while the Mind, from pleasure less,
> Withdraws into its happiness:
> The Mind, that Ocean where each kind
> Does streight its own resemblance find;
> Yet it creates, transcending these,
> Far other Worlds, and other Seas;
> Annihilating all that's made
> To a green Thought in a green Shade.[22]

Although Marvell is no doubt responding to the general epistemological crisis of his time, the problem he addresses and the solution he proposes are not primarily epistemological but theological. In short, the problem is the fallen state of the world, and the solution is the return to the original state of innocence found in Eden.

Throughout the minidrama of the poem, the mind remains a mirror, but the nature of the mirror, like the entire artificial world, is transformed. In the first half of the stanza quoted above, the mind appears to be that described by Aristotle. It has the power to receive each "kind," but what it contains is only a "resemblance"—Aristotle's *species*—of what it receives. But in the second half, that "Mind" turns out to be a place of transformation, an "Ocean" that, like the sea in Shakespeare, has the power to transform all that it takes in. Having annihilated "all that's made"—that is, the old, artificial world that is not created but "made"—the mind is left in a perfectly natural "green" world, which the mind itself generated. What it produces, when creation and annihilation are completed, is "a green thought in a green shade"—a condition in which there is a more perfect *adaequatio rei ad mentem* than is possible with the Aristotelian mind-as-mirror. Given

---

21. I am deeply indebted to Tayler, "The First Individual," who masterfully explains the transitional character of the stanza. See also his chapter "Marvell's Garden of the Mind" in Tayler, *Nature and Art*, 142–68.

22. *The Poems and Letters of Andrew Marvell*, 3d rev. ed., ed. Herschel Maurice Margoliouth (Oxford, U.K.: Clarendon Press, 1971), 49.

the identification of thought with shadows (handled most elegantly by Shakespeare, especially in *Richard II*), the "green thought" does not merely resemble the "green shade" of the garden, it *is* a "green shade." And the thought is no longer a shadow of the external world: the world is a shadow of the thought. That thought is, of course, a Neoplatonic "Idea," and the garden is an Edenic world produced by the transforming mind. And green, in Marvell's private vocabulary, is not only the color of nature (as opposed to artificial and seductive colors like pinks and reds), it is also, by way of a pun on *"vert"* in Latin and French, the color of turning, of conversion. For him, the creative mind is a green world with the power to generate other green worlds. Entering into the contemplative garden of the mind, one can take in the fallen world, annihilate it, and regenerate the Garden of Eden.

The bestowal on the creature of the faculties of creation and annihilation, powers formerly reserved to God alone, may seem an arrogation of divine creativity. However, what Marvell does is no more impious—and really little different from—the balancing act performed by poetic wit and Nature in the *Apology*. For Sidney, the poet's God-like abilities are reason to "give right honour to the heavenly Maker of that maker" (101); for Marvell, the annihilating and creating mind is the means by which it is possible to return to the Christian-Platonic Eden. For each, the fall into dualism is not essentially an epistemological problem, it is a problem as old as the original sin. Likewise, renewing the mind is for each a perennial project. Though innovative, both authors could hardly be more traditional. Each retains not only the form but also the substance of a deeply Christian view of the world.

Meyer Abrams has a great deal to say about the connection between creativity and conversion in the romantic period. He emphasizes in particular the importance of cyclical patterns and crisis or conversion narratives in shaping the romantic and, by extension, the modern mind. Although Abrams resembles Löwith in his account of the ways in which secular modern culture has incorporated the remains of a previously Christian culture, he refrains from evaluating the process and simply accepts as a fact such seepage from one age to the next. He is certainly right in arguing that "secular thinkers have no more been able to work free of the centuries-old Judeo-Christian culture than Christian theologians were able to work free of their inheritance of classical and pagan thought," though his characterization of the past as a constraint, something from which one would wish to "work free," does not convey the sense in which many Christian thinkers looked upon significant aspects of previous cultures as an inheritance. Nevertheless, Abrams's approach to secularization, in which religious ideas are reformulated and reframed rather than abandoned, must be credited for accommodating continuity as well as change in the culture.

For Abrams, "the secularization of inherited theological ideas and ways of thinking" "has not been the deletion and replacement of religious ideas but rather the assimilation and reinterpretation of religious ideas, as constitutive elements in a world view founded on secular premises."[23] According to Abrams, the romantic writers quite consciously set out to preserve Christian ideas by translating them into secular terms. In order to "save traditional concepts, schemes, and values which had been based on the relation of the Creator to his creature and creation," the romantics sought "to reformulate them within the prevailing two-term system of subject and object, ego and non-ego, the human mind or consciousness and its transactions with nature." Although displaced "from a supernatural to a natural frame of reference," "the ancient problems, terminology, and ways of thinking about human nature and history survived."[24] A prime example, which Abrams outlines, is the transformation of the Christian faith in revelation into the secular faith in political revolution into a faith in the human mind, with its powers of "imagination" and "cognition." For the romantic writers, "the mind of man confronts the old heaven and earth and possesses within itself the power . . . to transform them into a new heaven and new earth, by means of a total revolution of consciousness."[25]

Clearly, Abrams's description captures the structure and tenor of

---

23. *Natural Supernaturalism*, 13.
25. *Natural Supernaturalism*, 334.

24. *Natural Supernaturalism*, 13.

at least many forms of romanticism. As a causal account, however, it is open to question. It is not altogether clear, for example, how "secular" were the "premises" of the "world view" of Wordsworth or Coleridge, let alone Blake. It might be asked, for example, whether his story of the romantics starting with the "traditional concepts, schemes, and values" and "reformulat[ing] them within the prevailing two-term system of subject and object" might not be backward. If the "two-term system" was in fact the "prevailing" system, would it not make more sense to assume that this was the starting point, and that the incorporation of "traditional concepts" was a response to the significant problems that plagued the attempts to relate "subject and object, ego and non-ego, the human mind or consciousness and its transactions with nature"? If the development of Wordsworth's thought is any measure, it would seem that religion was not what he started with so much as what he turned toward. Furthermore, the romantic writers' disappointment with the French Revolution and subsequent faith in "a total revolution of consciousness" would seem to have been anticipated in some measure by Sidney, who wrote his work on the "zodiac" of the poet's "wit" when his hopes for political and military action were frustrated. An even more striking anticipation is the case of Marvell, who wrote "The Garden" in the shadow of the English Civil War.

Perhaps the test case for Abrams's secularization theory is that of Carlyle. In Carlyle's wish "to embody the divine Spirit of that Religion [Christianity] in a new Mythus," Abrams sees "the cardinal endeavor" of the romantic movement. This seems quite correct to me, insofar as Carlyle is explicitly rejecting the same enlightenment skepticism as the romantics. In calling for the "new Mythus," he is bidding farewell to Voltaire, who provides "only a torch for burning, no hammer for building."[26] The rejection of Voltaire, however, hardly seems to be a very good example of secularization; it suggests, rather, a rediscovery

---

26. Thomas Carlyle, *Sartor Resartus: The Life and Opinions of Herr Teufelsdröckh in Three Books*, ed. Rodger L. Tarr and Mark Engel (Berkeley and Los Angeles: University of California Press, 2000), 144.

of the spirit of Christianity. Indeed, Carlyle's "Natural Supernaturalism" is not a reclothing of Christianity but a "pierc[ing] through" the "Superannuated Symbols" and "world-embracing Phantasms" in order to look fixedly on "Existence." Stripped of its "hulls and garnitures," the "interior celestial Holy of Holies" will be exposed. Although the dialectic between the natural and the supernatural is, as Abrams argues, the fulcrum of romantic thought, the dynamic is not one that necessarily leads to secularization. Carlyle's paradoxical "Natural Supernaturalism" is not, as Abrams describes it, the outcome of the romantics' earlier endeavor "to naturalize the supernatural and to humanize the divine."[27] In fact, the quest to find in "Existence" the "interior celestial Holy of Holies" suggests precisely the opposite. Rather than translating Christian content into a new secular framework, Carlyle, like Wordsworth and Coleridge, is finding the supernatural in the natural and the divine in the human.

Of course, the secularization of the sacred or the sacralization of the secular can be very difficult to distinguish—they both may simply look like "spilt religion," to quote T. E. Hulme's famous definition of romanticism.[28] But the difference is critical. Keats's attempt to construct a "system of salvation" around the myth of Hyperion may fit Abrams's schema, but Carlyle's ecstatic discovery of the Book of Nature does not. What Carlyle discovers is what the medieval Neoplatonists had long before discovered, a "Volume" "whose Author and Writer is God." And he is struck by the fact that it is not a cookbook, as the enlightenment philosophers had imagined it, but a volume full of great mysteries, "written in celestial hieroglyphs, in the true Sacred-writing."[29] Indeed, the major movement of the period is not secularization but a reaction against the Enlightenment. Like Carlyle's bidding Voltaire adieu, Coleridge's rejection of associationism in favor of idealism was not a restructuring of religious ideas to fit the framework of secular premises. It was, rather, the trading in of a materialist

---

27. *Natural Supernaturalism*, 68.
28. "Romanticism and Classicism," in *Speculations*, ed. Herbert Read (London, 1936), 118, as quoted by Abrams, *Natural Supernaturalism*, 68.
29. Carlyle, *Sartor Resartus*, 189.

set of premises that he had found to be sterile for a more ample philosophical framework, one that would give the human spirit room to move and to encounter itself, the world, and God. Trying to solve the problems presented by the world and the culture's understanding of it, Carlyle, like Coleridge, took a step closer to the old Christian solutions and adapted his worldview accordingly, something Christians are perennially doing. This regenerative return was, for Carlyle, a rebirth, a *"palingenesia."* For him, as for Sidney, human progress is circular.

Whether the focus is Carlyle's "natural supernaturalism," Coleridge's creative imagination, or Sidney's "zodiac" of the "wit," to understand the origins of the concept one must consider both secularization and sacralization. More simply put, one must recognize the ongoing interplay of the sacred and the secular—something so obvious and yet so often overlooked. There is a deeply engrained habit in our culture of opposing the sacred and the secular. And for those trying to explain the discovery of human creativity, this habit exerts a prejudice in favor of reductive theories of secularization. Although the ordinary use of the term today shows that "creativity" has in fact been drained of its divine contents and put to everyday use, Sidney's thought in the *Apology*, properly understood, necessarily complicates this simple scenario. Fully aware of what he is doing, Sidney presents "making" as at once human and divine. In his thought, the sacred and secular realities are analogous rather than opposed. For the reader who is aware of this, no longer should it be possible to conceive of the origin of human creativity simply as part of a process of secularization. Nor should it be possible to overlook Sidney's religious commitments and theological interests when examining his justification of his "unelected vocation" of poetry.

The recognition of the interplay of sacred and secular in the *Apology* is also an effective remedy for the widespread habit of thinking of the transition from medieval to modern as a movement from an "Age of Faith" to an "Age of Reason." Although these rubrics were by-and-large discarded even before the limitations of periodization were commonly understood, the otherwise sophisticated accounts of modernity offered by Löwith and Blumenberg rely heavily, if implicitly, on the

Creativity and the Origins of Modernity 183

old-fashioned and reductive distinction between ages of faith and reason. Of course, hardly any specialized knowledge of the periods is necessary for one to realize that the separation of faith and reason is more honored in the breach than in the observance. The very forms of investigation in the Middle Ages, the *summa* and the *disputatio*, for example, show a great faith not only in God but in reason. And the spirit of the Enlightenment was not simply the antireligious secularism of the *philosophes*. The opposition to Voltaire was strong, and those like Vico in Italy and Wolff, Hamann, Herder, and Goethe in Germany would have considered it most unreasonable to exclude transcendence and mystery from their philosophical considerations. Indeed, formulating the relation between faith and reason was one of the great medieval projects, and in his great intellectual synthesis Aquinas carefully maintained their independence while articulating their subtle and complex interaction. So too the later thinkers I have discussed, from Sidney to Wordsworth and Coleridge, attempt the reconciliation of faith and reason, albeit in new and decidedly different contexts. Quite simply, at all points in history there have been thinkers who have tried, with greater or lesser success, to harmonize faith and reason; so too there have always been thinkers who have opposed these attempts. Ironically, in opposing faith and reason, the theorists of modernity—themselves secularists—resemble their opposites, the fideists of the Middle Ages.

It has always been difficult to give secular realities their due. They are forever being over- or undervalued—or both at the same time. One perennial temptation is to inflate the value of the one by artificially depressing the other. The disdain of worldly pursuits obviously has at times been a monkish or puritanical habit used to make a sterile life seem noble. On the other side, the denunciation of religion can be the secularist's trick for believing that liberalism provides a secure foundation for ethical and political judgments. In both cases, the tendency is to try to make either the secular or the sacred absolute, while making the other obsolete.

In his proposal that poetry replace religion, Matthew Arnold recognized this dynamic and awarded the victory to secularization (prematurely, it now appears). Placing each on opposite ends of the sacred-secular seesaw, Arnold predicted that "most of what now passes with us for religion and philosophy will be replaced by poetry." His motive for replacing religion and philosophy with poetry was not that he was a secularist, but rather that he saw Christianity in an enfeebled state, undermined by the application of the historical method to biblical studies and by scientific claims such as that of Darwin. Trying to fill the void created by the crisis in belief, he felt that "more and more mankind will discover that we have to turn to poetry to interpret life for us, to console us, to sustain us."[30] Arnold's formulation reveals something other than the obsolescence of religion. In attributing to poetry the power to fulfill the functions of religion—"to interpret life," "to console," and "to sustain"—it reveals that the two are not so much opposed as intertwined. Arnold's effort to fold religion into poetry is extended—and indeed reaches its pinnacle—with the poetic theory of Wallace Stevens. Having converted the search for God into the search for "a supreme fiction," Stevens looks to poetry as "a means of redemption."[31] Stevens argues that "we live in the mind." And "if we live in the mind, we live with the imagination." This imagination is the creative imagination described by Theseus, giving airy nothing a local habitation and a name. In Stevens's formulation, "the imagination is the faculty by which we import what is unreal into the real, . . . by which we project the idea of God into the idea of man."[32] In the "Final Soliloquy of the Interior Paramour" the identification is clear: "We say God and the imagination are one."[33] The only qualification—simple and profound—is the prefix, "we say."

The folding of the sacred into the secular or the secular into the sa-

---

30. Matthew Arnold, *The Portable Matthew Arnold*, ed. Lionel Trilling (New York: Viking Press, 1962), 300.
31. Wallace Stevens, *Opus Posthumous*, ed. Samuel French Morse (New York: Knopf, 1957), 160.
32. "Imagination as Value," in *The Necessary Angel: Essays on Reality and the Imagination*, in Wallace Stevens, *Collected Poetry and Prose* (New York: Library of America, 1997), 729.
33. Wallace Stevens, *The Collected Poems of Wallace Stevens* (New York: Knopf, 1965), 524.

cred did not, to be sure, start in the nineteenth century. In the Middle Ages as well as in the Renaissance, it can be seen in radical secularists (e.g., Siger of Brabant and Giordano Bruno) as well as in utopian thinkers (e.g., Joachim of Fiore and Tommaso Campanella). But this kind of identification of sacred and secular is the exception rather than the rule. The standard practice was to hold the sacred and the secular each in tension with the other. It is evident in Augustine's use of the *Aeneid* as a subtext for his own story in the *Confessions*. In his conversion to Christianity—effected by opening the Christian Scriptures at random—can be seen both his indebtedness to and rejection of the pagan practice of the *sortes Virgilianae*. Moving in just the opposite direction, Dante invents a poetics that is decidedly secular and yet constantly evokes the practices of allegorical interpretation traditionally applied to Sacred Scripture. It is precisely this tension and interplay between the sacred and the secular that enables the titillating (and facetious) blasphemy of many stories in the *Decameron*. And in the twentieth century, the habit of understanding human and divine love in terms of one another, which dates at least to the Song of Songs, can still be used for fresh effect by J. V. Cunningham in his witty epigram "History of Ideas":

> God is love. Then by inversion
> Love is God, and sex conversion.[34]

In contrast to these examples, in which the tensions between the sacred and the secular are exploited for effect, is the attempt to reconcile the two, without compromising either. This ambition to find the just proportion between the sacred and the secular unites two otherwise very different figures, Aquinas and Sidney, both of whom sought to provide a compelling presentation of the harmony of faith and reason. Entering deeply into the newly rediscovered works of Aristotle, Aquinas saw the possibility, and indeed the necessity, of respecting the value and autonomy of secular realities while asserting the superiori-

---

34. "A Century of Epigrams," 29, in J. V. Cunningham, *The Poems of J. V. Cunningham*, ed. Timothy Steele (Athens, Ohio: Swallow Press, 1997).

ty of the supernatural order. In a later period, taking up the ideal of the Renaissance courtier, Sidney reconciles courtly self-fashioning with the imitation of Christ. Of course, the differences separating Aquinas and Sidney are too numerous to detail. Most obvious, no doubt, is the contrast in style between Aquinas's systematic summa and Sidney's witty mock oration. The cultural divide is, at most points, unbridgeable. In the High Middle Ages, it would have been a practical absurdity for Aquinas to argue for the superiority of the active life over the contemplative life. So too for Sidney to advocate the contemplative life would have required him to step well beyond his historical place, if not his historical time. Nevertheless, each was zealous for seeing what he believed to be the true faith spread and take deeper root in the lives of individuals and of societies. Since they are arguably closer to one another in this respect than either would be to an adherent of one of the many forms of secularism today, it would be a mistake to let their differences occlude a basic and important similarity: each takes a bold step toward a more just appreciation of secular activities, and toward an understanding of the importance of the secular in the fulfillment of the sacred.[35]

It is tempting to place the *Apology*—and the Renaissance as a whole—within the context of a progression toward modern secularism and utopianism. Having taken the step of affirming the value of the temporal order, Sidney may appear one step closer to seeing *only* the value of the temporal order. Presenting the way ahead by looking back—to Eden, to the "golden" world—he may seem to prepare the way for Hobbes and Rousseau, who also would have mankind im-

---

[35]. Spenser and Milton, like Sidney, emphasize the role of the imagination in trying to reconcile the secular and the sacred. For an example of a study that too starkly opposes the sacred and the secular while trying to understand these authors, see John Guillory, *Poetic Authority: Spenser, Milton, and Literary History* (New York: Columbia University Press, 1983). Although Guillory makes some interesting observations about Sidney's role in "moralizing imagination," his opposition of sacred and secular leads him to believe that Sidney delivers "a view of poetry emptied of divinity." The supposed "secularity" of Sidney's view of the imagination becomes, for Guillory, "the stage upon which Spenser and Milton will play out the anxieties of the religious poet" (11).

prove its condition by looking back to its original state, "the state of nature." But Sidney's primitivism is, of course, something quite different from their respective versions. Neither "soft" nor "hard," it is, rather, "Christian." Although from one perspective Sidney may seem to prepare the way for Hobbes and Rousseau, from another he is that from which they broke away. Whereas Sidney's idea of renewal was explicitly Christian, the notions of Hobbes and Rousseau were essentially naturalistic. Unlike Sidney, these successors find secular substitutes for the object of Christian faith and place their trust, respectively, in the state and in the goodness of human nature. If there is to be a fence between the Christian past and the secularist and utopian present, Sidney would be on the opposite side from Hobbes and Rousseau.

In Sidney, the spirit of reform is still Christian. It is both the spirit of the Protestant reformers of religion and the Renaissance reformers of artistic and intellectual culture. In his poetic theory, Sidney would have his contemporaries enter fully into the heroic ideals of classical culture and, doing so, fulfill them, revealing the Christian truth that until then had remained hidden in the pagan ideals. The true Christians would imitate Cyrus, and in resembling him they would reveal the truth about Cyrus: that he is the type of Christ. This relationship is typological, and the process incarnational. The effect is a regeneration that turns the postlapsarian "brazen" world into an Edenic "golden" world, making the "too much loved earth more lovely" (100).

Despite the fact that the experience of countless readers attests to the reality of regeneration through literature, and despite the central place of the *Apology* in the history of literature, it nevertheless remains easy to label Sidney's "saucy" claim as an ideological construct. But even if poetic creativity is a manifestation of a false consciousness, there can be little argument with the assessment of J. Hillis Miller that "it is a severe limitation of literary and cultural study today that a good bit of it tends not to interest itself much in what might be called the religious or ontological dimension of writers' and cultures' ideologies." Reaffirming his opinion of a generation ago, that "religious questions are the most important," Miller goes so far as to argue that even when an ideology excludes God from the world, that absence unavoidably takes on a central and defining position. Indeed, he has demonstrated as much in his admirable study of the literature of the Victorian period. Steiner makes virtually the same point in relation to the grand sweep of Western literature, carrying out what amounts to an exquisite literary version of negative theology.[36] What holds for God holds for the sacred in general: its presence is often most powerfully experienced through its absence.[37]

In the end, however, knowing that the birth of human creativity occupies a central position in literary history and that it is bound up with the emergence of modernity is not enough. The question remains: Was human creativity discovered or invented? Is it real, or is it a symptom of a false consciousness? On one end of the spectrum is Löwith, who considers creativity, whether human or divine, a false consciousness. On the other is Blumenberg, who defends human creativity as a legitimate reality and considers only divine creativity to be an ideological construct. These, however, are not the only explanations available. For those who do not rule out the possibility of the existence of divine creativity, another possibility presents itself: namely, that the metaphor of human creativity is simply that, a metaphor—something like "computer memory" or the "leg of a table." If human creativity is a figure of speech, perhaps we should simply expect it to do more or less the work for which Aristotle thought it suited: to show a striking similarity between two different things. To the extent that human creativity has become a "dead" metaphor, it would seem that the comparison is so fitting that it has become invisible. This interpre-

36. J. Hillis Miller, *The Disappearance of God: Five Nineteenth-Century Authors* (Urbana: University of Illinois Press, 2000), xi; George Steiner, *Real Presences* (Chicago: University of Chicago, 1989).

37. Recognizing that neither the sacred nor the secular can do without the other, Christopher Dawson, *Religion and the Rise of Western Culture* (London: Sheed & Ward, 1950), 16, maintains that "[n]owhere is the dynamism of Western religion more strikingly manifested than in the indirect and unconscious influence it has exercised on the social and intellectual movements which were avowedly secular." The religious underpinnings of the development of scientific thought in the West is a perfect illustration of the point, and is discussed fully by Stanley L. Jaki in *The Road of Science and the Ways to God* (Edinburgh, U.K.: Scottish Academic Press, 1978), the Gifford lectures for 1974–1975 and 1975–1976.

tive approach—which treats human making and divine creating as independent and legitimate realities, but realities that can be more fully understood in light of one another—is so old that it may once again offer a fresh insight.

Still, there is yet another understanding of human creativity, which is to admit the possibility not only that human and divine creativity exist but also that there is a real relationship between them. This approach, which happens to be that of Sidney, treats human creativity not as a metaphorical but as an analogical expression. The relationship of divine creativity and human making, according to this understanding, is discovered, not devised. "Made" by the "heavenly Maker" in "His own likeness," the human "maker" exercises a regenerative creativity that is the image and likeness of divine creativity. Though "too saucy a comparison" to gain wide acceptance among Sidney's contemporaries or, indeed, among audiences of any time, this is Sidney's argument (101). For Sidney, literature has a regenerative power. Because they are truly different, neither reading and regeneration nor writing and creation are simply interchangeable; but because they are related, each helps explain the other. To fail to consider the analogy to divine creation is to circumscribe any exploration of the rich, varied, and often profound human reality that is writing. Similarly, to exclude the analogy to the regeneration in grace limits and indeed skews any account of the experience of reading. Sidney places no such limits on his theory of literature. Understanding human realities in light of the corresponding divine realities, Sidney presents in the *Apology* a compelling picture of literary regeneration. Seeing it, let us hope that at least our "erected wit" will allow us to "know what perfection is" even if "our infected will keepeth us from reaching unto it."

APPENDIX

The Text

In 1595 two editions of the *Apology* were published. Although Henry Olney's edition, *An Apologie for Poetrie*, appeared first, William Ponsonby had entered his edition, *The Defence of Poesie*, in the Stationers' Register on 29 November 1594, four months before Olney. The entry for Olney, on 12 April 1595, bears the annotation "This belongeth to Master Ponsonby by a former Entrance and an agrement is made between them wherby Master Ponsonby is to enjoy the copie according to the former Entrance."[1] As well as printing his own edition, Ponsonby took over the copies already printed by Olney, selling them after substituting his own title page. Having previously printed the *Arcadia* and Mary Sidney's *A Discourse of Life and Death* (a translation of a work by Philip Mornay), Ponsonby was already connected with the Sidneys. And it was Ponsonby who published the folio of Sidney's works in 1598. Since the folio includes Ponsonby's original version of the *Defence*, this text is presumed to have been preferred by Mary Sidney. Giving it added authority is the close resemblance it bears to the Penshurst manuscript, which was Robert Sidney's copy. Although Ponsonby's edition apparently has greater authority, Olney's edition is far more polished. It was clearly prepared with far greater care, and for this reason it has been favored by many modern editors (including Geoffrey Shepherd) despite its inferior claim to authority.

The only critical edition of the text is that of Katherine Duncan-Jones and Jan van Dorsten in *Miscellaneous Prose of Sir Philip Sidney* (Oxford, U.K.: Clarendon Press, 1973). Their introduction should be consulted, especially for its discussions of the authority of the Penshurst MS and of the lack of authority of the Norwich MS. Whereas Duncan-Jones and van Dorsten follow Ponsonby (checking it against the Penshurst MS) for their edition, I have followed Olney, except where Ponsonby's text is obviously superior. Although I rarely

---

1. See Sidney, *Prose Works*, 3.6.

decide in favor of Ponsonby's text, I record all variants. Except for silently substituting v's and u's and s's for f's, I have retained the original spelling, capitalization, and punctuation. Both the Olney and Ponsonby editions are available in facsimile for those wishing to investigate. For the Olney edition, *An Apologie for Poetrie*, see volume 413 in *The English Experience, Its Record in Early Printed Books Published in Facsimile* (Amsterdam: Theatrum Orbis Terrarum; New York: Da Capo Press, 1971); for the Ponsonby edition, see *The Defence of Poesie* (London: Noel Douglas, 1928).

From *An Apologie for Poetrie* / *The Defence of Poesie*

But now, let us see how the Greekes named it, and howe they deemed of it. The Greekes called him a Poet, which name, hath as the most excellent, gone thorough other Languages. It commeth of this word *Poiein*, which is, to make: wherein I know not, whether by lucke or wisedome, wee Englishmen have mette with the Greekes, in calling
5 him a maker: which name, how high and incomparable a title it is, I had rather were knowne by marking the scope of other Sciences, then by my partiall allegation. There is no Arte delivered unto mankinde, that hath not the workes of Nature for his principall object, without which they could not consist, & on which they so depend, as they become Actors and Players as it were, of what Nature will have set foorth. So doth
10 the *Astronomer* looke upon the starres, and by that hee seeth, setteth downe what order Nature hath taken therein. So doe the Geometrician, & Arithmetician, in their diverse sorts of quantities. So doth the Musitian in times, tel you which by nature agree, which not. The naturall Philosopher thereon hath his name, and the Morrall Philosopher standeth

---

P = Ponsonby's edition, *The Defence of Poesie*
O = Olney's edition, *An Apologie for Poetrie*
1 named] have named P; howe] how P
2 called] named P; a Poet] ποιητήν P
3 Languages] languages P; *Poiein*] ποιεῖν P; is,] is P; wherein] wherin P; not,] not P
4 lucke] luck P; wee] we P; mette] met P; Greekes,] Greekes P
5 maker:] Maker. P; which] Which P;
6 Sciences] sciences P; my] any P, partiall] partial P
7 Arte] Art P; unto] to O; mankinde,] mankind P; Nature] nature P
8 &] and P
9 and Players] & Plaiers, P; Nature] nature P; foorth] forth P
10 Astronomer] *Astronomer* P; hee] he P; setteth] set P
11 Nature] nature P; doe] doth P; Geometrician, & Arithmetician] *Geometritian & Arithmititian* P; diverse] divers
12 Musitian] *Musitians* P; times,] times P, you] you, P
13 naturall] natural P; Philosopher] *Philosopher* P; thereon] theron O; Morrall Philosopher] (morall *Philosopher* P

Appendix   193

upon the naturall vertues, vices, and passions of man; and followe Nature (saith hee)
therein, & thou shalt not erre. The Lawyer sayth what men have determined. The
Historian what men have done. The Grammarian speaketh onely of the rules of speech,
and the Rethorician, and Logitian, considering what in Nature will soonest prove and
perswade, thereon give artificial rules, which still are compassed within the circle of a
question, according to the proposed matter. The Phisition waigheth the nature of a mans
bodie, and the nature of things helpeful, or hurtefull unto it. And the Metaphisick, though
it be in the seconde and abstract notions, and therefore be counted supernaturall: yet doth
hee indeede builde upon the depth of Nature: onely the Poet, disdayning to be tied to any
such subjection, lifted up with the vigor of his owne invention, dooth growe in effect,
another nature, in making things either better then Nature bringeth forth, or quite a newe
formes such as never were in Nature, as the *Heroes, Demigods, Cyclops, Chimeras,
Furies,* & such like: so as hee goeth hand in hand with Nature, not inclosed within the
narrow warrant of her gifts, but freely ranging onely within the Zodiac of his owne wit.
Nature never set forth the earth in so rich tapistry, as divers Poets have done,
neither with so pleasant rivers, fruitful trees, sweet smelling flowers: nor whatsoever els may
make the too much loved earth more lovely. Her world is brazen, the Poets only deliver a
golden: but let those things alone and goe to man, for whom as the other things are, so it
seemeth in him her uttermost cunning is imployed, and knowe whether shee have brought

14 upon] uppon; and] or P; man;] man: P followe Nature] follow nature P; (saith hee)] saith he P
15 &] and P; Lawyer sayth] *Lawier* saith, P
16 Historian] *Historian,* P, Grammarian] *Gramarian,* P
17 Rethorician, and Logitian] *Rhetoritian* and *Logitian* P; Nature wil] will P; prove] proove,
18 perswade, thereon] perswade thereon, P artificial] artificiall P
19 Phisition waigheth] *Phisitian* wayeth P; of] of P
20 and] & P; helpeful] helpful P; hurtefull] hurtfull P; Metaphisick,] *Metaphisicke*
21 seconde and] second & P; notions] Notions P; supernaturall:] supernaturall
22 indeede builde] indeed build P; Nature:] nature P; onely] Only P; Poet] Poet P; disdayning] disdeining P
23 dooth growe] doth grow P; effect,] effect P
24 another;] into another P; nature,] nature: P; Nature] nature P; forth] foorth P; newe] new, P
25 Nature] nature P; *Chimeras*] *Chymeras* P
26 &] and P; like:] like; P; hee] he P; Nature] nature P
27 gifts] guifts O; ranging onely] raunging P
28 forth] foorth P; in] into P; tapistry,] Tapistry P; divers] diverse P
29 so pleasant] plesant O; fruitful] fruitfull P; sweet] sweete P; flowers:] flowers, P
30 lovely. Her] lovely: her P; brazen] brasen O
31 golden: but] golden. But P
32 cunning] comming P; imployed, and know] imploied: & know P shee] she P

foorth so true a lover as *Theagines*, so constant a friende as *Pilades*, so valiant a man as *Orlando*, so right a Prince as *Xenophons Cyrus:* so excellent a man every way, as *Virgils Aeneas:* neither let this be jestingly conceived, because the works of the one be essentiall: the other, in imitation or fiction: for any understanding knoweth the skil of the Artificer, standeth in that *Idea* or fore-conceite of the work, & not in the work it selfe. And that the Poet hath that *Idea*, is manifest, by delivering them forth in such excellencie as hee hath imagined them. Which delivering forth also, is not wholie imaginative, as we are wont to say by them that build Castles in the ayre: but so farr substantially it worketh, not onely to make a *Cyrus*, which had been but a particular excellencie, as Nature might have done, but to bestow a *Cyrus* upon the worlde, to make many *Cyrusses*, if they will learn aright, why, and how that Maker made him.

Neither let it be deemed too sawcie a comparison to balance the highest poynt of mans wit with the efficacie of Nature: but rather give right honor to the heavenly Maker of that maker: who having made man to his owne likeness, set him beyond & over all the workes of that second nature, which in nothing hee sheweth so much as in Poetrie: when with the force of a divine breath, he bringeth things forth far surpassing her dooings, with no small argument to the incredulous of that first accursed fall of *Adam:* sith our erected wit maketh us know what perfection is, and yet our infected will, keepeth us from reaching unto it. But these arguments wil by fewe be understood, and by fewer granted. Thus much (I hope) will be given me, that the Greekes with some probabilite of reason, gave him the name above all names of learning.

---

33 Theagines] Theagenes P; friende] friend P; Pilades] Pylades
34 *Cyrus:*] *Cyrus*, P
35 *Aeneas:* neither] *Aeneas.* Neither P; because] bicause P; essentiall] essenciall P
36 other,] other P; understanding] understanding, P; skil] skill P; the Artificer,] ech Artificer
37 *Idea* or fore-conceite] *Idea*, or fore conceit P; work] worke P; &] and P; work] worke P
38 forth] foorth P; hee hath] he had P
39 them. Which] them: which P; forth also,] foorth, also P; wholie] wholly P
40 ayre] aire P; substantially] substancially P
41 been] bene P; particular] particuler O; excellencie,] excellency P; Nature] nature P
42 worlde,] world P; *Cyrusses*] *Cyrus's* O; will learn] wil learne O
43 why,] why P; Maker] maker P
44 Neither] Neyther O; sawcie] sawcy P; comparison] comparison, P; point] poynt O
45 wit] wit, P Nature] nature P; Maker] maker P;
46 maker:] maker, P; likeness] likenes O; &] and P
47 hee] he P; Poetrie:] Poetry; P
48 the force] force P; forth] foorth P; far surpassing] surpassing P; dooings,] doings:
49 argument] arguments P; sith] since P
50 wit] wit, O; will] wil P
51 wil] will P; fewe] few P granted.] graunted: P
52 Thus] thus in P; (I hope)] I hope P; Greekes] Greeks P; probabilite] probability P

BIBLIOGRAPHY

I. Editions of Sidney's Works

Sidney, Philip, Sir. *An Apology for Poetrie*. Edited by Edward Arber. London, 1868. [Reprint of the Olney edition.]
———. *An Apology for Poetry*. Edited by Geoffrey Shepherd. London: T. Nelson, 1965. [Excellent introduction and notes; edition most often cited in recent studies.]
———. *An Apology for Poetry*. Edited by Forrest Robinson. New York: Macmillan, 1970.
———. *A Defence of Poetry*. Edited by J. A. van Dorsten. London: Oxford University Press, 1966.
———. *The Defence of Poesie*. London: Noel Douglas, 1928. [Reprint of the Ponsonby edition.]
———. *Miscellaneous Prose of Sir Philip Sidney*. Edited by Katherine Duncan-Jones and J. A. van Dorsten. Oxford, U.K.: Clarendon Press, 1973. [The most carefully edited modern edition.]
———. *The Prose Works of Sir Philip Sidney*. Edited by Albert Feuillerat. 4 vols. Cambridge, U.K.: Cambridge University Press, 1962. [Includes Sidney's translation of Mornay.]
———. *Sir Philip Sidney's Defense of Poesy*. Edited by Lewis Soens. Lincoln: University of Nebraska Press, 1970. [Very good introduction.]
Sidney, Philip, and Arthur Golding, trans. *A Work Concerning the Trewnesse of the Christian Religion*, by Philippe Mornay. Edited by F. J. Sypher. Delmar, N.Y.: Scholars' Facsimiles and Reprints, 1976.

II. Secondary Sources

Abrams, Meyer. *The Mirror and the Lamp: Romantic Theory and the Critical Tradition*. New York: Norton, 1958.
———. *Natural Supernaturalism: Tradition and Revolution in Romantic Literature*. New York: Norton, 1971.
Aguzzi-Barbagli, Danilo. "Humanism and Poetics." In *Renaissance Humanism:*

Foundations, Forms, and Legacy, edited by Albert Rabil Jr., 85–169. Philadelphia: University of Pennsylvania Press, 1988.

Allen, Don Cameron. *Image and Meaning: Metaphoric Traditions in Renaissance Poetry*. Baltimore: Johns Hopkins University Press, 1960.

———. *Mysteriously Meant: The Rediscovery of Pagan Symbolism and Allegorical Interpretation in the Renaissance*. Baltimore: Johns Hopkins University Press, 1970.

Allen, M. J. B. "Renaissance Neoplatonism." In *The Cambridge History of Literary Criticism*, edited by Glyn P. Norton, 435–41. Cambridge, U.K.: Cambridge University Press, 1999.

———. "Sidney's *Defence* and the Image Making of Plato's Sophist." In *Sir Philip Sidney's Achievements*, 93–108. New York: AMS Press, 1990.

Allen, M. J. B., Dominic Baker-Smith, Arthur F. Kinney, and Margaret Sullivan. *Sir Philip Sidney's Achievements*. New York: AMS Press, 1990.

Ariew, Roger, and Marjorie Grene. "Ideas, in and before Descartes." *Journal of the History of Ideas* 56 (1995): 87–106.

Atkins, J. W. H. *English Literary Criticism: The Renascence*. New York: Barnes & Noble, 1968.

Attridge, Derek. "Puttenham's Perplexity: Nature, Art, and the Supplement in Renaissance Poetic Theory." In *Literary Theory/Renaissance Texts*, edited by Patricia Parker and David Quint, 257–79. Baltimore: Johns Hopkins University Press, 1986.

Avis, Paul D. L. *God and the Creative Imagination: Metaphor, Symbol, and Myth in Religion and Theology*. London: Routledge, 1999.

Balthasar, Hans Urs von. *Presence and Thought: An Essay on the Religious Philosophy of Gregory of Nyssa*. Edited by Mark Sebanc. San Francisco: Ignatius Press, 1995.

Barnes, Catherine. "The Hidden Persuader: The Complex Speaking Voice of Sidney's *Defence of Poetry*." *PMLA* 86 (1971): 422–27.

Barry, Gerald Reid. *Man the Artist: His Creative Imagination*. London: Macdonald, 1964.

Beach, D. M. "The Poetry of Idea: Sir Philip Sidney and the Theory of Allegory." *Texas Studies in Literature and Language: A Journal of the Humanities* 13 (1971): 365–89.

Belting, Hans. *Likeness and Presence: A History of the Image before the Era of Art*. Chicago: University of Chicago Press, 1994.

Benson, Donald. "Idea and the Problem of Knowledge in Seventeenth-Century Aesthetics." *English Miscellany* 19 (1968): 83–104.

Bercovitch, Sacvan. *Typology and Early American Literature*. Amherst: University of Massachusetts Press, 1972.

Berger, Harry Jr. *Second World and Green World: Studies in Renaissance Fiction-Making*. Berkeley and Los Angeles: University of California Press, 1988.

Bergvall, Ake. "'The Poets Deliver': Procreation, Communication, and Incarnation in Sidney and Wordsworth." *Connotations: A Journal for Critical Debate* 8 (1998): 283–93.

———. "Reason in Luther, Calvin, and Sidney." *Sixteenth Century Journal* 23 (1992): 115–27.
Berkouwer, G. C. *Man: The Image of God*. Edited by Dirk Jellema. Grand Rapids, Mich.: Eerdmans, 1962.
Berley, Marc. *Reading the Renaissance: Ideas and Idioms from Shakespeare to Milton*. Pittsburgh, Pa.: Duquesne University Press, 2002.
Berry, Edward. *The Making of Sir Philip Sidney*. Toronto: University of Toronto Press, 1998.
———. "The Poet as Warrior in Sidney's *Defence of Poetry*." *Studies in English Literature 1500–1900* 29 (1989): 21–34.
Bieman, Elizabeth. *Plato Baptized: Towards the Interpretation of Spenser's Mimetic Fictions*. Toronto: University of Toronto Press, 1988.
Blumenberg, Hans. *The Legitimacy of the Modern Age*. Edited by Robert M. Wallace. Cambridge, Mass.: Harvard University Press, 1983.
Boas, Frederick S. *Sir Philip Sidney, Representative Elizabethan: His Life and Writings*. New York: Russell & Russell, 1970.
Bober, Harry. "*In Principio*: Creation before Time." In *Essays in Honor of Erwin Panofsky*, 13–28. New York: New York University Press, 1961.
Bolgar, R. R. *The Classical Heritage and Its Beneficiaries*. Cambridge, U.K.: Cambridge University Press, 1954.
Borris, Kenneth. *Allegory and Epic in English Renaissance Literature: Heroic Form in Sidney, Spenser, and Milton*. Cambridge, U.K.: Cambridge University Press, 2000.
Bouwsma, William. "The Renaissance Discovery of Human Creativity." In *Humanity and Divinity in the Renaissance and Reformation: Essays in Honor of Charles Trinkaus*, 17–33. Leiden, The Netherlands: E. J. Brill, 1993.
Bowra, Maurice. *The Romantic Imagination*. Cambridge, Mass.: Harvard University Press, 1949.
Boyd, John. *The Function of Mimesis and Its Decline*. Cambridge, Mass.: Harvard University Press, 1968.
Brient, Elizabeth. *The Immanence of the Infinite: Hans Blumenberg and the Threshold to Modernity*. Washington, D.C.: The Catholic University of America Press, 2001.
Brink, Jean R. "Philosophical Poetry: The Contrasting Poetics of Sidney and Scaliger." *Explorations in Renaissance Culture* 8–9 (1982–83): 45–53.
Bronowski, Jacob. *The Poet's Defence*. Westport, Conn.: Hyperion Press, 1979.
Bullard, Mellissa Meriam. "'The Inward Zodiac': A Development in Ficino's Thought on Astrology." *Renaissance Quarterly* 43 (1990): 687–707.
Bundy, Murray. *The Theory of the Imagination in Classical and Medieval Thought*. Urbana: University of Illinois Press, 1927.
Buxton, John. "Sidney and Theophrastus." *English Literary Renaissance* 2 (1972): 79–82.
———. *Sir Philip Sidney and the English Renaissance*. London: Macmillan, 1964.

Cairns, David. *The Image of God in Man*. London: S. C. M. Press, 1953.
Callahan, John. *Greek Philosophy and the Cappodocian Cosmology*. Cambridge, Mass.: Harvard University Press, 1958.
Campbell, Lily. *Divine Poetry and Drama in Sixteenth-Century England*. Berkeley and Los Angeles: University of California Press, 1959.
———. "Sidney as 'the Learned Soldier.'" *Huntington Library Quarterly* 7 (1944): 175–78.
Candido, Joseph. "Fulke Greville's Biography of Sir Philip Sidney and the 'Architectonic' Tudor Life." *South Central Bulletin* 2 (1985): 3–12.
Cantalupo, Charles. "Religio Poetae." *Renascence* 36 (1983–1984): 139–46.
Caputo, John. *More Radical Hermeneutics: On Not Knowing Who We Are*. Bloomington: Indiana University Press, 2000.
Carruthers, Mary. *The Book of Memory: A Study of Memory in Medieval Culture*. Cambridge, U.K.: Cambridge University Press, 1990.
Cassirer, Ernst. *The Individual and the Cosmos in Renaissance Philosophy*. Translated by Mario Domandi. New York: Harper & Row, 1963.
Castor, Grahame. *Pléiade Poetics*. Cambridge, U.K.: Cambridge University Press, 1964.
Charity, A. C. *Events and Their Afterlife: The Dialectics of Christian Typology in the Bible and Dante*. Cambridge, U.K.: Cambridge University Press, 1966.
Chaudhuri, Sukanta. *Infirm Glory: Shakespeare and the Renaissance Image of Man*. Oxford, U.K.: Clarendon Press, 1981.
Cheadle, B. D. "'The Truest Poetry Is the Most Feigning': Sidney on the Poet as Maker." *Theoria: A Journal of Studies in the Arts, Humanities and Social Sciences* 52 (1979): 39–49.
Chenu, Marie-Dominique. *Nature, Man, and Society in the Twelfth Century: Essays on New Theological Perspectives in the Latin West*. Chicago: University of Chicago Press, 1968.
Cherniss, Harold. *The Platonism of Gregory of Nyssa*. Berkeley and Los Angeles: University of California Press, 1930.
Clark, D. L. *Rhetoric and Poetry in the Renaissance*. New York: Columbia University Press, 1922.
Clark, Eleanor Grace. *Ralegh and Marlowe: A Study in Elizabethan Fustian*. New York: Fordham University Press, 1941.
Clements, Robert. *Critical Theory and Practice of the Pléiade*. Cambridge, Mass.: Harvard University Press, 1942.
Clifford, Gay. *The Transformations of Allegory*. London: Routledge and Kegan Paul, 1974.
Coleridge, Samuel Taylor. *Biographia Literaria*. 2 vols. Edited by James Engell and W. Jackson Bate. Princeton, N.J.: Princeton University Press, 1983.
———. *Biographia Literaria, with Aesthetic Essays*. 2 vols. Edited by John Shawcross. Oxford, U.K.: Clarendon Press, 1907.

———. *Imagination in Coleridge*. Edited by John Spencer Hill. Totowa, N.J.: Rowman & Littlefield, 1978.
———. *Lay Sermons*. Edited by R. J. White. Vol. 6 of the *Collected Works*. Princeton, N.J.: Princeton University Press, 1972.
———. *Lectures 1808–1819: On Literature*. Edited by R. A. Foakes. Princeton, N.J.: Princeton University Press, 1987.
Connell, Dorothy. *Sir Philip Sidney: The Maker's Mind*. Oxford, U.K.: Oxford University Press, 1977.
Coogan, Robert. "More Dais than Dock: Greek Rhetoric and Sidney's Encomium on Poetry." *Studies in the Literary Imagination* 15 (1982): 99–113.
———. "The Triumph of Reason: Sidney's Defense and Aristotle's Rhetoric." *Papers on Language and Literature* 17 (1981): 255–70.
Craft, William. *Labyrinth of Desire: Invention and Culture in the Work of Sir Philip Sidney*. Newark: University of Delaware Press, 1994.
Craig, D. H. "A Hybrid Growth: Sidney's Theory of Poetry in *An Apology for Poetry*." In *Sidney in Retrospect: Selections from "English Literary Renaissance,"* edited by Arthur F. Kinney, 62–80. Amherst: University of Massachusetts Press, 1988.
Crane, William. *Wit and Rhetoric in the Renaissance*. New York: Columbia University Press, 1937.
Curtius, Ernst Robert. *European Literature and the Latin Middle Ages*. Edited by Willard Trask. New York: Pantheon Books, 1953.
Curtright, Travis. "Sidney's *Defense of Poetry*: Ethos and the Ideas." *Ben Jonson Journal* 10 (2003): 101–16.
Damon, Phillip. "History and Idea in Renaissance Criticism." In *Literary Criticism and Historical Understanding*, edited by Phillip Damon, 25–51. New York: Columbia University Press, 1967.
Danby, J. F. *Poets on Fortune's Hill: Studies in Sidney, Shakespeare, Beaumont and Fletcher*. London: Faber & Faber, 1952.
Daniélou, Jean. *From Shadows to Reality*. Translated by D. W. Hibberd. London: Burns and Oates, 1960.
Davis, W. R. *Idea and Act in Elizabethan Fiction*. Princeton, N.J.: Princeton University Press, 1969.
Dawson, Christopher. *Religion and the Rise of Western Culture*. London: Sheed & Ward, 1950.
Debus, Allen. *Man and Nature in the Renaissance*. Cambridge, U.K.: Cambridge University Press, 1978.
Delumeau, Jean. *History of Paradise*. New York: Continuum, 1995.
De Man, Paul. *Blindness and Insight: Essays in the Rhetoric of Contemporary Criticism*. Minneapolis: University of Minnesota Press, 1983.
DeNeef, A. Leigh. "Rereading Sidney's *Apology*." *Journal of Medieval and Renaissance Studies* 10 (1980): 155–91.
———. *Spenser and the Motives of Metaphor*. Durham, N.C.: Duke University Press, 1982.

Devereux, James A. "The Meaning of Delight in Sidney's *Defence of Poesy*." *Studies in the Literary Imagination* 15 (1982): 85–97.
Ditlevsen, Torben. "'Truth's Journey to Word': On the Concept of Imitation in Sidney's *Apology for Poetry*." *Linguistica et Litteraria* 2 (1973): 54–70.
Doherty, M. J. *The Mistress-Knowledge: Sir Philip Sidney's "Defence of Poesie" and Literary Architectonics in the English Renaissance*. Nashville, Tenn.: Vanderbilt University Press, 1991.
Donno, Elizabeth S. "Old Mouse-Eaten Records: History in Sidney's *Apology*." *Studies in Philology* 72 (1975): 275–98.
D'Onofrio, Giulio, ed. *History of Theology: The Renaissance*. Vol. 3. Collegeville, Minn.: Liturgical Press, 1996.
Donow, Herbert S., and Trevor J. Swanson. *A Concordance to the Poems of Sir Philip Sidney*. Ithaca, N.Y.: Cornell University Press, 1975.
Dorsten, J. A. van. *Poets, Patrons, and Professors: Sir Philip Sidney, Daniel Rogers, and the Leiden Humanists*. Leiden, The Netherlands: Leiden University Press, 1962.
———. "Sidney and Franciscus Junius the Elder." *Huntington Library Quarterly* 42 (1978–79): 1–13.
Dorsten, J. A. van, Dominic Baker-Smith, and Arthur F. Kinney. *Sir Philip Sidney: 1586 and the Creation of a Legend*. Leiden, The Netherlands: E. J. Brill and Leiden University Press, 1986.
Dowlin, Cornell March. "Sidney and Other Men's Thought." *Review of English Studies* 20 (1944): 257–71.
———. "Sidney's Two Definitions of Poetry." *Modern Language Quarterly* 3 (1942): 573–81.
Duncan-Jones, Katherine. *Sir Philip Sidney: Courtier Poet*. New Haven, Conn.: Yale University Press, 1991.
Dupré, Louis. *The Passage to Modernity: An Essay in the Hermeneutics of Nature and Culture*. New Haven, Conn.: Yale University Press, 1993.
Economou, George. *The Goddess Natura in Medieval Literature*. Cambridge, Mass.: Harvard University Press, 1972.
Eden, Kathy. *Poetic and Legal Fiction in the Aristotelian Tradition*. Princeton, N.J.: Princeton University Press, 1986.
Elia, R. L. "Platonic Irony in Sidney's an *Apology for Poetrie*." *Revue des Langues Vivantes* 36 (1970): 401–5.
Engell, James. *The Creative Imagination: Enlightenment to Romanticism*. Cambridge, Mass.: Harvard University Press, 1981.
Evans, Frank. "The Concept of the Fall in Sidney's *Apology*." *Renaissance Papers* (1969): 9–14.
Evans, Maurice. "Sir Philip Sidney: The Maker." *New Lugano Review* 1 (1979): 36–44.
Evans, R. J. W. *Rudolf II and His World: A Study in Intellectual History 1576–1612*. Oxford, U.K: Clarendon Press, 1973.
Fargnoli, Joseph. "Patterns of Renaissance Imagination in Sir Philip Sidney's *Defence of Poesie*." *Massachusetts Studies in English* 8 (1982): 36–42.

Bibliography 201

Farmer, Norman K. *Poets and the Visual Arts in Renaissance England*. Austin: University of Texas Press, 1984.
Ferguson, Margaret W. *Trials of Desire: Renaissance Defenses of Poetry*. New Haven, Conn.: Yale University Press, 1983.
Fletcher, Angus John Stewart. *Allegory: The Theory of a Symbolic Mode*. Ithaca, N.Y.: Cornell University Press, 1964.
Foster, Leslie D. "'I Speak of the Art, and Not of the Artificer': The Logical Structure of Sidney's *Defence of Poetry* and the Concessive Arguments." *Hebrew University Studies in Literature* 5 (1977): 155–81.
Frank, Robert Worth Jr. "The Art of Reading Medieval Personification-Allegory." *English Literary History* 20 (1953): 237–50.
Fraser, Russell A. "Sidney the Humanist." *South Atlantic Quarterly* 66 (1967): 87–91.
Garces Garcia, Pilar. "The Place of Man in the Chain of Being According to Sidney's *Defence of Poesie*." *Sederi: Journal of the Spanish Society for English Renaissance Studies* 4 (1993): 63–68.
Garrett, Martin. *Sidney: The Critical Heritage*. London: Routledge, 1996.
Gauchet, Marcel. *The Disenchantment of the World: A Political History of Religion*. Princeton, N.J.: Princeton University Press, 1997.
Gent, Lucy. *Picture and Poetry 1560–1620: Relations between Literature and the Visual Arts in the English Renaissance*. Leamington Spa, Warwickshire, U.K.: James Hall, 1981.
Gersh, Stephen. *Middle Platonism and Neo-Platonism: The Latin Tradition*. South Bend, Ind.: University of Notre Dame Press, 1986.
Gilson, Etienne. *The Christian Philosophy of Saint Augustine*. New York: Octagon Books, 1983.
———. *History of Christian Philosophy in the Middle Ages*. New York: Random House, 1940.
Gleason, John B. *John Colet*. Berkeley and Los Angeles: University of California Press, 1989.
Gombrich, E. H. "*Icones Symbolicae*: The Visual Image in Neo-Platonic Thought." *Journal of the Warburg Institute* 11 (1948): 163–88.
Goodenough, Erwin Ramsdell. *An Introduction to Philo Judaeus*. Lanham, Md.: University Press of America, 1986.
Greenblatt, Stephen. *Renaissance Self-Fashioning: From More to Shakespeare*. Chicago: University of Chicago Press, 1980.
Greene, Roland. "Fictions of Immanence, Fictions of Embassy." In *The Project of Prose in Early Modern Europe and the New World*, edited by Elizabeth Fowler and Roland Greene, 176–202. Cambridge, U.K.: Cambridge University Press, 1997.
Greene, Thomas. *The Light in Troy: Imitation and Discovery in Renaissance Poetry*. New Haven, Conn.: Yale University Press, 1982.
Gregory, E. R. Jr. "Du Bartas, Sidney, and Spenser." *Comparative Literature Studies* 7 (1970): 437–49.
Groenveld, Simon. "'In the Course of His God and True Religion': Sidney and the

Dutch Revolt." In *Sir Philip Sydney's Achievements*, edited by M. J. B. Allen, 57–67. New York: AMS Press, 1990.

Gross, Jules. *La Divinisation du Chrétien d'après les Pères Grecs*. Paris: Librairie Lecoffre, 1938.

Guillory, John. *Poetic Authority: Spenser, Milton, and Literary History*. New York: Columbia University Press, 1983.

Hager, Alan. *Dazzling Images: The Masks of Sir Philip Sidney*. Newark: University of Delaware Press, 1991.

Halio, Jay. "The Metaphor of Conception and Elizabethan Theories of the Imagination." *Neophilologus* 50 (1966): 454–61.

Hall, Vernon. "Preface to Scaliger's *Poetices Libri Septem*." *Modern Language Notes* 40 (1945): 445–543.

———. *Renaissance Literary Criticism: A Study of Its Social Context*. New York: Columbia University Press, 1945.

Hamilton, A. C. "Sidney and Agrippa." *Review of English Studies*, n.s., 7 (1956): 151–57.

———. "Sidney's Humanism." In *Sir Philip Sidney's Achievements*. New York: AMS Press, 1990.

———. "Sidney's Idea of the 'Right Poet.'" *Comparative Literature* 9 (1957): 51–59.

———. *Sir Philip Sidney: A Study of His Life and Works*. Cambridge, U.K.: Cambridge University Press, 1977.

———. *The Structure of Allegory in the "Faerie Queene."* Oxford, U.K.: Clarendon Press, 1961.

Hanning, Robert. "'Ut Enim Faber . . . Sic Creator': Divine Creation as Context for Human Creativity in the Twelfth Century." In *Word, Picture, and Spectacle*, edited by Clifford Davidson, 95–149. Kalamazoo: Medieval Institute Publications, Western Michigan University, 1984.

Hardison, O. B. Jr., ed. *English Literary Criticism: The Renaissance*. New York: Appleton-Century-Crofts, 1963.

———. "The Two Voices of Sidney's *Apology for Poetry*." In *Sidney in Retrospect: Selections from "English Literary Renaissance,"* edited by Arthur F. Kinney, 45–61. Amherst: University of Massachusetts Press, 1988.

Harrier, Richard. "Invention in Tudor Literature: Historical Perspectives." In *Philosophy and Humanism: Renaissance Essays in Honor of Paul Oskar Kristeller*, edited by Edward P. Mahoney, 370–86. New York: Columbia University Press, 1976.

Hathaway, Baxter. *The Age of Criticism: The Late Renaissance in Italy*. Westport, Conn.: Greenwood Press, 1972.

Haugaard, William. "Renaissance Patristic Scholarship and Theology in Sixteenth-Century England." *Sixteenth Century Journal* 10 (1979): 37–60.

Hayden, John O. *Polestar of the Ancients: The Aristotelian Tradition in Classical and English Literary Criticism*. Newark: University of Delaware Press, 1979.

Heninger, S. K. Jr. "'Metaphor' and Sidney's *Defence of Poesie*." *John Donne Journal: Studies in the Age of Donne* 1 (1982): 117–49.

———. "Sidney and Milton: The Poet as Maker." In *Milton and the Line of Vision*, edited by Joseph Anthony Wittreich, 57–95. Madison: University of Wisconsin Press, 1975.

———. "Sidney and Serranus' Plato." In *Sidney in Retrospect: Selections from "English Literary Renaissance,"* edited by Arthur F. Kinney, 27–44. Amherst: University of Massachusetts Press, 1988.

———. *Sidney and Spenser: The Poet as Maker*. University Park: Pennsylvania State University Press, 1989.

———. "Speaking Pictures: Sidney's Rapprochement between Poetry and Painting." In *Sir Philip Sidney and the Interpretation of Renaissance Culture: The Poet in His Time and in Ours: A Collection of Critical and Scholarly Essays*, edited by Gary F. Waller, 3–16. London: Croom Helm, 1984.

———. "Spenser and Sidney at Leicester House." *Spenser Studies: A Renaissance Poetry Annual* 8 (1987): 239–49.

———. "Spenser, Sidney, and Poetic Form." *Studies in Philology* 88 (1991): 140–52.

———. *Touches of Sweet Harmony: Pythagorean Cosmology and Renaissance Poetics*. San Marino, Calif.: Huntington Library, 1974.

Herman, Peter C. *Squitter-Wits and Muse-Haters: Sidney, Spenser, Milton and Renaissance Antipoetic Sentiment*. Detroit, Mich.: Wayne State University Press, 1996.

Herrick, Marvin Theodore. *The Fusion of Horatian and Aristotelian Literary Criticism, 1531–1555*. Urbana: University of Illinois Press, 1946.

Hollander, Robert. "Typology and Secular Literature: Some Medieval Problems and Examples." In *Literary Uses of Typology from the Late Middle Ages to the Present*, edited by Earl Miner, 3–19. Princeton, N.J.: Princeton University Press, 1976.

Honig, Edwin. *Dark Conceit: The Making of Allegory*. Evanston, Ill.: Northwestern University Press, 1959.

Howell, Roger Jr. "The Sidney Circle and the Protestant Cause in Elizabethan Foreign Policy." *Renaissance and Modern Studies* 19 (1975): 31–46.

Howell, Wilbur. *Logic and Rhetoric in England, 1500–1700*. Princeton, N.J.: Princeton University Press, 1956.

———. *Poetics, Rhetoric, and Logic: Studies in the Basic Disciplines of Criticism*. Ithaca, N.Y.: Cornell University Press, 1975.

Hulse, Clark. *The Rule of Art: Literature and Painting in the Renaissance*. Chicago: University of Chicago Press, 1990.

Hunsaker, Steven V. "Perspectives on the Poetics of the Conceit." *Lucero: A Journal of Iberian and Latin American Studies* 2 (1991): 102–11.

Hunt, John. "Allusive Coherence in Sidney's *Apology for Poetry*." *Studies in English Literature* 27 (1987): 1–16.

Hunter, C. Stuart. "Erected Wit and Infected Will: Sidney's Poetic Theory and Poetic Practice." *Sidney Newsletter and Journal* 5 (1984): 3–10.

Hunter, William Bridges, C. A. Patrides, and Jack H. Adamson. *Bright Essence: Studies in Milton's Theology*. Salt Lake City: University of Utah Press, 1971.

Hyden, Hiram. *The Counter-Renaissance*. Gloucester, Mass.: Peter Smith, 1966.
Hyman, Virginia R. "Sidney's Definition of Poetry." *Studies in English Literature 1500–1900* 10 (1970): 49–62.
Jacobson, Daniel. "Sir Philip Sidney's Dilemma: On the Ethical Function of Narrative Art." *Journal of Aesthetics and Art Criticism* 54 (1996): 327–36.
Jaki, Stanley. *Genesis 1 through the Ages*. London: Thomas More Press, 1992.
Jayne, Sears. "Ficino and the Platonism of the English Renaissance." *Comparative Literature* 4 (1952): 214–38.
———. "Introduction." In *Commentary on Plato's "Symposium on Love,"* edited by Sears Jayne. Dallas, Tex.: Spring Publications, 1985.
———. *John Colet and Marsilio Ficino*. Oxford, U.K.: Oxford University Press, 1963.
Jeanneret, Michel. "Renaissance Exegesis." In *The Cambridge History of Literary Criticism*, edited by Glyn P. Norton, 36–43. Cambridge, U.K.: Cambridge University Press, 1999.
Johnson, Carol. *Reason's Double Agents*. Chapel Hill: University of North Carolina Press, 1966.
Kalstone, David. *Sidney's Poetry: Contexts and Poetics*. New York: Norton, 1970.
Kantorowicz, Ernst. "'Deus Per Naturam, Deus Per Gratiam': A Note on Medieval Political Theology." *Harvard Theological Review* 45 (1952): 253–77.
———. *The King's Two Bodies: A Study in Medieval Political Theology*. Princeton, N.J.: Princeton University Press, 1957.
———. "The Sovereignty of the Artist: A Note on Legal Maxims and Renaissance Theories of Art." In *Essays in Honor of Erwin Panofsky*, 261–79. New York: New York University Press, 1961.
Kay, Dennis, ed. *Sir Philip Sidney: An Anthology of Modern Criticism*. Oxford, U.K.: Clarendon Press, 1987.
Kermode, Frank. *English Pastoral Poetry*. New York: Barnes & Noble, 1953.
Kimbrough, Robert. "Sidney's Invention: The Fiction of Discovery." *Aligarh Journal of English Studies* 12 (1987): 256–62.
———. *Sir Philip Sidney*. New York: Twayne, 1971.
Kinney, Arthur F. *Essential Articles for the Study of Sir Philip Sidney*. Hamden, Conn.: Archon, 1986.
———. "Humanist Poetics and Elizabethan Fiction." *Renaissance Papers* (1978): 31–45.
———. "Parody and Its Implications in Sidney's *Defense of Poesie*." *Studies in English Literature 1500–1900* 12 (1972): 1–19.
———. "Rhetoric and Fiction in Elizabethan England." In *Renaissance Eloquence: Studies in the Theory and Practice of Renaissance Rhetoric*, edited by James J. Murphy, 385–93. Berkeley and Los Angeles: University of California Press, 1983.
———, ed. *Sidney in Retrospect: Selections from "English Literary Renaissance."* Amherst: University of Massachusetts Press, 1988.
Kishler, T. C. "Aristotle and Sidney on Imitation." *Classical Journal* 54 (1963): 63–64.

Klibansky, Raymond. *The Continuity of the Platonic Tradition during the Middle Ages.* Millwood, N.Y.: Krauss, 1982.

Kolnai, Aurel. *The Utopian Mind.* London: Athlone, 1995.

Krieger, Murray. "An Apology for Poetics." In *Words about Words about Words: Theory, Criticism, and the Literary Text.* Baltimore: Johns Hopkins University Press, 1988.

———. *Poetic Presence and Illusion: Essays in Critical History and Theory.* Baltimore: Johns Hopkins University Press, 1979.

Krouse, F. Michael. "Plato and Sidney's *Defense of Poesie.*" *Comparative Literature* 6 (1954): 138–47.

Kuin, Roger. "Scholars, Critics, and Sir Philip Sidney, 1945–70." *British Studies Monitor* 2 (1972): 3–22.

Lawry, Jon S. *Sidney's Two "Arcadias": Pattern and Proceeding.* Ithaca, N.Y.: Cornell University Press, 1972.

Levao, Ronald. *Renaissance Minds and Their Fictions: Cusanus, Sidney, Shakespeare.* Berkeley and Los Angeles: University of California Press, 1985.

———. "Sidney's Feigned Apology." In *Sir Philip Sidney: An Anthology of Modern Criticism.* Oxford, U.K.: Clarendon Press, 1987.

Levin, Harry. "The Golden Age and the Renaissance." In *Literary Views: Critical and Historical Essays*, edited by Carroll Camden, 1–14. Chicago: University of Chicago Press, 1964.

Levy, Fred J. "Philip Sidney Reconsidered." *English Literary Renaissance* 2 (1972): 5–18.

Lewis, C. S. *English Literature in the Sixteenth Century.* New York: Oxford University Press, 1954.

———. *Studies in Words.* Cambridge, U.K.: Cambridge University Press, 1967.

Lindenbaum, Peter. "Sidney and the Active Life." In *Sir Philip Sydney's Achievements*, edited by M. J. B. Allen, 176–93. New York: AMS Press, 1990.

Lloyd, A. C. "Introduction to Later Neoplatonism." In *The Cambridge History of Later Greek and Early Medieval Philosophy*, edited by A. H. Armstrong, 272–301. Cambridge, U.K.: Cambridge University Press, 1970.

Lovejoy, Arthur O., and George Boas. *Primitivism and Related Ideas in Antiquity.* Baltimore: Johns Hopkins University Press, 1935.

Löwith, Karl. *Meaning in History.* Chicago: University of Chicago Press, 1949.

MacIntyre, Alasdair C. *After Virtue: A Study in Moral Theory.* South Bend, Ind.: University of Notre Dame Press, 1981.

Mahoney, John L. "The Problem of Imitation in Neoclassical and Romantic Aesthetics and Criticism." In *Proceedings of the Xth Congress of the International Comparative Literature Association*, Vol. 1. New York: Garland, 1985.

Malloch, A. E. "'Architectonic' Knowledge and Sidney's *Apologie.*" *English Literary History* 20 (1953): 181–85.

Matz, Robert. *Defending Literature in Early Modern England: Renaissance Literary Theory in Social Context.* New York: Cambridge University Press, 2000.

McDannell, Collen, and Bernhard Lang. *Heaven: A History*. New York: Vintage Books, 1990.
McGrath, Lynette. "John Donne's Apology for Poetry." *Studies in English Literature 1500–1900* 20 (1980): 73–89.
McIntyre, John P., S. J. *Poetry as Gnosis: The Literary Theory of Sir Philip Sidney*. Toronto: University of Toronto, 1969.
———. "Sidney's 'Golden World.'" *Comparative Literature* 14 (1962): 356–65.
McLeod, Frederick. *The Image of God in the Antiochene Tradition*. Washington, D.C.: The Catholic University of America Press, 1999.
McNight, Stephen A. *The Modern Age and the Recovery of Ancient Wisdom: A Reconsideration of Historical Consciousness, 1450–1650*. Columbia: University of Missouri Press, 1991.
Miles, Leland. *John Colet and the Platonic Tradition*. La Salle, Ill.: Open Court, 1961.
Miller, Anthony. "Sidney's *Apology for Poetry* and Plutarch's *Moralia*." *English Literary Renaissance* 17 (1987): 259–75.
Mirollo, James. *Mannerism and Renaissance Poetry: Concept, Mode, Inner Design*. New Haven, Conn.: Yale University Press, 1984.
Montgomery, Robert L. *The Reader's Eye: Studies in Didactic Literary Theory from Dante to Tasso*. Berkeley and Los Angeles: University of California Press, 1979.
Muir, Kenneth. *Sir Philip Sidney*. London, Longmans, Green, 1960.
Mulryan, John. "Sir Philip and the Scholars: A Review Article." *Cithara: Essays in the Judeo-Christian Tradition* 13 (1974): 76–82.
Murrin, Michael. *The Allegorical Epic: Essays in Its Rise and Decline*. Chicago: University of Chicago Press, 1980.
———. *The Veil of Allegory: Some Notes toward a Theory of Allegorical Rhetoric in the English Renaissance*. Chicago: University of Chicago Press, 1969.
Myrick, Kenneth. *Sir Philip Sidney as a Literary Craftsman*. Lincoln: University of Nebraska Press, 1965.
Nahm, Milton. *The Artist as Creator: An Essay on Human Freedom*. Baltimore: Johns Hopkins University Press, 1956.
———. "The Theological Background of the Theory of the Artist as Creator." *Journal of the History of Ideas* 8 (1947): 363–72.
Nash, Ronald. *The Light of the Mind: St. Augustine's Theory of Knowledge*. Lexington: University Press of Kentucky, 1969.
Nauert, Charles. *Agrippa and the Crisis of Renaissance Thought*. Urbana: University of Illinois Press, 1965.
Nuttall, A. D. *A New Mimesis*. London: Methuen, 1983.
Panofsky, Erwin. "Artist, Scientist, Genius: Notes on the 'Renaissance-Dämmerung.'" In *The Renaissance: Six Essays*, 123–82. New York: Harper, 1962.
———. *Idea: A Concept in Art Theory*. Edited by Joseph Peake. Columbia: University of South Carolina Press, 1968.
Partee, Morriss H. "Anti-Platonism in Sidney's *Defence*." *English Miscellany: A Symposium of History, Literature and the Arts* 22 (1971): 7–29.

———. "Sir Philip Sidney and the Renaissance Knowledge of Plato." *English Studies* 51 (1970): 411–24.
Patrides, C. A. *The Grand Design of God: The Literary Form of the Christian View of History*. London: Routledge, 1972.
Pelikan, Jaroslav. *Christianity and Classical Culture: The Metamorphosis of Natural Theology in the Christian Encounter with Hellenism*. New Haven, Conn.: Yale University Press, 1993.
———. *Reformation of Church and Dogma (1300–1700)*. Chicago: University of Chicago Press, 1984.
Potter, Jean. "Introduction." In *On the Division of Nature*, edited by Myra Uhlfelder and Jean Potter, i–xliii. Indianapolis, Ind.: Bobbs-Merrill, 1976.
Prescott, Anne Lake. *French Poets and the English Renaissance: Studies in Fame and Transformation*. New Haven, Conn.: Yale University Press, 1978.
———. "King David as a 'Right Poet': Sidney and the Psalmist." *English Literary Renaissance* 19 (1989): 131–51.
Raiger, Michael. "Sidney's Defense of Plato." *Religion and Literature* 30 (1998): 21–57.
Raitiere, Martin N. "The Unity of Sidney's *Apology for Poetry*." *Studies in English Literature 1500–1900* 21 (1981): 37–57.
Raitt, Jill. "Elizabeth of England, John Casimir, and the Protestant League." In *Controversy and Conciliation: The Reformation and the Palatinate, 1559–1583*, edited by Derk Visser and Richard P. Richter, 117–45. Allison Park, Pa.: Pickwick, 1986.
Rees, Joan. "Fulke Greville's Epitaph on Sidney." *Review of English Studies* 19 (1968): 47–51.
Rice, Eugene. *The Renaissance Idea of Wisdom*. Cambridge, Mass.: Harvard University Press, 1958.
Rist, John M. *Plotinus: The Road to Reality*. Cambridge, U.K.: Cambridge University Press, 1967.
Rivers, Isabel. *Classical and Christian Ideas in English Renaissance Poetry: A Student's Guide*. 2nd ed. London: Routledge, 1994.
Roberts, Mark. "The Pill and the Cherries: Sidney and the Neo-Classical Tradition." *Essays in Criticism* 16 (1966): 22–31.
Robinson, Forrest G. *The Shape of Things Known: Sidney's "Apology" in Its Philosophical Tradition*. Cambridge, Mass.: Harvard University Press, 1972.
Rorty, Richard. *Philosophy and the Mirror of Nature*. Princeton, N.J.: Princeton University Press, 1979.
Rosand, David. "Dialogues and Apologies: Sidney and Venice." *Studies in Philology* 88 (1991): 236–49.
Rosenberg, Eleanor. *Leicester, Patron of Letters*. New York: Columbia University Press, 1955.
Rossky, William. "Imagination in the English Renaissance: Psychology and Poetic." *Studies in the Renaissance* 5 (1958): 49–73.

Roston, Murray. "The Perfect Knight." In *Sixteenth-Century English Literature*, 139–53. New York: Shocken Books, 1982.

Rudenstine, Neil L. *Sidney's Poetic Development*. Cambridge, Mass.: Harvard University Press, 1967.

Rutenber, Culber. *Doctrine of the Imitation of God in Plato*. New York: King's Crown Press, 1946.

Ruthven, K. K. "The Poet as Etymologist." *Critical Quarterly* 10 (1968): 9–37.

Said, Edward. *Beginnings: Intention and Method*. New York: Basic Books, 1975.

Samuel, Irene. "The Influence of Plato on Sir Philip Sidney's *Defense of Poesy*." *Modern Language Quarterly* 1 (1940): 383–91.

Sasek, L. *The Literary Temper of the English Puritans*. Baton Rouge: Louisiana State University Press, 1961.

Sinfield, Alan. "The Cultural Politics of the *Defence of Poetry*." In *Sir Philip Sidney and the Interpretation of Renaissance Culture: The Poet in His Time and in Ours: A Collection of Critical and Scholarly Essays*, edited by Gary F. Waller, 124–43. London: Croom Helm, 1984.

———. *Literature in Protestant England, 1560–1660*. London: Croom Helm, 1983.

———. "Sidney and Du Bartas." *Comparative Literature* 27 (1975): 8–20.

———. "Sidney, Du Plessis-Mornay and the Pagans." *Philological Quarterly* 58 (1979): 26–39.

Spellmeyer, Kurt. "Plotinus and Seventeenth-Century Literature: A Prolegomenon to Further Study." *Pacific Coast Philology* 17 (1982): 50–58.

Spies, Marijke. *Rhetoric, Rhetoricians, and Poets: Studies in Renaissance Poetry and Poetics*. Edited by H. Duits and A. van Strien. Amsterdam: Amsterdam University Press, 1999.

Spingarn, Joel. *A History of Literary Criticism in the Renaissance*. London: Macmillan, 1899.

Steadman, John M. *The Lamb and the Elephant: Ideal Imitation and the Context of Renaissance Allegory*. San Marino, Calif.: Huntington Library, 1974.

Steiner, George. *Grammars of Creation*. New Haven, Conn.: Yale University Press, 2001.

Stillman, Robert. "Deadly Stinging Adders: Sidney's Piety, Philipism, and the *Defence of Poesy*." *Spenser Studies* 16 (2002): 231–39.

Strozier, Robert M. "Poetic Conception in Sir Philip Sidney's *An Apology for Poetry*." *Yearbook of English Studies* 2 (1972): 49–60.

Sullivan, John. *The Image of God: The Doctrine of St. Augustine and Its Influence*. Dubuque, Iowa: Priory Press, 1963.

Summers, David. *The Judgement of Sense: Renaissance Naturalism and the Rise of Aesthetics*. Cambridge, U.K.: Cambridge University Press, 1987.

Tayler, Edward W. *Donne's Idea of a Woman: Structure and Meaning in the "Anniversaries."* New York: Columbia University Press, 1991.

———. "The First Individual." In *Soundings of Things Done: Essays in Early Modern*

Literature in Honor of S. K. Heninger, Jr., edited by Peter Medine, 251–59. Newark: University of Delaware Press, 1997.
———. *Nature and Art in Renaissance Literature*. New York: Columbia University Press, 1964.
Tester, S. J. *A History of Western Astrology*. Woodbridge, Suffolk, U.K.: Boydell Press, 1987.
Thaler, Alwin. *Shakespeare and Sir Philip Sidney: The Influence of the "Defense of Poesy."* New York: Russell & Russell, 1967.
Thomas, Keith. *Religion and the Decline of Magic: Studies in Popular Beliefs in Sixteenth- and Seventeenth-Century England*. London: Weidenfeld, 1971.
Tigerstedt, E. N. *The Decline and Fall of the Neo-Platonic Interpretation of Plato: An Outline and Some Observations*. Helsinki, Finland: Societas Scientiarum Fennica, 1974.
———. "The Poet as Creator: Origins of a Metaphor." *Comparative Literature Studies* (1968): 455–88.
Torrance, T. F. *Calvin's Doctrine of Man*. Grand Rapids, Mich.: Eerdmans, 1957.
Treip, Mindele Anne. *Allegorical Poetics and the Epic: The Renaissance Tradition to "Paradise Lost."* Lexington: University Press of Kentucky, 1994.
Trimpi, Wesley. "Sir Philip Sidney's an *Apology for Poetry*." In *The Cambridge History of Literary Criticism: The Renaissance*, edited by Glyn P. Norton, 187–98. Cambridge, U.K.: Cambridge University Press, 1999.
Trinkaus, Charles. *"In Our Image and Likeness": Humanity and Divinity in Italian Humanist Thought*. 2 vols. Chicago: University of Chicago Press, 1970.
Tuve, Rosemund. *Allegorical Imagery*. Princeton, N.J.: Princeton University Press, 1966.
———. "Introduction." In *The Zodiake of Life*, edited by Rosemund Tuve. New York: Scholars' Facsimiles and Reprints, 1947.
Ulreich, John. "'The Poets Only Deliver': Sidney's Conception of Mimesis." *Studies in the Literary Imagination* 15 (1982): 67–84.
Vignaux, Paul, ed. *"In Principio": Interprétations des premiers versets de la Genèse*. Paris: Études Augustiniennes, 1973.
Voegelin, Eric. *Order and History*. Baton Rouge: Louisiana State University Press, 1956.
Waller, G. F. "'This Matching of Contraries': Bruno, Calvin and the Sidney Circle." *Neophilologus* 56 (1972): 331–43.
Waller, Gary F., and Michael D. Moore, eds. *Sir Philip Sidney and the Interpretation of Renaissance Culture: The Poet in His Time and in Ours: A Collection of Critical and Scholarly Essays*. London: Croom Helm, 1984.
Wallis, R. T. *Neoplatonism*. New York: Scribner's, 1972.
Watts, Pauline Moffitt. *Nicolaus Cusanus: A Fifteenth-Century Vision of Man*. Leiden, The Netherlands: E. J. Brill, 1982.
Weatherby, Harold. *Mirrors of Celestial Grace: Patristic Theology in Spenser's Allegory*. Toronto: University of Toronto Press, 1994.

Webster, John. "Temple's Neo-Latin Commentary on Sidney's *Apology*: Two Strategies for a Defense." In *Acta Conventus Neo-Latini Bononiensis*, edited by Richard J. Schoeck, 317–24. Binghamton, N.Y.: Medieval and Renaissance Texts and Studies, 1985.

Weinberg, Bernard. *A History of Literary Criticism in the Italian Renaissance*. Chicago: University of Chicago Press, 1961.

Weiner, Andrew D. "Moving and Teaching: Sidney's *Defence of Poesie* as a Protestant Poetic." *Journal of Medieval and Renaissance Studies* 2 (1972): 259–78.

———. "Sidney, Protestantism, and Literary Critics: Reflections on Some Recent Criticism of the *Defence of Poetry*." In *Sir Philip Sidney's Achievements*, 117–26. New York: AMS Press, 1990.

———. "Sidney/Spenser/Shakespeare: Influence/Intertextuality/Intention." In *Influence and Intertextuality in Literary History*, edited by Jay Clayton and Eric Rothstein, 245–70. Madison: University of Wisconsin Press, 1991.

———. *Sir Philip Sidney and the Poetics of Protestantism: A Study of Contexts*. Minneapolis: University of Minnesota Press, 1978.

White, Alan R. *The Language of Imagination*. Oxford, U.K.: Blackwell, 1990.

Williams, Arnold. *The Common Expositor: An Account of the Commentaries on Genesis, 1527–1633*. Chapel Hill: University of North Carolina Press, 1948.

Williams, Bernard. *Descartes: The Project of Pure Enquiry*. Hassocks, U.K.: Harvester Press, 1978.

Wilson, Harold. "Some Meanings of 'Nature' in Renaissance Literary Theory." *Journal of the History of Ideas* 2 (1941): 430–48.

Wilson, Thomas. *The Arte of Rhetorique*. Gainesville, Fla.: Scholars' Facsimiles and Reprints, 1962.

Wimsatt, William K., and Cleanth Brooks. *Literary Criticism: A Short History*. New York: Knopf, 1957.

Wolfley, Lawrence C. "Sidney's Visual-Didactic Poetic: Some Complexities and Limitations." *Journal of Medieval and Renaissance Studies* 6 (1976): 217–42.

Worden, Blair. *The Sound of Virtue: Philip Sidney's "Arcadia" and Elizabethan Politics*. New Haven, Conn.: Yale Univesity Press, 1996.

Yates, Frances. *The Art of Memory*. Chicago: University of Chicago Press, 1966.

———. *The French Academies of the Sixteenth Century*. London: Warburg, 1947.

———. *Giordano Bruno and the Hermetic Tradition*. Chicago: University of Chicago Press, 1991.

———. *The Occult Philosophy in the Elizabethan Age*. London: Routledge, 1979.

INDEX

Abelard, 89 n24
Abrams, Meyer, 14-15, 178-81; mentioned, 32 n24, 41 n17, 82 n1, 110, 130, 134, 157
Addison, Joseph, 15 n24, 41 n17
Aeneas, 21, 139, 166. *See also* Virgil
Aesop, 38, 138. *See also* allegory, Sidney's examples
Agrippa, Heinrich Cornelius, 140
Agrippa, Menenius, 38-39, 138, 144. *See also* allegory, Sidney's examples
Alain de Lille, 122-23, 124
Alençon, Duke of, 1
allegory: allegorical poetics, 8, 33, 34-53; and divided audiences, 45-53, 46 n27; Sidney's examples, 34, 38-39, 138; typology, 41-45
Allen, Michael J. B., 12 n19
Ambrose, St., 89, 99
Aquinas, St. Thomas: on analogy of God and man, 26-27, 26 n16; on Ideas, 57-58; on Providence, 118, 147-48; on faith and reason, 183, 185-86; mentioned, 28, 47, 48 n30, 123 n35, 129, 149
Arcadia, 1
Ariosto, Lodovico, 143
Aristotle: Aristotelian poetics, 5-6, 8, 9, 34, 36, 110, 112, 156; on Ideas, 56-60, 62-63, 66, 147-49, 156; on nature, 123, 125 n39, 129; mentioned, 18, 20, 22, 27 n16, 37 n8, 54, 55, 64, 65, 66, 67, 69, 101, 103 n60, 111 n3, 120 n23, 123, 123 n35, 125 n39, 146 n11, 165 n7, 173, 175, 177, 185, 188

Arnold, Matthew, 183-84
Arthur, King, 42
Ascham, Roger, 9
Astrophil and Stella, 1
Athanasius, St.: on creation, 83, 84 n7, 86-88; on redemption, 115-17, 121; mentioned, 88, 90 n26, 122
Atkins, J. W. H., 10
Attridge, Derek, 10 n17
Augustine, St.: on analogy of God and man, 25-26, 149 n15; on creation, 83-84, 86; on Ideas, 67-68, 97-99; on rhetoric, 37; on secular order, 129, 185; mentioned, 27, 69, 85, 88, 102, 103, 104, 107, 122, 127, 150

Bacon, Sir Francis: as encyclopedist, 72-73, 172-73; on imagination, 15, 61-62; on poetry, 48; mentioned, 165 n7, 167, 174, 175, 176
Barnes, Catherine, 13 n22
Barney, Stephen, 42 n19
Bartholomaeus Anglicus, 73, 74 n37
Basil, St., 25 n13, 88, 89, 90 n26, 93
Bellier, Pierre, 100 n50
Bernardus Silvestris, 73, 117, 122-23, 124
Berry, Edward, 3 n5, 13 n22
Blake, William, 180
Blumenberg, Hans, 159-61, 174, 182-83, 188
Blundeville, Thomas, 58 n7
Boas, George, xii
Boccaccio, Giovanni, 5, 34, 110, 111 n3; on allegory, 38, 47-49, 185. *See also* humanist poetics

211

Boehme, Jacob, 76
Boethius, 117-18, 126
Bonaventure, St., 43
Borris, Kenneth, 37, 41 nn17-18
Bouwsma, William, 19 n3, 158-60, 163
Bovelle, Charles, 66 n23, 111 n4
Brabant, Siger of, 185
Brezhnev, Leonid, xii
Browne, Thomas: on creation, 102-3, 143-44; on providence, 118-19, 152-54
Bruno, Giordano, 74-76, 185
Bullinger, Heinreich, 150 n17
Burghley, William Cecil, Lord, 155

Calvin, Jean, 119 n20, 126 n43, 127, 150, 154 n27. See also Protestantism
Campanella, Tommaso, 185
Carlyle, Thomas, 180-82
Carruthers, Mary, 75 n39
Chalcidius, 85 n11, 89, 90. See also Timaeus
Chapman, George, 74, 109
Chartres, School of, 57, 99, 123-24
Chaucer, Geoffrey, 124
Chenu, Marie-Dominique, 128-29
Christ: as image of God, 25 n12, 94; as model, 42, 117, 119, 150-55, 186, 187; use of parables, 34, 38, 39, 51, 138
Cicero: on Ideas, 42, 43 n21, 55, 56, 58, 116 n13, 146; and imitation, 144 n8, 146; and rhetorical tradition, 10, 12, 34, 37, 113; mentioned, 42, 43 n21, 85 n11, 156
Clement of Alexandria, St., 88
Clement of Rome, St., 85, 87
Coleridge, Samuel Taylor: on allegory, 41 n17, 44; on analogy of poetry and creation, 84; on creative imagination, xiv, 31-33, 130-32, 135; on secular order, 181, 182, 183
Colet, John, 100-101
Cooper, Thomas, 58
Craft, William, 13 n22, 119 n20
Craig, D. H., 54
Crashaw, Richard, 169
creation: biblical accounts, 23, 25, 76, 81-85, 88-90, 111, 113-14, 142, 148, 162; and emanation (see Plotinus; Scotus Eriugena); hermetic doctrines, 76 n43, 101, 102-3, 105; medieval theories, 18-20, 26, 43-44, 83, 117-18, 121-24, 128-29; patristic theories, 25-26, 83-88, 92-100, 108, 114-17; Renaissance theories, 21-23, 27-28, 65-68, 76-80, 91, 100-108, 118-21, 124-28, 142; romantic theories, 31-33, 129-33. See also demiurge; hexameral tradition; Idea; poetry, as creation; poetry, poet as maker; Timaeus
Cummings, Brian, 4 n7
Cunningham, J. V., 185
Curtius, Ernst Robert, 85 n11
Curtright, Travis, 55
Cusa, Nicholas of, 13, 14, 18-20
Cyrus, 7, 39, 42-43, 43 n21, 52-53, 135, 139-56, 176, 187

Dante Alighieri, 5, 34, 52, 143, 185
Daniel, the prophet, 155
Darwin, Charles, 184
David, King (of Israel), 39, 127, 138, 145, 154 nn27-28
Davies, Sir John, 113
Davis, Walter, 40 n15, 46
Dawson, Christopher, 188 n37
demiurge, 82, 84, 85-93, 96, 99, 103, 115-17. See also Plato, cosmogony; Timaeus
Deneef, A. Leigh, 55, 110 n2
Descartes, Réne: and hexameral tradition, 167-71; on Ideas, 61, 68; mentioned, 107, 165 n7, 167, 172, 174, 175, 176
Dionysius the Pseudo-Areopagite, 102
Doherty, M. J., 55, 144 n8
Dollimore, Jonathan, xi
Donne, John, 27-28, 59-60 n9, 78 n50, 95, 103-4, 113, 169
Dorsten, J. A. van, 191
Dove, John, 103
Drayton, Michael, 61, 75 n41
Du Bartas, Guillaume Saluste, 3, 76-80, 97, 102, 105, 112, 161

Index 213

Duncan-Jones, Katherine, 1 n2, 9 n12, 100 nn50-51, 191
Dupré, Louis, 165 n7
Dürer, Albrecht, 110, 153

Ecclesiastes, 175
Eden, Kathy, 149 n16
Edwards, Jonathan, 119
Eliot, T. S., 176
Elizabeth I, 1, 2 n4, 120 n23, 155
Erasmus, 51, 90 n26

fables. *See* allegory, Sidney's examples
Ferguson, Margaret, 13 n22
Feuillerat, Albert, 100 n51
Ficino, Marsilio: on creativity, 17, 109; on Ideas, 64-69, 71-72, 75; influence, 101; mentioned, 21 n4, 50 n36, 57, 89 n24, 107
Fiore, Joachim of, 185
Fletcher, Angus, 41 n18
Flood, Robert, 123
Fowler, Alastair, 72 n32
Fracastoro, Girolamo, 34

Galileo, 171
Garrett, Martin, 2 n3
Gascoigne, George, 8, 35-37
Gauchet, Marcel, 165 n7
Genesis. *See* creation, biblical accounts
Gilbert de la Porrée, 128
Gilson, Etienne, 67 n24
"golden" world, 6, 28, 43, 70, 112, 121, 124-26, 125 n40, 128, 132, 139-40, 143, 145, 156, 166-67, 186-87
Golding, Arthur, 49, 100 n51, 106, 125 n40
Googe, Barnabe, 73
Gorboduc, 156
Gosson, Stephen, 8
Greenblatt, Stephen, xii
Greene, Thomas, 135 n55
Gregory the Great, 34, 47, 48 n30, 49
Gregory of Nazianzus, 25 n13, 90 n26
Gregory of Nyssa, 25, 89, 93-94
Greville, Fulke, 3, 76 n44
Gross, Jules, 24 n11

Guillory, John, 186 n35

Hamann, Johann Georg, 183
Hamilton, A. C., 2 n3, 38, 40-41
Hanning, Robert, 18 n1
Hardison, O. B., 4 n9, 13
Harrington, John, Sir, 49, 143-44
Hartley, David, 130
Hathaway, Baxter, 43 n21
Hayden, John, 13 n21
Haydn, Hiram, 140
Heninger, S. K., Jr., 13, 16 n26, 55, 74 n37, 77-78, 77-78 nn46-48, 82-83, 105 n66, 146 n10
Herbert, George, 169
Hercules, 52
Herder, Johann, Gottfried, 183
Herman, Peter, 2 n3, 9 n12
Hermes Trismegistus, 101
hermeticism, 49-50
hexameral tradition, 76-80, 168-73
Hilliard, Nicholas, 64
history of ideas, x, 15-16
Hobbes, Thomas, 62, 167, 171-72, 174, 176, 186-87
Homer, 175
Horace, 52; influence, 5, 8, 12, 34, 36, 36-37 nn6-7, 48, 50
Howell, Wilbur, 35 n2
Hugh of St. Victor, 44-45, 126
Hulme, T. E., 181
humanist poetics, 5, 13, 34, 39-40 n14, 46 n27, 47, 110-11, 110-11 n3. *See also* Boccaccio; Dante; Petrarch; poetry, and theology
Hume, David, 130
Hunt, John, 13 n22

Idea, 17, 19-20, 56-80, 92, 95 n40, 96 n43, 97-99, 102-4, 112, 116 n13, 117-21, 126, 143-44, 146 n10, 171, 178; in Sidney, 5, 6, 7, 8, 33, 35, 37, 39, 43-45, 43 n21, 53, 54-56, 81-83, 106, 107, 140, 144-45, 147-52, 176
Ignatius of Loyola, St., 169-70
image of God, ix, xiii, 24, 25-33, 67, 94-96, 105, 115, 117, 119 n20, 120-21, 126,

image of God, *(Continued)*
126 n43, 142, 149 n15, 151-52, 162, 189.
See also Christ, as image of God; poetry, poet as maker
imagination, 15, 31-33, 41 n17, 58-63, 92, 106, 125-26, 129-31, 179, 182, 184, 186 n35
imitation: artistic, ix, 5-6, 9-10, 14-15, 18-24, 32-33, 34, 63, 69-71, 92, 119 n20, 121, 129, 131, 145; world as, 25, 63, 69-71, 145; ethical, 7, 29, 39, 43 n21, 86, 87, 116 n13, 134-35, 139, 145-46, 148, 149, 149 n15, 151, 152-53, 155, 156, 169; of Christ, 151-53, 186, 187; of God, 23-24, 29, 32-33, 51, 121, 124-27, 169, 171-72
invention, 8
Irenaeus, St., 86
Isaiah, 154-55

Jaki, Stanley, 188 n37
Jayne, Sears, 50 n36, 101
Jerome, St., 49
John, St. (the apostle), 105
Johnson, Samuel, 62
Joyce, James, 175

Kant, Immanuel, 130
Kantorowicz, Ernst, xii, 18
Keats, John, 181
Kempis, Thomas à, 152
Kinney, Arthur, 9 n12, 12 n19
Klibansky, Raymond, 89 n24

Lactantius, 8
Lamb, Mary Ellen, 14 n22
Landino, Cristoforo, 20-22
Languet, Hubert, 4
Larsen, Kenneth, 60, 61 n12
Leicester, earl of, 120 n23
Levao, Ronald, 12-13, 55
Lewis, C. S., 45-46, 137
Locke, John, 61-62, 170
Lodge, Thomas, 8
Logos, 104-8, 148-49
Lomazzo, Giovanni Paolo, 64
Lombard, Peter, 83
Lovejoy, A. O., xii

Löwith, Karl, 159-61, 163, 174, 178, 182-83, 188
Luther, Martin, 119 n20, 165 n7

Machiavelli, Nicolo, 165 n7
Macintyre, Alasdair, 165 n7
MacKenna, Stephen, 69 n27
Marlowe, Christopher, 74
Martz, Louis, 169
Marvell, Andrew, 119 n22, 130, 132, 176-78, 180
Matz, Robert, 4 n7, 9 n12, 14 n22
Melanchthon, Philipp, 4, 58 n7
Miller, Anthony, 12
Miller, J. Hillis, 187-88
Milton, John, 30, 41 n17, 52, 74 n37, 89, 103, 112, 119 n22, 125, 133-34, 140, 141, 186 n35
Minturno, Antonio, 11, 34, 112, 113 n6
Mirollo, James, 64 n20
modernity. *See* secular order, and modernity
Moerbeke, William of, 27 n16, 57
Moffett, Thomas, 75
Montaigne, Michel de, 140
Mornay, Philippe de, 3, 100-102, 105-7, 112, 148, 161, 191
Murrin, Michael, 38, 39
Myrick, Kenneth, 6 n11, 13

Nahm, Milton, 82 n1, 84 n7
Nathan (the prophet), 39
Nature, xii n3, 11 n17, 18-20, 22-23, 28, 41 n17, 67, 69-70, 95-96, 106, 121-24, 128-29 n46, 131-34, 131-32 n52, 142-43, 171-72, 187; human nature, ix, xi, 16, 25, 28-29, 30, 52, 109, 126-27, 135, 140-43, 152, 165, 168, 177-78, 179-81, 187 (*see also* image of God); in Sidney, 6-7, 14-15, 31-33, 70-71, 112, 124-29, 134-36, 162
Navarre, 65-66, 112
neoclassical poetics, 5-6, 13, 34, 46 n27. *See also* Aristotle, Aristotelian poetics
Neoplatonism. *See* Plato, Platonic and Neoplatonic traditions

New Historicism, x-xii, 3-5, 13, 14
Newton, Sir Isaac, 32 n22
Northumberland, earl of, 74

Oberman, Heiko, 165 n7
Ockham, William of, 19, 165 n7
Olney, Henry, 2, 50, 191-92
Origen, 78 n48, 86, 89, 93, 99, 100, 101, 148
Orpheus, 102
Ovid, 125 n40
Oxford, earl of, 1, 100 n51

Palingenius, Marcellus, 73-74, 76
Panofsky, Erwin, xii, 56, 82 n1, 120 n23, 121, 153
parables, *See* allegory, Sidney's examples
Patrides, C. A., 118 n17
Paul, St., 25-26, 27, 60-61, 93 n33, 102, 113, 114, 116 n13, 150-52
Pelikan, Jaroslav, 88 n21, 150 n17
Petrarch, Francesco, 110, 111 n3
Philo, 78 n48, 89, 94-97, 100-101, 105, 116-17
Pico della Mirandola, 16, 28-29, 141, 164
Plato, 12 n19, 17, 42, 55; on art, 22; 62, 63, 69, 71; cosmogony, 13, 25, 81-83; on Ideas, 43 n21, 54-59, 58 n7, 116 n13, 143 n5, 147; influence, 12, 16, 17, 25 n13, 28, 30, 37 n7, 43, 49, 50, 50 n36, 53 n38, 60-80, 83-107, 109-10, 112, 114, 115-16, 117, 118, 122, 125, 126, 128, 129, 140, 150, 176, 178, 181. *See also* demiurge; Idea; *Timaeus*
Pléiade, 34, 49, 112
Plotinus, 55, 69-71, 122, 150
Plutarch, 12 n19, 38, 146
poetry: as creation, ix, xiii-iv, 5-6, 10-11, 14-16, 17-33, 37, 41 n17, 55, 81-84, 91-92, 109-11, 129-33, 157-64, 182, 187-89 (*see also* creation); as fiction, 6-7, 21, 35, 39-45, 47, 48, 52, 113, 125-26, 132, 136, 138, 184; and philosophy, 12, 27, 34, 35, 38-39, 39-40 n14, 47, 128, 138; poet as maker, ix, 7, 10, 23-24, 29, 40, 81-82, 91-92, 119 n20, 147, 149, 151-52, 162, 189 (*see also* creation); and poetic inspiration, 7, 10, 23-24, 39, 109-14, 135-36; and poetic genres, 137-39; as a speaking picture, 22, 23, 34, 79; and theology, ix-x, 5, 24, 26, 30-33, 39, 47, 55, 110-11, 110-11 n3, 128-29, 137, 176, 179-80, 182, 183-84, 188 (*see also* humanist poetics; Protestantism);
Ponsonby, William, 2, 50, 191-92
Pope, Alexander, 146
Prescott, Anne Lake, 47 n29, 53 n38, 127 n44
Protestantism, 1-4, 4 n7, 13, 14, 24, 50, 55, 144 n7, 151, 152, 155-56, 161-62, 165 n7, 187
Pugliano, John Pietro, 7
Purchas, Samuel, 90
Puttenham, George (?), 10-11, 24, 92

Raitiere, Martin, 13 n22
Raleigh, Sir Walter, 74-75, 76 n43, 118, 155
Ramism, 12, 14
Rembrandt van Rijn, 155
Renaissance, 5
rhetorical poetics, 5, 9, 33, 34-37, 40, 43, 82, 87, 110, 113
"right poet," 46-47
Robortello, Francesco, 43
Robinson, Forrest, 12, 54, 146 n11
romanticism, 5, 14, 15, 30-33, 45, 62, 109-10, 129-36, 157, 178-81. *See also* individual authors
Rorty, Richard, 61 n13
Ross, Alexander, 148-49
Rousseau, Jean Jacques, 186-87
Rousselet, Jean, 94 n38

Salisbury, John of, 73
Savanarola, 140
Scaliger, Julius Caesar, 11, 22-23, 34, 63-64, 90-92, 113, 156
Schelling, Friedrich, 130
Schmitt, Carl, 159
Scotus Eriugena, John, 57, 99, 122-23
secular order: and modernity, 157-60, 164-75, 165 n7, 182-83, 188; relation to the sacred, 26-33, 110-11, 127-30, 134-35, 152-53, 157-65, 178-89

self-knowledge, 105-7, 137-39, 140, 144-50, 153, 176
Seneca, 55-56, 85 n11
Septuagint, 84-85
serio-ludere, 51
Shakespeare, William, 21, 30, 31, 59, 62, 63, 74, 177, 178; use of "idea," 59; on nature, 124-25, 129, 132, 139-42
Shelley, Percy Bysshe, 30-31, 130
Shepherd, Geoffrey, 1 n2, 9, 9 n12, 12 n20, 14, 38, 82 n1, 120 n23, 146, 191
Sherwood, Terry, 113 n7
Shrewsbury, 146
Sidney, Mary, 50, 191
Sidney, Robert, Sir, 144 n9, 191
Silvestris, Bernard, 73
Simonides, 34
Sinfield, Alan, xi-xii, 3-4, 13, 24 n9
Soens, Lewis, 127 n44
Spellmeyer, Kurt, 55, 69-70
Spenser, Edmund, 30, 42, 60-61, 63, 74, 74 n37, 77 n46, 103, 141, 186 n35
Spies, Jarijke, 63 n17
Spingarn, Joel, 5, 11-12
Steiner, George, 188
Steuco, Agostino, 76
Stevens, Wallace, 184
Stillman, Robert, 4, 24
Summers, David, 56 n2, 64 n18
Sylvester, Joshua, 49, 76 n44, 78-80, 102

Tasso, Torquato, 31, 43 n21
Tatian, 87
Tayler, Edward, 15 n25, 58 nn6-7, 59-60 n10, 125 n39, 177 n21
Theophilus of Antioch, St., 87
Tigerstedt, E. N., 20 n4
Tillyard, E. M. W., xi
Timaeus, 75 n40, 82-85, 89-90, 95, 99-100, 102, 116-17, 116 n13, 123, 128. *See also* demiurge; Plato, cosmogony

Treip, Mindele Anne, 37, 41 nn17-18
Trimpi, Wesley, 55, 57 n3
Trinkaus, Charles, 16 n27
Tuve, Rosemund, 37, 41-42

Ulreich, John, 55, 103 n60
Vasari, Giorgio, 63-64, 66, 121, 175
Vico, Giambattista, 183
Viperano, Giovanni Antonio, 91-92
Virgil, 21, 41 n17, 52, 111 n3, 127, 133, 143-44, 166, 185
Vives, Juan Luis, 16, 28
Voegelin, Eric, 165 n7
Voltaire, 180, 183

Walker, Alice, 10 n14
Walsingham, Sir Francis, 2 n4
Weatherby, Harold, 90 n26
Weber, Max, 165 n7
Weinberg, Bernard, 36 n6, 113 n6
Weiner, Andrew, 13, 24, 55
Willcock, Gladys Doidge, 10 n14
William of Conches, 99
William of Orange, 3
Williams, Arnold, 89, 99-100
Willis, Richard, 9-10
Wilson, Thomas, 37
Wolff, Christian, 183
Woolton, John, 126 n43
Worden, Blair, 4 n8
Wordsworth, William, 32-33, 45, 110, 130-36, 175, 180, 181, 183

Xenophon. *See* Cyrus

Yates, Frances, 75 n39

zodiac, 72-80, 114, 123-24; of the "wit," 46, 63, 72, 76, 77, 82, 97, 135, 146-47, 180, 182
Zuccaro, Federico, 120-21

Sidney's Poetics: Imitating Creation was designed and composed in Dante with Caslon display by Kachergis Book Design of Pittsboro, North Carolina.

www.ingramcontent.com/pod-product-compliance
Lightning Source LLC
Chambersburg PA
CBHW032034290426
44110CB00012B/794